# The Activist Investor Campaign
## A Board and Executive Survival Guide

Brian R. Miller

2026

# Contents

## Chapter 11:  When the Letter Arrives – The First 72 Hours                                                      131

## Chapter 12:  Evaluating the Activist's Demands – Substance Over Reflexive Defense                             143

## Chapter 13: Defense Mechanisms – What Works, What Doesn't, and What Backfires                                 153

## Appendix B: The 13D Filing – Anatomy and Analysis Guide                                                           281

## Appendix C: Campaign Materials Templates              291

## Appendix D: The Activist Investor Tabletop Exercise Kit 305

## Appendix E: Key Governance and Activism Research Sources                                                          319

# The Activist Investor Campaign

# The Activist Investor Campaign

## A Board and Executive Survival Guide

Brian R. Miller

SYNTHETIC INSIGHTS PUBLISHING

First Edition · 2026

Published by Synthetic Insights Publishing

ISBN: 979-8-9946737-7-5 (Paperback)
ISBN: 979-8-9946737-9-9 (Hardcover)

Printed in the United States of America

First Edition

# Preface: Why This Book Had to Be Written

In September 2025, I sat in a conference room with thirty other professionals – lawyers, executives, consultants, and aspiring board directors – and listened to a man who had spent more than three decades on the other side of the boardroom table. Andrew Shapiro, a veteran activist investor with thirteen campaigns to his name, had been invited to speak to our cohort in the SLGI Board Readiness Program. He was not there to scare us. He was there to educate us. And what he said that afternoon changed the way I think about corporate governance.

"Boards and directors are like subatomic particles," Shapiro told us, borrowing an analogy from governance legend Nell Minnow. "When you put them under observation, they behave quite different."

That single sentence captures the fundamental truth of shareholder activism – a truth that most boards never internalize until it is too late. The mere presence of an activist investor changes board behavior. Not the proxy fight. Not the public letter. Not the media campaign. The *observation itself* is the catalyst.

Over the following weeks and months, I would learn just how much I did not know about this corner of corporate governance. And I was not alone. In a room full of accomplished professionals preparing for board service, the knowledge gap around activist investing was staggering. Most of us understood governance in the abstract – fiduciary duties, audit committee responsibilities, executive compensation structures. But when it came to the mechanics of an actual activist campaign – how targets are selected, how positions are accumulated, how demand letters are crafted, how proxy fights are waged, and how settlements are negotiated – we were starting from nearly zero.

That gap is not unique to our cohort. It is endemic across corporate boardrooms.

## The Preparedness Problem

Here is the reality: most boards learn about shareholder activism from their lawyers, and they learn it at the worst possible moment – after a Schedule 13D has already been filed. By then, the activist has spent months conducting research, building a position, assembling director candidates, and drafting campaign materials. The board, meanwhile, is scrambling to retain advisors, assess the situation, and craft a response – all while managing the daily demands of running a company.

This asymmetry is not accidental. Activist investors are professionals. Running campaigns is what they do. For boards and management teams, an activist engagement is an extraordinary event – one that most directors will face only once or twice in their careers, if ever. The result is a preparedness gap that consistently favors the activist.

The numbers underscore the urgency. In 2024, 243 activist campaigns were launched globally, with 119 board seats won and a record 27 CEO resignations at targeted companies. In 2025, activity surged to an all-time record of 297 campaigns, with 32 CEO casualties and 120 board seats changing hands. No company is too large to be targeted – Elliott Management took a $5 billion-plus stake in Honeywell and built a roughly $4 billion position in PepsiCo. No sector is immune – technology companies now represent nearly a quarter of all activist targets.

And yet, the vast majority of boards have never conducted an activist vulnerability assessment. They have never run an activist simulation. They have never asked themselves the question that every activist investor asks before committing capital: *Is this company's underperformance improvable?*

# The Journey That Produced This Book

This book did not begin as a book. It began as an education.

In August 2025, I enrolled in the SLGI Board Readiness Program – an intensive governance education program designed to prepare professionals for corporate board service. Over the following four months, I was immersed in every dimension of board governance: fiduciary duties, audit oversight, executive compensation, strategic planning, risk management, and yes, shareholder activism.

The activism component was different from everything else in the program. It was not a lecture followed by a case discussion. It was a full-contact, eight-week tabletop simulation.

Our cohort was divided into three teams: the activist investors, the company's management team, and the company's board of directors. The target company was Flowers Foods – a real, publicly traded consumer packaged goods company. Each team was given access to the company's actual SEC filings, financial data, governance structure, and competitive positioning. The activist team was tasked with building a complete campaign: a corporate analysis, an investment thesis, a demand letter, an investor presentation, proposed director candidates, a campaign website, press releases, and a negotiation strategy. The management and board teams had to evaluate the activist's demands and decide how to respond.

I co-led the tabletop exercise and served on the activist investor team, which was led by Taylor Price.

For eight weeks, our team did what real activists do. We analyzed Flowers Foods' financial performance against its peers. We scrutinized its governance structure – board composition, director tenure, committee assignments, executive compensation. We identified what Shapiro calls "improvable problems" – areas where the company's underperformance could be attributed to specific, fixable issues. We drafted a thirteen-page demand letter. We built a comprehensive investor presentation. We prepared talking points, FAQs, and media strategies. We identified and proposed independent director candidates.

Then, in a capstone session in December 2025, we sat across the table from the management and board teams and negotiated. We presented our case. They pushed back. We offered settlement terms. They countered. The dynamics were remarkably similar to what practitioners describe in real campaigns – the posturing, the calculation of leverage, the search for face-saving compromises, the fundamental tension between a board defending its position and an activist pressing for change. The experience was intense, adversarial, and deeply educational – not just for the activist team, but for everyone involved.

Sheryl Palmer – the CEO and board chair of Taylor Morrison – joined us and provided a perspective that complemented Shapiro's perfectly. Where Shapiro described how activists build pressure, Palmer described how boards feel that pressure and how the best leaders respond. Her emphasis on the critical importance of having a skilled investor relations function, on the danger of the bunker mentality, and on the need for boards to honestly evaluate whether the activist has a point – these insights were invaluable, and they are woven throughout this book.

What struck me most was not the tactical knowledge I gained – though that was substantial. It was the realization that this kind of preparation should not be reserved for the small number of professionals fortunate enough to participate in a program like SLGI. Every board director, every CEO, every general counsel, and every investor relations professional needs to understand how activist campaigns work – from both sides of the table.

Andrew Shapiro reinforced this point when he described his approach to activist defense consulting – what he calls the "activist vaccine." His argument is elegant: the best defense against activism is not a poison pill or a classified board. It is governance so sound that activism becomes unnecessary. But to build that kind of governance, you first have to understand what the activist sees when they look at your company.

That is what this book delivers.

## What This Book Is – and What It Is Not

This is a practical guide. It is written for board directors, C-suite executives, general counsel, and investor relations professionals who need to understand shareholder activism in its entirety – not just the legal mechanics, not just the financial analysis, but the complete lifecycle of an activist campaign from initial screening through resolution.

What makes this book different from the handful of other treatments of this subject is its completeness and its perspective. Most books on activism are written either from the activist's viewpoint (aimed at investors) or from the legal defense perspective (aimed at lawyers). This book covers both sides of the table with equal depth. You will learn how activists select targets, build campaigns, and create leverage – and you will learn how boards should evaluate demands, engage constructively, and negotiate settlements. You will understand the economics of activism, the role of institutional investors, and the influence of proxy advisory firms. And you will learn how to build the governance framework that makes your company resistant to activist intervention in the first place.

This book draws on three primary sources. First, the insights and frameworks of Andrew Shapiro – a thirty-year veteran of activist investing who has the rare combination of deep experience and a willingness to share his playbook with the people he usually sits across from. Second, the real campaign materials and simulation experience from the Flowers Foods tabletop exercise – a multi-week exercise that produced hundreds of pages of campaign artifacts. Third, extensive research on recent campaigns, regulatory developments, and governance trends through 2025.

What this book is *not* is an academic treatise. You will not find regression analyses or theoretical frameworks disconnected from practice. Every concept in this book is tied to real-world application. Every framework is designed to be used, not just understood.

## How to Use This Book

This book is structured in five parts, and it can be read in two ways.

**Sequential reading** takes you through the complete lifecycle of an activist campaign. Part I establishes the landscape – what activism is, how it evolved, who the activists are, and what they look for. Part II opens the activist's playbook – target selection, position building, the 13D filing, campaign materials, and proxy fights. Part III shifts to the board's response – the first seventy-two hours, evaluating demands, defense mechanisms, and settlement negotiations. Part IV examines campaigns in action through case studies and the role of institutional investors and proxy advisory firms. Part V focuses on prevention and preparedness – the activist vaccine, running your own tabletop simulation, and post-campaign governance transformation.

**Targeted reference** lets you go directly to the section you need. If you have just received a 13D filing, start with Chapter 11. If you want to assess your company's vulnerability, go to Chapter 4. If you are preparing for a board seat and want to understand the landscape, begin with Chapter 1. If you want to run an activist simulation for your board, turn to Chapter 19.

Whichever approach you choose, I encourage you to read with a specific company in mind – your own, if you serve on a board, or one you are evaluating. The concepts in this book become most powerful when applied to a real situation.

## A Note on Sources and Attribution

Throughout this book, I quote Andrew Shapiro extensively. His insights come from a keynote address and subsequent discussions during the SLGI Board Readiness Program in the fall of 2025. I also reference insights from Sheryl Palmer, the CEO and board chair of Taylor Morrison, who provided invaluable perspective on activist defense from the management side. The Flowers Foods tabletop materials are used as illustrative examples of how activist campaigns are constructed in practice.

The statistics and data in this book reflect the most current publicly available information through the end of 2025. Shareholder activism is a dynamic field – the numbers will continue to evolve. But the strategic frameworks, the governance principles, and the practical playbooks in these pages are built to endure well beyond any single proxy season.

This book had to be written because the preparedness gap is real, the stakes are high, and the existing resources are insufficient. If even one board avoids the catastrophic mistake of treating a legitimate activist as a hostile raider – or one company builds the governance practices that prevent activism from being necessary in the first place – then this book will have accomplished its purpose.

Let us begin.

---

*Brian R. Miller February 2026*

# Acknowledgments

This book would not exist without the SLGI Board Readiness Program and the people who made it extraordinary.

Roosevelt Giles designed a program that does what most governance education does not — it forces participants to apply what they have learned under pressure, against intelligent opposition, with real data and real consequences. His philosophy that "the process is the key" pervades every chapter of this book.

Andrew Shapiro gave us something rare: an activist investor willing to open his playbook to the people he usually sits across from. His thirty years of experience, his candor about how activists think, and his concept of the "activist vaccine" form the intellectual backbone of this book. The fact that he shared these insights freely — with the explicit goal of making boards better — says everything about his commitment to good governance.

Sheryl Palmer brought the perspective that completed the picture. Where Shapiro showed us how activists build pressure, Palmer showed us how the best leaders respond to it — with intellectual honesty, strategic clarity, and the understanding that an activist who has done their homework deserves a substantive answer, not a dismissal.

Taylor Price was my partner in crime throughout this entire process. He led the activist team in our Flowers Foods tabletop exercise with the kind of rigor and strategic thinking that made the simulation feel genuinely real, and his thoughtful, deliberate perspective allowed me to drive forward, build, and create with confidence. Beyond the exercise, his editorial contributions and insights made this a better book.

The entire SLGI cohort — the management team, the board team, and the activist team — brought a level of preparation and engagement that produced one of the most valuable learning experiences of my professional life. The quality of this book is a direct reflection of the quality of the people in that room.

Finally, to my family, who endured months of conversations about proxy contests, 13D filings, and standstill agreements with more patience than any reasonable person should be expected to provide.

---

I owe a particular acknowledgment to Flowers Foods. Their company served as the foundation of our tabletop exercise, and the governance questions we explored were genuine, nuanced, and instructive precisely because Flowers Foods is a real company operating in a complex competitive environment.

At the time of this book's publication, Flowers Foods has begun implementing many of the improvements our exercise identified — governance reforms and strategic adjustments that closely mirror the recommendations our activist team developed. They are less than a year into consolidating a significant acquisition and are in the middle of executing a longer-term business strategy that will reshape their competitive position. This is precisely the point in a company's trajectory where business judgment is most consequential and least provable — the results will only become clear as they consolidate the acquisition and complete execution on their strategic objectives.

What is already clear is the positive impact Flowers Foods has in the communities it serves, most visibly through Dave's Killer Bread — a brand built on the conviction that everyone deserves a second chance. A company whose most recognizable product embodies that principle is a company worth rooting for.

I wish them well as they work to drive value to their shareholders, employees, customers, and broader society.

# Chapter 1: The Subatomic Particle Effect – Why Activism Changes Everything

## PART I: UNDERSTANDING THE LANDSCAPE

I remember the exact moment the analogy landed.

It was September 2025, and I was sitting in a room full of aspiring board directors – lawyers, executives, consultants – listening to Andrew Shapiro, a veteran activist investor with thirty years and thirteen campaigns behind him. Shapiro had been invited to address our cohort in the SLGI Board Readiness Program, and he was describing Nell Minnow, the governance legend who has spent decades tracking, analyzing, and publicly grading the governance practices of America's largest companies. Then Shapiro shared one of Minnow's observations. The analogy was drawn from physics, but its implications were purely corporate:

"Boards and directors are like subatomic particles. When you put them under observation, they behave quite different."

In quantum mechanics, the observer effect describes how the act of measurement changes the state of the system being measured. A particle that would behave one way when unobserved behaves differently the moment someone watches. The observation itself – not any force applied, not any energy expended – alters the outcome.

Shareholder activism works the same way.

An activist investor does not need to win a proxy fight to change a company. In fact, most activists never fight a proxy contest at all. The vast majority of campaigns are resolved through settlements – the rate climbed from roughly seventy-five percent in 2023 to ninety-two percent in 2025 – and many of those settlements happen so quickly that the public never even learns a campaign existed. In 2025, the average time from an activist's first engagement to a settlement agreement dropped to just sixteen and a half days. Some companies announced settlements before anyone outside the boardroom knew an activist had taken a position.

The mere act of observation changes behavior. A director who was coasting through board meetings suddenly pays attention. A committee that was rubber-stamping management's proposals begins asking questions. A CEO who had operated without meaningful oversight discovers that someone is watching – and that the watcher has both the capital and the sophistication to force accountability.

This is the subatomic particle effect. And it is the foundational principle of this entire book.

## The Fundamental Premise

Shareholder activism, at its core, rests on a simple premise: shareholders own the company, and they have the right to hold the board of directors accountable for how that company is governed.

That premise sounds uncontroversial. In practice, it is anything but.

For most of the history of the public corporation, the relationship between shareholders and boards has been characterized by what governance scholars call "rational apathy." Individual shareholders, each holding a tiny fraction of a company's outstanding shares, have little economic incentive to invest the time and money required to monitor board performance. The costs of engagement – analyzing financials, attending annual meetings, filing shareholder proposals, running proxy contests – far exceed the benefits any single shareholder can expect to capture. So most shareholders do nothing. They vote with their feet, selling shares if they are unhappy rather than try-ing to change the company from within.

Activist investors break this model. They accumulate positions large enough that the economics of engagement become favorable. They invest the resources to conduct deep analysis of a company's gover-nance, strategy, and financial performance. And they use the tools available to shareholders – SEC filings, proxy contests, public letters, media campaigns, and litigation – to force boards to confront issues they might prefer to ignore.

The question is not whether this dynamic is comfortable for boards – it is not. The question is whether it produces better governance outcomes. And the evidence, accumulated over decades of academic research and practical experience, overwhelmingly suggests that it does.

Companies targeted by activists tend to experience governance improvements in the years following a campaign. Board com-position improves. Capital allocation becomes more disciplined. Transparency increases. In many cases, financial performance improves as well – not because activists are better operators than management, but because the act of observation forces boards to do the work they should have been doing all along.

This is not to say that all activism is constructive, or that every campaign produces positive outcomes. Some activists are genuinely short-term, opportunistic operators who extract value rather than creating it. Some campaigns are motivated more by fund marketing than by genuine governance concerns. And even well-intentioned activists can be wrong – about strategy, about timing, about the capabilities of their proposed director nominees. The question for boards is not whether to embrace all activism uncritically. It is whether to take the activist's diagnostic framework seriously, regardless of whether you ultimately agree with their prescriptions. The diagnosis and the remedy are separate conversations – and boards that conflate them often reject valuable insights because they do not like the source.

# Why Every Director Needs to Understand Activism

If you serve on a corporate board – or aspire to – you might be tempted to view shareholder activism as someone else's problem. Your company is well-run. Your board is engaged. Your shareholders are satisfied. Why spend time studying a dynamic that may never affect you?

Here is why: even if an activist never targets your company, understanding activism will make you a better director.

The activist's analytical framework – the questions they ask, the metrics they scrutinize, the governance weaknesses they identify – is precisely the framework that every effective director should be applying to their own board. When an activist evaluates a company, they ask: Is the board truly independent, or has it been captured by the CEO? Is capital being allocated with discipline, or is it being wasted on empire-building acquisitions and vanity projects? Is the company communicating its strategy effectively, or has it retreated into a bunker? Are directors adding value, or are they collecting fees for attendance?

These are not hostile questions. They are the questions that fiduciary duty demands.

Andrew Shapiro put it directly: "I am the independent director's friend as an activist. I am the nemesis of co-conspirators and co-opted directors of the Imperial CEO – and the Imperial CEO." His point is worth sitting with. The activist's interests are aligned with the interests of truly independent directors – those who take their oversight role seriously, who push back on management when warranted, and who prioritize shareholder value over board collegiality. The activist is the enemy only of directors who have stopped doing their jobs.

Understanding the activist's perspective, then, is not about preparing for an attack. It is about internalizing the discipline that effective governance requires. A director who can see their company through an activist's eyes – who can identify the vulnerabilities, the underperformance, the governance gaps – will be a more valuable member of any board.

# The Misconception: Raiders vs. Reformers

One of the most persistent obstacles to productive engagement with activists is the lingering image of the corporate raider.

The term evokes the 1980s – hostile takeovers, leveraged buyouts, the aggressive financial engineering of figures like Carl Icahn, T. Boone Pickens, and the fictional Gordon Gekko. In the popular imagination, an activist investor is someone who shows up uninvited, demands radical change for short-term profit, and leaves destruction in their wake. The word "activist" itself carries a confrontational connotation that colors how boards respond to even the most constructive engagement.

This image is decades out of date.

Modern shareholder activism encompasses a wide spectrum of approaches, motivations, and time horizons. At one end are economic activists – investors who take substantial positions in undervalued companies and push for governance improvements that they believe will create long-term shareholder value. These investors often hold their positions for years, not months. They prefer private engagement over public confrontation. They seek board seats not to disrupt but to contribute. At the other end are short-term operators and occasional agitators – but they represent a minority of the activism landscape, and their campaigns tend to be the least successful.

The distinction matters because it determines how boards should respond. A company that treats every activist as a raider will default to entrenchment – calling the lawyers, adopting defensive measures, refusing to engage. This response is often the worst possible strategy, because it gives a constructive activist exactly the narrative they need: a board that will not listen to its own shareholders.

Consider the contrast. When Elliott Management took its $5 billion position in Honeywell in late 2024, the activist arrived with a detailed analysis of the company's conglomerate structure, a specific thesis about the value that could be unlocked through separation, and a credible plan for execution. Within months, Honeywell announced it would split into three independent companies – essentially adopting Elliott's recommendation. This was not a raid. It was a governance intervention that the market endorsed: Honeywell's shareholders benefited from a strategic transformation that the incumbent board had resisted for years.

Now consider the alternative: a board that treats such an engagement as a hostile attack, refuses to meet with the activist, retains defensive advisors, and issues press releases about the company's "strong strategic direction." That response does not make the activist go away. It makes them more determined – and it provides them with a compelling public narrative about a board that prioritizes its own continuity over shareholder interests.

In my experience, the boards that navigate activism most effectively are those that begin by evaluating the substance of the activist's claims rather than reacting to the fact that an activist has appeared. Is the company actually underperforming its peers? Are there legitimate governance concerns? Is the capital allocation strategy defensible? These are the questions that should drive the response – not the reflexive instinct to circle the wagons.

Andrew Shapiro captured the dynamic succinctly: "In many instances, if a company's been targeted by an activist, more likely than not, I'm probably going to agree with the activist – that the board deserves it." That observation, coming from a veteran of the governance wars, should give every director pause. The uncomfortable truth is that most activism is provoked by genuine governance failures – and the sooner boards accept that reality, the better prepared they will be to respond constructively.

## The Stakes

The numbers alone should command attention: 297 activist campaigns launched globally in 2025 – an all-time record, and the third consecutive year of new highs. Thirty-two CEOs forced out. One hundred twenty board seats changing hands. No company is too large – Elliott Management took a $5 billion-plus stake in Honeywell and pushed successfully for a three-way breakup. No sector is safe – technology, industrials, consumer products, energy, and healthcare have all seen significant activity.

The full scope of these numbers – and the structural forces driving them – is examined in detail in the next chapter. But the headline is this: activism has reached industrial scale, and the pace is accelerating.

The question is not whether your company might face an activist. The question is whether your governance is strong enough to withstand the scrutiny – and whether you would want it to be.

# What Happens When Boards Are Unprepared

The consequences of the preparedness gap are not theoretical. Consider the board that receives a 13D filing and has no response plan: the first seventy-two hours are consumed by panic while the activist – who has spent months preparing – is already executing. Or consider the board with a defensive playbook but not a governance playbook: they know how to adopt a poison pill but not how to evaluate whether the activist has a point. Their defensive reflexes make them look exactly like the entrenched board the activist described in their public letter. The worst outcome is not losing a proxy fight. It is losing the confidence of your institutional shareholder base – the quiet majority that has been watching the same underperformance metrics the activist identified. When that confidence breaks, the proxy fight is already lost. The formal vote is merely a confirmation.

# The New Reality: Activism as Permanent Condition

Perhaps the most important shift that directors need to understand is that activism is no longer a cyclical phenomenon. It is not something that surges during periods of market distress and recedes during bull markets. It has become a permanent structural feature of corporate governance – as embedded in the system as the proxy statement, the annual meeting, and the independent audit.

Several factors have made this permanence inevitable. The universal proxy card is a structural change that will not be reversed. The growth of institutional stewardship teams at the largest asset managers is an investment that creates its own demand for engagement. The technology infrastructure that supports activist research – SEC filing databases, governance scoring platforms, peer benchmarking tools – becomes more accessible every year. And the economics of activism continue to attract new entrants: as long as there are companies with improvable underperformance, there will be investors willing to commit capital and reputational resources to fix them.

The implication for boards is profound. You cannot prepare for activism as a contingency – something that might happen someday and probably will not. You must prepare for it as a condition – an ongoing reality that shapes how you govern, how you communicate, and how you allocate capital, every day. The boards that internalize this reality will be better governed even if an activist never appears. The boards that do not will be perpetually vulnerable.

Shapiro captured this ethos with a line that has stayed with me since his keynote: "There's a lot of activist defense advisors who advise companies: think like an activist. But the one thing they can't do – they can't think like an activist. They've never been an investor or an activist investor." The defense advisors can teach you the mechanics. This book will teach you the mindset.

# The Observation Has Already Begun

Here is the uncomfortable truth that every board needs to internalize: you are already being observed.

Activist investors are screening your company right now. They are running your financials through models that compare your returns on assets and equity against your peers. They are analyzing your proxy statement for governance weaknesses – staggered boards, overboarded directors, CEO-chair duality, excessive compensation without corresponding performance. They are reading your earnings calls and your investor presentations, looking for the gap between what you say and what you deliver.

They may never appear. But the discipline of assuming they are watching – of governing as though every decision will be scrutinized by a sophisticated investor with a magnifying glass – is the discipline that makes companies better.

The subatomic particle effect is not a threat. It is a standard. And the boards that embrace it will not only survive the era of activism.

They will thrive in it.

The observation has begun. Let us make sure your board is ready.

# Chapter 2: The Evolution of Shareholder Activism – From Raiders to Reformers

In late 1985, Carl Icahn won control of Trans World Airlines, completing the acquisition in January 1986. He had not set out to run an airline. He had set out to make money – and TWA, with its valuable route network, real estate holdings, and depressed stock price, looked like an undervalued asset ripe for extraction. Over the next decade, Icahn would strip TWA of its most valuable assets, load it with debt, and ultimately drive it into bankruptcy – twice. When it was over, thousands of employees had lost their jobs, creditors had been decimated, and Icahn had walked away with hundreds of millions of dollars in profit.

This is the image that still haunts the term "activist investor" – and it is the image that boards must move beyond if they want to navigate the modern activism landscape effectively.

The evolution of shareholder activism from the corporate raids of the 1980s to the governance-focused campaigns of the 2020s is not simply a story of changing tactics. It is a story of fundamental transformation in who activists are, what they want, how they operate, and how the broader investment community responds to them.

Andrew Shapiro has lived through nearly all of it. "Back in 1993 when I formed my funds," he told us, "I had a thirty-two-year term limit – the longest the IRS allowed. I was thirty-one years old. I didn't really think or imagine what thirty-two years meant because it was longer than I had been alive on earth." Three decades later, Shapiro had run the longest-running activist hedge fund in the small and micro-cap space – and had watched the entire practice transform from the province of corporate raiders into a mainstream governance mechanism. "I've been doing this since 1993," he noted, "and some of my best campaigns were done before you'll find stuff in Google or the internet."

Understanding this evolution is essential for any director or executive, because the way you respond to an activist today should be shaped not by the ghosts of the 1980s but by the reality of the present.

# The Age of the Raider: 1980s

The 1980s were the era of the hostile takeover, and the figures who dominated the headlines were as colorful as they were controversial.

Carl Icahn, T. Boone Pickens, Nelson Peltz, and a handful of other financiers developed a playbook that was brutally simple: identify a company trading below the value of its parts, accumulate a position, and then either force a sale, push for a breakup, or threaten a hostile takeover – often funded by the newly available instrument of junk bonds, pioneered by Michael Milken at Drexel Burnham Lambert. The term "greenmail" entered the corporate lexicon – the practice of accumulating a threatening position in a company and then selling it back to the company at a premium, essentially getting paid to go away.

T. Boone Pickens' campaign against Gulf Oil in 1984 was emblematic of the era. Pickens accumulated a significant stake in Gulf, one of the largest oil companies in the world, and launched a takeover bid. Gulf's board, unwilling to sell to Pickens, instead arranged a "white knight" acquisition by Chevron – a transaction that enriched Pickens and his fellow shareholders but eliminated Gulf Oil as an independent company. The transaction was worth $13.2 billion, making it the largest merger in U.S. history at the time.

The corporate response to this wave of raids produced some of the defensive mechanisms that persist today. The shareholder rights plan

– commonly known as the poison pill – was invented in 1982 by Martin Lipton of Wachtell, Lipton, Rosen & Katz specifically to combat hostile takeovers. Classified boards, which stagger director elections over three-year cycles to prevent a single-election sweep, became widespread. State legislatures passed anti-takeover statutes. And corporate boards – often with the enthusiastic support of management – adopted an arsenal of defensive provisions designed to make hostile acquisitions as difficult as possible.

The era also produced its share of excess. Michael Milken, whose junk bonds fueled many of the decade's largest takeovers, was indicted on racketeering and fraud charges in 1989 and ultimately sentenced to 10 years in prison. Drexel Burnham Lambert, his firm, collapsed into bankruptcy. Several of the decade's most prominent raiders found themselves on the wrong side of securities laws. The leveraged buyout of RJR Nabisco in 1988 – captured in the book *Barbarians at the Gate* – became a symbol of Wall Street excess, a $25 billion transaction driven more by ego and fees than by any compelling strategic logic.

The legacy of the 1980s is complicated. The raiders genuinely destroyed value in some cases – TWA being perhaps the most visible example. But they also exposed a real problem in American corporate governance: boards that were insulated from shareholder accountability, management teams that were entrenched and unaccountable, and capital structures that reflected management's comfort rather than shareholders' interests. The raiders were crude instruments, but they exposed weaknesses that more civilized tools would later address.

When I first encountered this history in the SLGI program, I made the mistake that most newcomers to governance make: I assumed the 1980s tools were obsolete. They are not. The defensive measures born in this era – poison pills, classified boards, state anti-takeover statutes – remain fixtures of corporate governance today. Understanding their origins is important, because it reveals their purpose: they were designed to combat hostile takeovers and asset stripping, not the governance-focused activism that characterizes the modern landscape. Boards that invoke these 1980s-era defenses against twenty-first-century governance activists are using tools designed for a different kind of threat – and the mismatch can be costly.

# The Institutional Turn: 1990s-2000s

The 1990s marked a turning point in the character of shareholder activism. The corporate raiders did not disappear, but they were increasingly joined – and eventually eclipsed – by a different kind of activist: the institutional investor.

CalPERS, the California Public Employees' Retirement System, became the bellwether of institutional activism. Managing hundreds of billions of dollars on behalf of state employees, CalPERS had both the economic motivation and the fiduciary obligation to push for better governance at the companies in its portfolio. Rather than threatening hostile takeovers, CalPERS published annual "focus lists" of underperforming companies, engaged directly with boards and management teams, and used its voting power to influence director elections and shareholder proposals.

This institutional activism was fundamentally different from the raider model in three respects. First, institutional activists could not simply sell their positions if they were unhappy – large index fund positions are effectively permanent, making voice the only alternative to exit. Second, institutional activists were motivated by long-term performance rather than short-term extraction. Third, their legitimacy as fiduciaries representing millions of beneficiaries gave their governance demands a moral authority that individual raiders could never claim.

The governance reforms of this period were substantial. The number of companies with majority-independent boards increased dramatically. Board-level committees – audit, compensation, nominating – became standard features of governance architecture. Say-on-pay advisory votes gave shareholders a direct voice on executive compensation. And the concept of "good governance" – previously a niche concern of academics and activists – entered the mainstream of corporate practice.

Yet institutional activism had limitations. Pension funds and mutual fund companies were generally reluctant to wage the kind of aggressive, public campaigns that produce immediate change. They preferred private engagement – letters, meetings, quiet diplomatic pressure. When that failed, they voted their shares, but they rarely escalated beyond that. The result was a governance landscape in which the most egregious abuses were curtailed but more subtle forms of underperformance and entrenchment persisted.

## The Golden Age Begins: 2010s

The 2010s saw the emergence of a new generation of activist hedge funds that combined the aggressive posture of the 1980s raiders with the governance sophistication of institutional investors. These funds were not looking to greenmail companies or strip assets. They were looking to unlock value through better governance, more disciplined capital allocation, and strategic transformation – and they had the analytical depth, the capital, and the patience to see their campaigns through.

The campaign that signaled the arrival of this new era was Pershing Square Capital Management's engagement with Canadian Pacific Railway in 2012. Bill Ackman, Pershing Square's founder, built a $1.4 billion position in Canadian Pacific and argued that the railroad's operating performance was drastically below its potential. When the board refused to engage, Ackman launched a proxy fight – and won. He replaced the CEO, installed a new management team led by E. Hunter Harrison, and over the next several years, Canadian Pacific's operating ratio improved dramatically and its stock price roughly tripled.

The Canadian Pacific campaign demonstrated something important: an activist could create enormous value not through financial engineering but through operational improvement driven by better governance. Ackman did not break up the company, leverage it with debt, or extract short-term profits. He installed better management and held the company accountable for results.

Carl Icahn, the quintessential 1980s raider, evolved with the times. His 2013 campaign at Apple – in which he pushed for increased share buybacks, arguing that Apple's massive cash hoard was being deployed too conservatively – was a far cry from the TWA takeover. Icahn was not trying to break up Apple or replace its management. He was making a capital allocation argument that many institutional investors shared. Apple eventually increased its buyback program to over $100 billion.

By the middle of the decade, activists were targeting some of the largest and most prominent companies in the world. Nelson Peltz's Trian Partners took on Procter & Gamble in what became the most expensive proxy fight in history. Elliott Management, under Paul Singer, became the most prolific and feared activist in the world, waging dozens of campaigns simultaneously across multiple continents. ValueAct Capital pioneered a more collaborative approach, taking board seats and working quietly with management rather than waging public campaigns.

The 2010s also saw a notable change in how activism was perceived by the broader investment community. Where institutional investors had once viewed activists with suspicion – seeing them as disruptive short-term operators – they increasingly recognized activists as a governance check that could benefit all shareholders. Academic research published during this period consistently found that companies targeted by activists experienced improved governance practices and, in many cases, superior financial performance in the years following a campaign. This research helped legitimize activism in the eyes of pension funds, endowments, and other long-term institutional investors who had previously been skeptical.

By the end of the decade, activism had been fully integrated into the governance ecosystem. Proxy advisory firms like ISS and Glass Lewis had developed sophisticated frameworks for evaluating activist campaigns. Investment stewardship teams at the largest asset managers had grown from a handful of analysts to departments of dozens. And the conversation had shifted from whether activism was legitimate to how it could be made more effective – both for activists pursuing change and for boards seeking to engage constructively.

The 2010s established activism as a permanent feature of the governance landscape – not a cyclical phenomenon or a fringe activity, but a mainstream mechanism for shareholder accountability.

# The Watershed: Engine No. 1 vs. ExxonMobil (2021)

If there is a single event that defines the modern era of shareholder activism, it is the Engine No. 1 proxy fight against ExxonMobil in May 2021.

The numbers alone are staggering. Engine No. 1, a hedge fund managing approximately $250 million in assets, took on ExxonMobil, a company with a market capitalization exceeding $250 billion. The fund owned a negligible fraction of ExxonMobil's shares. By every conventional measure, Engine No. 1 had no business challenging one of the world's largest and most powerful companies.

But Engine No. 1 had something more powerful than capital: a thesis that resonated with the institutional investor base.

The fund's argument was straightforward. ExxonMobil's board had failed to adapt the company's strategy to the energy transition. Total shareholder return had dramatically lagged peers over every meaningful time horizon. The board lacked directors with the energy industry expertise needed to oversee a strategic pivot. And the company's resistance to engaging constructively with shareholders on climate-related risks had eroded institutional confidence.

Engine No. 1 nominated four director candidates and launched a proxy solicitation. ExxonMobil fought back aggressively, spending tens of millions of dollars on the defense. The outcome hinged on the votes of the three largest asset managers in the world: BlackRock, Vanguard, and State Street.

All three voted for at least some of Engine No. 1's nominees. When the votes were tallied, the tiny fund had won three of four contested board seats at one of the world's largest companies.

When Shapiro described this campaign to our cohort, you could feel the room shift. This was not theory anymore – this was a $250 million fund defeating a $250 billion company with nothing but a better argument. The ExxonMobil campaign shattered several assumptions that had previously governed board thinking about activism. First, the assumption that size provides protection – it does not. Second, the assumption that an activist needs a large ownership stake to be credible – Engine No. 1 proved that a compelling thesis matters more than shareholding size. Third, and most importantly, the assumption that institutional investors will reflexively support the incumbent board – they will not, when the board has demonstrably failed to deliver results and adapt to changing circumstances.

# The Universal Proxy Card: The Rule Change That Changed Everything (2022)

On September 1, 2022, the SEC's universal proxy card rules took effect. This single regulatory change has done more to reshape the dynamics of activism than any development since the invention of the poison pill.

Before the universal proxy, shareholders voting by proxy had to choose between two competing slates: the company's nominees or the activist's nominees. They could not mix and match. If an activist nominated three candidates and the company nominated eight for an eight-seat board, the shareholder had to choose one card or the other. This structural advantage overwhelmingly favored companies, because shareholders who supported even one of the activist's nominees had to reject the entire company slate to vote for them.

The universal proxy card eliminated this constraint. Now shareholders can vote for any combination of company-nominated and activist-nominated directors, just as they could if they attended the meeting in person. A shareholder who likes seven of the company's nominees but prefers one of the activist's candidates can construct exactly that ballot.

The predicted impact was a surge in proxy fights. The actual impact has been far more interesting – and far more consequential for boards.

Rather than an explosion of contested elections, the universal proxy card has accelerated the pace of settlements to an extraordinary degree. The logic is simple: under the old rules, companies could calculate that the structural advantage of the binary slate choice made proxy fights winnable even against activists with legitimate grievances. Under the universal proxy, that calculation has reversed.

When institutional investors can cherry-pick the best candidates from either side, a company with weak directors on its slate is at a severe disadvantage. The rational response, for most companies, is to settle before the fight – and that is exactly what has happened.

The data tells the story. In 2022, the first year of the universal proxy, the average time from activist engagement to settlement was approximately 77 days. By 2024, that figure had dropped to roughly 34 days. In 2025, it plummeted further – to just 16.5 days in the second quarter. The number of settlements without prior public agitation – cases where the first public indication of activist involvement was the settlement announcement itself – has surged. In 2025, a record 52 U.S. settlements were reached, up from 35 the prior year.

The universal proxy card has not merely changed tactics. It has changed the fundamental power dynamic between activists and boards. Companies that previously could afford to stonewall constructive engagement now face a stark calculation: settle early on reasonable terms, or risk losing seats in a vote where shareholders can freely select the strongest candidates regardless of which side nominated them.

For directors, the implication is clear: governance quality is no longer just a matter of principle. It is a matter of survival. A board with genuinely strong, qualified directors has nothing to fear from the universal proxy card. A board populated with cronies, the disengaged, and the overboarded has everything to fear – because shareholders can now surgically remove the weakest links.

# Activism by the Numbers: The Modern Landscape

The acceleration of activism in the 2020s has been relentless, and the data from 2023 through 2025 paints a picture of a governance mechanism that has reached industrial scale.

In 2023, activists launched 252 campaigns globally and won 122 board seats. The year saw a continuation of the trend toward constructive activism, with the majority of seats won through settlement rather than proxy fights.

In 2024, the pace increased further. Global campaign activity rose to 243 – the highest since 2018. In the United States alone, 115 campaigns were launched, up six percent year-over-year. A record 160 unique investors participated in activism campaigns, and 45 of them – twenty-eight percent – were first-timers who had never before launched a public campaign. For the first time in history, first-time activists were responsible for a larger share of campaigns (eighteen percent) than the major established firms (seventeen percent) – an extraordinary inversion that would have been unthinkable a decade earlier.

This democratization of activism is one of the most significant trends of the decade. Activism is no longer the exclusive province of a handful of large hedge funds. It is a tool available to any investor with a credible thesis, the analytical resources to support it, and the willingness to engage. Many first-time activists bring deep sector expertise – former executives, industry specialists, or operational consultants who understand the target company's business better than most traditional activist funds.

The year 2024 also saw activism move up-market. Roughly thirty percent of target companies had market capitalizations exceeding $25 billion, a share that had been steadily climbing. Technology companies attracted an all-time high proportion of campaigns – approaching twenty-five percent – as activists targeted underperforming software companies, semiconductor firms, and digital platform businesses.

Then came 2025 – the year that rewrote the record books. With 297 campaigns, global activity hit an all-time high, marking the third consecutive record year. A record 32 U.S. CEOs resigned within a year of an activist campaign, a sixty percent increase over the four-year average. Ninety-two percent of board seats won by activists came through settlement rather than proxy fights. The quality of activist-nominated directors reached new highs, with thirty-one percent having CEO or CFO experience and sixty percent having prior board experience.

These numbers are not abstract. Each campaign represents a real company – with real employees, real customers, and a real board – confronting the most intense governance scrutiny it has ever faced. For the directors and executives reading this book, the message is unavoidable: activism is not a temporary trend. It is the new permanent condition of corporate governance.

# The Globalization of Activism

For decades, shareholder activism was predominantly an American phenomenon. The concentration of dispersed ownership, robust shareholder rights, accessible proxy mechanics, and an active market for corporate control made the United States the natural habitat for activist campaigns.

That is changing – and changing rapidly.

European activism has grown substantially, driven by governance reforms in the UK, Germany, France, and the Nordic countries. The United Kingdom, with its shareholder-friendly corporate governance code and tradition of institutional engagement, has become the second-largest market for activism after the United States. Germany, historically resistant to Anglo-Saxon governance norms, has seen a wave of campaigns targeting underperforming industrial conglomerates. French companies, once protected by a web of cross-shareholdings and government relationships, have found themselves increasingly vulnerable to activist demands for improved capital efficiency.

Asian markets have experienced the most dramatic transformation. Japan, where entrenched management and cross-shareholdings had long insulated companies from shareholder pressure, has become one of the fastest-growing activism markets in the world. The Tokyo Stock Exchange's own reforms – including pressure on companies to improve return on equity and reduce cross-shareholdings – have created an environment in which activist campaigns are not just tolerated but implicitly encouraged. South Korea's corporate governance reform movement has produced both domestic activists and attracted international funds looking to unlock value in Korea's historically discounted conglomerates.

Elliott Management alone has waged high-profile campaigns across Europe and Asia, taking a multi-billion-dollar position in BP in 2025 and conducting campaigns in South Korea, Japan, and Australia. Starboard Value, Jana Partners, and other U.S.-based activists have similarly expanded their geographic reach. As Shapiro told our cohort – with characteristic understatement – "I've done thirteen different 13Ds. Read what's called Item 4 and my exhibits. They will include some entertaining love letters." Those love letters now travel across borders.

The globalization of activism means that non-U.S. companies can no longer assume that their governance structures insulate them from activist pressure. Cross-border campaigns are becoming routine, and the playbooks developed in the American market are being adapted and applied worldwide. The universal proxy card may be a U.S. regulatory innovation, but the governance accountability it represents is a global phenomenon.

For directors on the boards of multinational companies, this expansion is particularly relevant. Your company's shareholder base increasingly includes global investors who apply activist frameworks regardless of where the company is domiciled. The governance expectations of a BlackRock or a State Street do not stop at national borders. And the activist firms that have mastered the American market are now looking for opportunities wherever governance failures create value gaps – from London to Tokyo to Seoul.

## The Structural Forces Behind the Acceleration

Several forces are driving this sustained acceleration, and none show signs of reversing: the universal proxy card has tilted the playing field toward activists; institutional stewardship teams have grown more assertive and willing to vote against incumbent directors; technology has reduced the cost and speed of activist research; and the barriers to launching a campaign have fallen so far that first-time activists now represent a larger share of campaigns than established firms.

But the most consequential shift is one that boards often miss entirely: the move from proxy fights to settlements as the primary resolution mechanism.

By 2025, ninety-two percent of board seats won by activists came through settlement – agreed-upon transitions negotiated between the parties, often before the public knew a campaign existed. The average time to settlement compressed from months to weeks to, in many cases, days. A record number of settlements that year were announced without any prior public disclosure of activist involvement.

This shift has profound implications for how boards should prepare. The traditional defensive playbook – retain advisors, adopt defensive measures, prepare for a proxy fight – is designed for a confrontation that increasingly never happens. The boards that succeed are the ones that can evaluate an activist's thesis quickly, engage substantively within days of first contact, and negotiate a resolution that serves shareholder interests without the time, expense, and distraction of a public battle.

The settlement revolution also means the most effective activism is the campaign you never hear about – the one that produces board changes and strategic pivots through private negotiation rather than public confrontation. For directors, this invisibility can be deceptive. The absence of headline-grabbing proxy fights does not mean activism is declining. It means activism is becoming more efficient – and harder to see until it arrives at your boardroom door.

## What This Means for You

If the history of shareholder activism teaches one lesson, it is this: every era produces a new set of assumptions about what boards can get away with, and every era eventually overturns those assumptions.

In the 1980s, boards assumed that corporate raiders could be bought off with greenmail or blocked with poison pills. The institutional investors of the 1990s proved that governance reform could come from within the shareholder base. In the 2010s, activist hedge funds demonstrated that even the largest companies were vulnerable to well-researched, well-funded campaigns. In the 2020s, the universal proxy card and the rise of settlement-driven activism have shown that the traditional defensive playbook is no longer sufficient.

The boards that thrive in this environment are not the ones with the strongest defenses. They are the ones with the strongest governance.

In the next chapter, we will examine the people behind the campaigns – the different types of activists, their motivations, their operating models, and the economics that drive their decisions. Understanding who activists are – and what they actually want – is the first step toward engaging with them effectively.

# Chapter 3: Who Are the Activists? – Profiles, Motivations, and Operating Models

When I was preparing for the Flowers Foods tabletop simulation – building an activist campaign from scratch against a real public company – I made an assumption that many board directors share: I assumed that activist investors are essentially alike. They buy stock, they write demanding letters, they threaten proxy fights, and they try to make a quick profit. The specifics might vary, but the basic model was the same.

I was wrong. And that misunderstanding, had I carried it into an actual boardroom, would have led me to respond to every activist the same way – which is to say, badly.

Andrew Shapiro, during his keynote to our cohort, dismantled this assumption with characteristic directness. He laid out a taxonomy of activist investors that immediately clarified why the board's response must be calibrated to the type of activist it is facing. A governance reformer with a five-year time horizon requires a fundamentally different approach than a short-term operator looking to flip a position. An ESG advocate pushing for climate disclosure has different goals and different leverage points than an economic activist focused on capital allocation. And a greenmailer – yes, they still exist – requires a response that would be entirely inappropriate for a constructive engagement.

This chapter profiles the major categories of activist investors, examines the firms and individuals who dominate the landscape, and explores the economic model that drives their decisions. By the end, you should be able to identify what type of activist you are dealing with within the first few pages of their 13D filing – and begin calibrating your response accordingly.

# The Activist Taxonomy

## Economic Activists

Shapiro placed himself squarely in this category, and he defined it with precision: "I'm an economic activist. I'm here for stock price. I'm here for shareholder value."

Economic activists are focused on one thing: making money by improving the company. They believe – and they typically have the analysis to support this belief – that the target company is undervalued because of fixable problems. Those problems might be operational (poor capital allocation, bloated cost structure, underperforming divisions), governance-related (a captured board, an entrenched CEO, cronyism in the nominating process), or communicative (a management team that refuses to explain its strategy to investors).

What distinguishes economic activists from other categories is their time horizon and their theory of value creation. They are not looking to extract short-term profit through financial engineering. They are looking to unlock long-term value through governance improvements that they believe the current board is either unable or unwilling to make.

Economic activists typically hold their positions for years. They invest substantial resources in understanding the target company's business – often developing analysis that rivals or exceeds what the company's own strategic planning team produces. They prefer private engagement to public confrontation, because public fights are expensive, distracting, and uncertain. But they are willing to escalate to proxy fights when private engagement fails.

This is the category that represents the majority of activist campaigns today, and it is the category that most often produces positive outcomes for all shareholders – not just the activist.

## Social and ESG Activists

The environmental, social, and governance (ESG) activism movement has grown from a niche concern into a substantial force in corporate governance. These activists push companies to address climate risk, diversity and inclusion, human rights in supply chains, political spending disclosure, and a range of other social and environmental issues.

Engine No. 1's ExxonMobil campaign is the most prominent example, though it is worth noting that Engine No. 1 framed its argument primarily in economic terms – the failure to adapt to the energy transition was destroying shareholder value – rather than purely environmental ones. As You Sow, the Interfaith Center on Corporate Responsibility, and numerous other organizations file dozens of shareholder proposals each proxy season targeting ESG issues.

But the ESG activism landscape has become more complicated in recent years. Shapiro noted a development that many governance professionals have been slow to recognize: "There are now social impact activists who are anti-DEI and anti-ESG."

The anti-ESG backlash has produced its own activist movement. Organizations like the National Legal and Policy Center and Strive Asset Management – founded by Vivek Ramaswamy – have launched campaigns arguing that companies have become too focused on social and environmental issues at the expense of shareholder returns. Anti-ESG shareholder proposals have surged: the number roughly quadrupled between 2021 and 2024, reaching approximately 112 proposals in the 2024 proxy season.

Here is the critical nuance for directors: despite the surge in volume, anti-ESG proposals have garnered almost no shareholder support. Average support hovers around two to three percent, and no anti-ESG proposal in 2024 received more than ten percent of the vote. This tells us something important about the institutional investor base: while there is significant political and media attention on the ESG backlash, the shareholders who actually control voting power remain broadly supportive of – or at least indifferent to – ESG disclosure and governance practices.

For boards, the practical implication is that ESG-related activism, whether pro or anti, tends to be about disclosure and policy rather than fundamental governance reform.  It requires a different response toolkit than economic activism – one focused on communication, stakeholder engagement, and the substance of ESG practices rather than board composition or capital allocation.

## Hit-and-Run Activists

Every industry has its opportunists, and activist investing is no exception.

Hit-and-run activists are short-term operators who accumulate a position, make noise – typically by filing a 13D with aggressive demands and issuing a public letter – and then look to profit from the short-term stock price movement that their campaign generates. Their time horizon is measured in weeks or months, not years. Their analysis tends to be superficial compared to economic activists. And their demands often prioritize immediate value extraction – a special dividend, an accelerated share buyback, a quick sale of the company – over sustainable governance improvement.

The distinguishing feature of hit-and-run activists is their motivation: they are not trying to fix the company. They are trying to make a name for themselves so they can raise more capital for their fund. A successful campaign that generates headlines and a quick stock pop is, from their perspective, an excellent marketing event – regardless of whether it creates lasting value.

Boards facing hit-and-run activists have a different calculus than those facing economic activists. Because hit-and-run operators have short time horizons and limited analytical depth, their campaigns are often less credible with institutional investors. The appropriate response is typically to engage with the substance of their claims – addressing any legitimate points while demonstrating to the broader shareholder base that the board has a credible long-term strategy.

The danger comes when boards treat economic activists as hit-and-run operators.  A constructive activist with legitimate governance concerns who is dismissed as a short-term opportunist will escalate – and when they do, the board's refusal to engage becomes the central narrative of the campaign.

## Greenmailers

Greenmail – the practice of accumulating a threatening position and then selling it back to the company at a premium – was the defining tactic of the 1980s raiders. It is less common today, partly because of regulatory changes and partly because it has fallen out of favor with institutional investors who view it as value extraction from their pockets.

But the greenmail model has not entirely disappeared. It has evolved into more sophisticated forms. An activist might accumulate a position, push for a share buyback program that disproportionately benefits large holders, and then exit during the buyback. Or they might push for a strategic sale of the company, knowing that the acquisition premium will deliver a quick return regardless of whether the sale is in the long-term interests of other stakeholders.

The key to identifying greenmail-style behavior is the mismatch between the activist's demands and the company's long-term interests. An activist pushing for a sale of the company might be right – the company might genuinely be worth more as an acquisition target – or they might simply be engineering their own exit. The board's job is to evaluate the substance independent of the motivation.

## White Paper Activists

White paper activists arrive with a detailed business plan – often running to dozens or hundreds of pages – that lays out a specific operational or strategic vision for the company. These campaigns are the most analytically intensive form of activism, and they can be the most difficult for boards to dismiss, because the activist has done their homework.

The Flowers Foods tabletop exercise that I co-led gave me firsthand experience with the white paper approach. Our activist team produced a comprehensive corporate analysis, a detailed investor letter identifying specific operational and governance concerns, a full-length investor presentation, proposed director candidates with relevant industry experience, and a complete campaign website with FAQs and press materials. The volume and quality of material we produced – and we were a student team running a simulation – gave me a profound appreciation for what a well-resourced activist hedge fund can bring to bear against a target company.

For boards, white paper activists present both a challenge and an opportunity. The challenge is that their analysis may be more detailed and more current than the board's own strategic review. The opportunity is that a substantive, well-researched campaign can serve as a catalyst for improvements that the board should have been pursuing independently.

# The Major Firms: Profiles in Activism

## Elliott Management

If there is a single name that dominates modern shareholder activism, it is Elliott Management.

Founded by Paul Singer in 1977, Elliott has grown into a roughly $76 billion behemoth that wages fourteen to fifteen campaigns per year across multiple continents. Elliott's approach combines aggressive financial analysis with a willingness to deploy extraordinary resources – including litigation, public campaigns, and sustained multi-year engagements – to achieve its objectives.

Elliott's scale allows it to take positions that would be impossible for smaller funds. The firm's $5 billion-plus stake in Honeywell in late 2024 – which successfully pushed the industrial conglomerate to split into three independent companies – was among the largest individual activist positions in history. Its roughly $4 billion position in PepsiCo in 2025 was even more audacious, targeting one of the world's most iconic consumer brands.

Elliott's campaign against Southwest Airlines in 2024 illustrates the firm's approach. After building a $1.9 billion position, Elliott published a detailed analysis arguing that Southwest's leadership had failed to evolve the airline's business model. The campaign resulted in the resignation of the CEO, the CFO, and the chief administrative officer, along with the appointment of five new board members – a comprehensive leadership transformation driven by a single activist engagement.

What makes Elliott distinctive is not just its size but its breadth. The firm operates globally, waging campaigns in Europe, Asia, and Latin America as well as the United States. It is equally comfortable targeting $5 billion mid-caps and $250 billion mega-caps. And it has a reputation for tenacity – once Elliott commits to a campaign, it rarely backs down.

## Starboard Value

Jeff Smith's Starboard Value has earned a reputation as one of the most operationally focused activists in the market. Founded in 2011, Starboard manages approximately $9 billion in assets and takes a deeply analytical approach to identifying operational improvements at target companies.

Starboard's most famous campaign was its 2014 engagement with Darden Restaurants, the parent of Olive Garden and other casual dining chains. Smith and his team produced a 294-page presentation detailing operational failures at the company – a document that included the now-legendary analysis of Olive Garden's breadstick and salad policies. Starboard won a proxy fight and replaced the entire board, and Smith personally served as chairman. Darden's stock rose approximately sixty percent in the year following the activist's intervention.

What distinguishes Starboard from many other activists is Smith's willingness to take personal responsibility for the companies he targets. He has served on more than 17 corporate boards and chaired four – an unusual level of direct involvement that reflects his conviction that operational improvement requires hands-on oversight.

## Trian Partners

Nelson Peltz's Trian Partners occupies a unique position in the activist landscape. Founded in 2005, Trian manages approximately $6.2 billion and practices what might be called "operational activism" – a philosophy rooted in Peltz's fifty-plus years of experience running companies.

Before Peltz, most activists were financial engineers. They bought undervalued stocks, pushed for buybacks or dividends, and moved on. Peltz proved that operational expertise could create more sustainable value than financial manipulation. His campaigns at companies like Procter & Gamble – which at the time produced the most expensive proxy fight in corporate history, a record later surpassed by the Disney contest in 2024 – were grounded not in demands for financial engineering but in detailed prescriptions for operational improvement.

Peltz's approach reflects a distinctive theory of engagement: Trian takes large positions, works with management teams where possible, and pushes for changes that it believes will produce sustainable long-term value. The firm's patient, operational focus has earned it a degree of credibility with institutional investors that more aggressive activists sometimes lack.

## ValueAct Capital

ValueAct Capital represents the constructive end of the activist spectrum. The firm is known for taking positions and then working collaboratively with management – often from a board seat – rather than waging public campaigns. ValueAct's approach is quiet, long-term, and focused on strategic repositioning rather than financial engineering.

ValueAct posted strong returns of approximately twenty-one percent in 2024, underscoring the effectiveness of its collaborative model. The firm's success suggests that not all activism requires confrontation – and that some of the most effective governance improvements come from activists who bring expertise and perspective to the boardroom rather than ultimatums.

## Jana Partners

Jana Partners occupies a middle ground between aggressive and constructive activism. The firm has waged campaigns across multiple sectors and is known for combining financial analysis with operational prescriptions. Jana's campaigns tend to be well-researched and analytically rigorous, earning credibility with institutional investors who evaluate activist proposals on their merits.

## Ancora Holdings

Ancora Holdings represents the sector-specialist approach to activism. The firm has concentrated its campaigns in specific industries – most notably transportation – where it brings deep sector expertise and established relationships. Ancora's 2024 campaign against Norfolk Southern, which ultimately produced a CEO replacement, illustrates how sector-focused activists can leverage industry knowledge to build compelling cases for change.

# The Fall of an Icon: Carl Icahn

No chapter on activist investors would be complete without addressing the dramatic fall of Carl Icahn – the figure who, more than any other individual, defined shareholder activism for four decades.

In May 2023, Hindenburg Research – a short-selling firm specializing in exposing corporate fraud and mismanagement – published a report accusing Icahn Enterprises of operating a structure that masked years of poor performance. The impact was immediate and devastating. Icahn Enterprises' market capitalization collapsed by more than half – from approximately $18 billion to roughly $7 billion – as investors fled.

The SEC investigated and, in August 2024, reached a settlement with Icahn and Icahn Enterprises. The charges were not fraud – the SEC found no evidence of the most serious allegations in the Hindenburg report. Instead, the settlement addressed Icahn's failure to disclose that he had pledged between fifty-one and eighty-two percent of Icahn Enterprises' outstanding securities as collateral for personal margin loans – a disclosure violation dating back to at least 2005. The total settlement was $2 million: $500,000 from Icahn personally and $1.5 million from Icahn Enterprises.

Icahn characterized the settlement as vindication, noting that the SEC found no fraud and no inflation of asset values. And technically, he was right – the disclosure violations were regulatory, not substantive. But the reputational damage was profound. The man who had built his career holding boards accountable for governance failures had been caught failing to disclose fundamental information about his own financial arrangements.

The Icahn episode is instructive for several reasons. It demonstrates that activists themselves are not immune to the governance failures they attack. It shows the power of short-selling research firms as a check on activist funds – an ironic inversion of the traditional activism dynamic. And it serves as a reminder that the activist landscape is constantly evolving: the dominant figures of one era do not necessarily carry their credibility into the next.

# The Operating Model: How Activist Funds Work

Understanding the economic model of activist investing is essential for directors, because it explains both the incentives and the constraints that shape activist behavior.

## Fund Structure and Economics

Most activist funds are structured as limited partnerships, with the activist firm serving as general partner and outside investors – pension funds, endowments, family offices, and high-net-worth individuals – as limited partners. The standard fee structure is "2 and 20": a two percent annual management fee on assets under management, plus a twenty percent performance allocation (often called "carry") on investment profits above a hurdle rate.

This fee structure creates powerful incentives. The management fee provides a stable revenue base, but the real money is in the carry. An activist fund managing $5 billion that generates a twenty percent return in a year earns $200 million in performance fees – on top of $100 million in management fees. These economics attract talented analysts and investors, and they fund the extraordinary resources that large activist campaigns require.

## Campaign Economics

Running an activist campaign is expensive. The costs include legal fees (often millions of dollars), proxy solicitation expenses, public relations advisors, investment banking fees, printing and mailing costs for proxy materials, and the opportunity cost of dedicating senior professionals to a single engagement for months or years.

A major proxy fight can cost $10 million to $30 million or more. Even a campaign that resolves through settlement typically runs into the millions when legal, advisory, and research costs are included. These economics create a natural screen: activists are unlikely to target companies unless the potential upside significantly exceeds the campaign costs.

For a fund managing $5 billion, a $200 million position in a target company represents four percent of assets. If the activist believes the stock is thirty percent undervalued and that their campaign can close that gap, the potential profit on the position is $60 million – more than enough to justify campaign costs of $5 million to $15 million. This math explains why activists tend to concentrate on situations where the value gap is large and the governance failures are clear.

## The Incentive Alignment Question

One of the most important questions for directors evaluating an activist campaign is whether the activist's interests are aligned with those of other shareholders.

The answer is nuanced. On one hand, activists profit only if the stock price goes up – which means their financial interests are fundamentally aligned with those of other shareholders. An activist who destroys value while extracting fees would quickly lose investors and credibility.

On the other hand, time horizons may differ. An activist with a two-year investment horizon might push for changes that boost the stock price in the medium term but are not in the company's long-term interest – a leveraged recapitalization that increases near-term returns but saddles the company with debt, for example, or a sale of a division that produces a one-time gain but weakens the company's competitive position.

The most sophisticated boards evaluate not just *what* the activist is proposing but *when* they expect to realize their return. An activist willing to hold through a multi-year transformation is a fundamentally different counterparty than one looking to exit within six months.

## How Funds Raise Capital

Activist funds raise capital from institutional limited partners – pension funds, sovereign wealth funds, endowments, and family offices – who allocate a portion of their portfolios to alternative investments. The fundraising pitch is straightforward: activism generates returns that are uncorrelated with the broader market, because the value creation comes from governance changes rather than market movements.

The ability to raise capital is directly tied to the fund's track record. This creates a virtuous cycle for successful activists: strong returns attract more capital, which enables larger campaigns, which target larger companies, which generates higher returns. It also explains why first-time activists, despite their growing numbers, typically start with smaller targets – they need to build a track record before they can attract the capital required for mega-cap campaigns.

# Reading the 13D: Identifying What You Are Dealing With

When a 13D lands on the board's table, the first analytical task is to determine what type of activist you are facing. The filing itself provides critical clues.

**Item 4 – Purpose of Transaction** is the most important section. An economic activist will typically describe specific governance, strategic, or capital allocation concerns and propose concrete changes. A hit-and-run operator will use more generic language about "enhancing shareholder value" without much analytical depth. A white paper activist will attach extensive exhibits detailing their analysis.

**The exhibits** – letters to the board, investor presentations, analysis documents – reveal the quality and depth of the activist's work. Detailed, company-specific analysis suggests a serious, well-resourced engagement. Generic demands suggest a less substantive campaign.

**The ownership level** matters. A five percent position indicates minimum disclosure-triggered reporting. A ten to fifteen percent position indicates significant commitment and resources. Elliott's multi-billion-dollar positions signal a level of conviction and staying power that demands a different response than a fund that barely cleared the five percent threshold.

**The fund's track record** is publicly available. Has this activist waged successful campaigns before? What were the outcomes? Did they hold through settlements, or did they exit quickly? A director who invests an hour researching the activist's history will be far better prepared than one who reacts to the filing in isolation.

Understanding who is on the other side of the table is the first step toward an effective response. The chapters that follow will examine what these activists look for when they screen for targets – and how you can see your own company through their eyes before they do.

# Chapter 4: What Activists Look For – The Four Improvable Problems

In the fall of 2025, my team sat in a conference room with financial statements spread across every surface – annual reports, proxy filings, earnings transcripts, peer comparison spreadsheets, and analyst reports. We were eight weeks into the Flowers Foods tabletop simulation, and our job as the activist investor team was to answer a single question: Where is this company's underperformance improvable?

Not just where is the company underperforming – that was the easy part. Any analyst with access to a Bloomberg terminal can identify a stock that trails its peers. The harder question, and the one that separates serious activists from noise, is whether the underperformance stems from problems that a different board or a different strategy could actually fix.

Andrew Shapiro distilled this diagnostic framework with the clarity of someone who has spent three decades applying it to real companies with real moncy at stake: "What we look for is where underperformance is improvable. The focus is on determining the problem. And these four problems are not mutually exclusive, but they're four different types of problems and they're all improvable."

That formulation is the activist's entire research methodology. Everything else – the financial screens, the governance analysis, the peer benchmarking, the proxy statement review – is in service of answering that one question: which of these four problems is present, and can a different board or strategy fix it? These are not academic abstractions. They are the lens through which every serious activist evaluates every potential target.

# Problem 1: Low Return on Assets

The first problem an activist looks for lives on the left-hand side of the balance sheet. It is a problem of assets – what the company owns and how productively those assets are being deployed.

A company with a low return on assets is one that has more resources than it is effectively using. The symptoms are varied but recognizable: excess cash sitting on the balance sheet earning minimal returns, money-losing divisions that persist year after year without a credible turnaround plan, real estate holdings that are underutilized or unrelated to the core business, or investment portfolios that generate returns well below the company's cost of capital.

Consider the cash question. When a company accumulates cash far beyond what is needed for operations, investment, and a reasonable strategic reserve, every dollar sitting idle is a dollar that is earning less than shareholders could earn by deploying it elsewhere. The activist looks at that cash pile and sees a quantifiable value gap. If the company has $3 billion in excess cash and is earning one percent on it while the cost of equity is ten percent, the opportunity cost to shareholders is enormous – and fixable.

Money-losing divisions present a similar logic. Every company has businesses that underperform, but disciplined boards force management to confront the question: is this division worth more to us than it would be to someone else? A division losing $50 million a year might have significant value to an acquirer who can integrate it into a larger platform or restructure its cost base. The activist sees that $50 million annual drain and asks: why is the board allowing this to continue?

Fallow real estate is another variant. Companies that have accumulated properties over decades – manufacturing facilities, office buildings, distribution centers, retail locations – may be sitting on assets whose market value far exceeds their value to the business. The activist identifies these assets, estimates their realizable value, and argues that selling, leasing, or otherwise monetizing them would create more shareholder value than continuing to hold them.

The fix for low return on assets is operational: sell, restructure, or redeploy. Divest underperforming divisions. Monetize non-core real estate. Return excess cash to shareholders through dividends or buybacks. Each of these actions is within the board's authority and can typically be executed within a reasonable timeframe – which is precisely why activists target this problem. It is improvable, and the timeline to improvement is measurable.

When we analyzed Flowers Foods through this lens, we asked straightforward questions: Are there asset categories – brands, facilities, distribution networks – that are generating returns below the cost of capital? Is there excess cash or underutilized capacity? Are there businesses within the portfolio that would be worth more to a different owner?

Roosevelt Giles offered a provocative observation about how companies sometimes use capital returns to mask asset productivity problems: "I think that they have been paying that dividend to deflect the operational aspects of the company. So they should not be paying the dividend. But I think that is air cover not to look at the operation, not to look at the composition of the board and management." In other words, a generous dividend can function as a governance smokescreen – keeping shareholders content enough to stop asking uncomfortable questions about asset returns. The answers to these questions form the foundation of the activist's investment thesis on asset productivity.

# Problem 2: Low Return on Equity with Adequate Return on Assets

The second problem is subtler, and boards that do not understand it often find themselves blindsided by activists who do.

A company can have an adequate return on assets – its operations are reasonably productive, its divisions are generating acceptable returns on the capital invested in them – and still have a low return on equity. When this happens, the problem is not on the left-hand side of the balance sheet. It is on the right-hand side. It is a capital structure problem.

Return on equity is a function of profit margin, asset turnover, and financial leverage. If a company's margins and asset utilization are competitive with peers but its return on equity lags, the most likely culprit is leverage – specifically, too little of it. This may seem counterintuitive – most governance discussions emphasize the dangers of excessive debt. But under-leverage is also a governance failure, because it means the company is not optimizing its cost of capital. A company with competitive operating returns but no debt is leaving shareholder value on the table – the same profits spread across a smaller equity base (after prudent borrowing and buybacks) would generate higher returns for every remaining shareholder.

Activists look at this gap between return on assets and return on equity and see an optimization opportunity. The fix is financial: share repurchases, special dividends, or a recapitalization that moves the company toward a more efficient capital structure. These are not radical proposals – they are the tools of standard corporate finance – but they require boards to think about capital structure as an active governance decision rather than something that management handles.

The most sophisticated activists will present detailed capital structure analyses comparing the target company to its peers. If the peer group averages a debt-to-equity ratio of 0.8 and the target company is at 0.2, the activist has a clear and quantifiable argument that the company's shareholders are being penalized by an overly conservative financial policy.

Boards encountering this argument need to understand it well enough to respond substantively. Simply asserting that a conservative balance sheet provides "strategic flexibility" is insufficient if the company has not articulated what that flexibility is needed for. An activist will immediately ask: What acquisition are you planning? What investment requires this level of dry powder? If the answer is "nothing specific," the activist's case for returning capital to shareholders becomes very difficult to rebut.

The fundamental question an activist is asking with this analysis is deceptively simple: how is this company deploying its equity, and is it generating an adequate return on that deployment? Equity is not free capital – it is the most expensive capital a company has, because shareholders bear the residual risk and expect returns that compensate them for it. When a company sits on a large equity base without putting it to productive use, it is effectively asking shareholders to accept lower returns than they could earn elsewhere. The activist's proposed remedies – leveraged recapitalizations, accelerated buyback programs, special dividends – are all mechanisms for right-sizing the equity base to match the company's actual capital needs. A company that needs $2 billion in equity to run its operations but carries $4 billion is asking shareholders to fund $2 billion in idle capital at the cost of equity, which might be 10 or 12 percent. That $2 billion returned to shareholders through buybacks does two things simultaneously: it increases earnings per share for remaining shareholders by reducing the share count, and it increases return on equity by shrinking the denominator. The math is straightforward, which is why this is one of the activist's most powerful arguments – it is difficult to dispute with anything other than a specific, credible plan for deploying the excess capital at returns that exceed the cost of equity. Boards that cannot articulate such a plan are, in the activist's framing, destroying shareholder value through inaction.

# Problem 3: Governance and Management Problems

The third problem moves from the financial to the institutional. When an activist identifies governance and management problems as the primary source of underperformance, they are saying something that boards rarely want to hear: the board itself is the problem.

This is the most confrontational of the four categories, because it challenges not just the company's strategy or financial structure but the competence and independence of the people in the boardroom. And yet, it is frequently the most important problem – because governance failures are often the root cause of the other three.

A company with a captured board – one that has been co-opted by the CEO, populated with friends and associates, and insulated from shareholder accountability – is a company that is unlikely to make the difficult decisions that create shareholder value. It will not divest underperforming divisions because the CEO does not want to manage a smaller company. It will not optimize the capital structure because management prefers the comfort of excess cash. It will not communicate transparently because that would invite the scrutiny that entrenchment is designed to avoid.

Activists screen for governance problems using publicly available data, primarily from the proxy statement. The signals they look for include:

**Board composition.** Are the directors genuinely independent, or do they have material relationships with the CEO or the company? How were they recruited? Did they come through a rigorous nominating process that assessed skills and capabilities, or were they selected by the CEO from a network of personal and professional connections?

**Director tenure.** Long-tenured directors are not inherently problematic, but boards where the average tenure exceeds ten or twelve years without meaningful refreshment raise questions about whether the directors have maintained their independence or have become part of the management establishment.

**CEO-Chair duality.** When the CEO also serves as board chair, the board's ability to provide independent oversight is structurally compromised. An effective lead independent director can mitigate this concern, but many boards treat the lead director role as ceremonial rather than substantive.

**Committee composition and activity.** Are the audit, compensation, and nominating committees staffed with genuinely independent directors who have the expertise to provide effective oversight? How often do they meet? What do their reports say?

**Executive compensation.** Does the compensation structure align management incentives with shareholder interests? Or does it reward management regardless of performance – through guaranteed bonuses, excessively generous change-of-control provisions, or metrics that management can game?

Shapiro described his role in addressing governance problems with the directness of someone who has spent decades doing it: "I am the independent director's friend as an activist. I am the nemesis of co-conspirators and co-opted directors of the Imperial CEO – and the Imperial CEO."

The fix for governance problems is board change. Replace directors who are captured, disengaged, or conflicted with independent directors who bring relevant expertise and an investor mindset. And the fix, while conceptually simple, is the most difficult to implement – because the people who need to be replaced are the people who control the process.

This is precisely why activism exists. When the internal governance mechanisms fail – when the nominating committee does not refresh the board, when the lead director does not challenge the CEO, when compensation is not tied to performance – the external mechanism of shareholder activism provides the accountability that the board was supposed to deliver.

# Problem 4: Transparency and Communication Failures

The fourth problem is, in some ways, the most avoidable – and the most frequently committed.

A company that is not communicating its strategy, its progress, and its response to challenges to its investor base is a company that is inviting activist attention. When investors cannot see the value that management claims exists, they have two choices: take management's word for it, or assume the worst. Activists, by nature and by profession, assume the worst.

Shapiro was emphatic on this point: "If you do that, I can only think the worst. I'm not going to imagine the best. So if I only think the worst, I'm more likely to escalate."

The "bunker mentality" – reducing disclosure, becoming less transparent, refusing to engage with shareholders who ask difficult questions – is the surest way to escalate an activist's concerns from curiosity to campaign. It signals either that management has something to

hide or that it is too arrogant to believe it owes shareholders an explanation. Either interpretation is damaging.

The transparency problem manifests in several ways:

**Inadequate strategic disclosure.** The company has a strategy,
but it has not communicated it in sufficient detail for investors to
evaluate whether it is working. Earnings calls consist of scripted
remarks and carefully managed Q&A sessions that avoid difficult
questions. The proxy statement provides boilerplate governance language without substantive explanation of board decisions.

**Refusal to engage with shareholders.** The company declines
meeting requests from significant shareholders, limits investor
access to management, and treats shareholder questions at annual
meetings as nuisances to be managed rather than information to be
considered.

**Opaque capital allocation.** The company makes significant
investment decisions – acquisitions, capital expenditure programs,
new business initiatives – without clearly explaining the expected
returns or the strategic rationale. When the investments underperform, management provides vague assurances rather than honest
assessments.

**Defensive posture.** When analysts or shareholders raise concerns, the company's response is defensive rather than substantive.
Management dismisses criticism rather than engaging with it. The
board is shielded from direct shareholder communication by layers
of investor relations and legal protocol.

The fix for transparency problems is the most straightforward of the
four: communicate. Engage with shareholders. Explain your strategy. Articulate your capital allocation framework. Acknowledge
challenges honestly and describe what you are doing to address
them. Listen to criticism rather than dismissing it.

This is not a difficult prescription, but it requires something that
many management teams and boards find genuinely uncomfortable:
vulnerability. Transparent communication means admitting that
not everything is going well, that some investments have not panned
out, that the competitive landscape has shifted in ways that require
a strategic response. Management teams that equate transparency

with weakness will resist it – and in doing so, they will create exactly
the opacity that activists exploit.

# The "Bad Boards" Framework: The Range of Culpability

One of the most valuable conceptual tools that Shapiro offered during his keynote was his framework for understanding board dysfunction. Rather than the simplistic binary of "good boards" and "bad boards," Shapiro described a spectrum – what he calls the "range of culpability."

"A bad board is not composed of 100 percent bad board members," Shapiro explained. "And a board member, it's not black and white. It's not a bright line. You're a bad board member or you're a good board member. The issue is a range. I call it the range of culpability."

This framework positions directors on a continuum based on their awareness of governance failures and their role in perpetuating them.

## Disengaged Directors

At the least culpable end of the spectrum are directors who have simply checked out. They may be overboarded – serving on so many boards that they cannot give adequate attention to any one. They may be first-time directors who were never properly onboarded and genuinely do not understand what effective oversight looks like. They may have been diligent when first appointed but have become complacent over years of unchallenging service.

The critical insight about disengaged directors is that they are reachable. They are not actively participating in governance failures – they are simply absent. And absence, while harmful, can be cured.

Shapiro described what happens when an activist appears at a company with disengaged directors: "When you file a 13D and you write a letter to the board, those who were asleep wake up pretty damn fast." The filing of a 13D is, for a disengaged director, a wake-up call. Suddenly, the consequences of inattention become concrete: reputational risk, personal liability, the possibility of being voted out by shareholders. Directors who were coasting realize that someone is watching – and many of them respond by doing the work they should have been doing all along.

This is the subatomic particle effect in its purest form. The disengaged director's behavior changes not because the activist applies force, but because the activist's observation makes the consequences of continued disengagement impossible to ignore.

## Co-opted Directors

Moving along the spectrum, co-opted directors present a more difficult challenge. These are not directors who are unaware of governance failures. They know what is right. They understand their fiduciary duties. They can see the problems that an activist would identify. But they have been captured – by their relationship with the CEO, by the financial benefits of board service, by the social dynamics of the boardroom, or by some combination of all three.

A co-opted director might have been recruited by the CEO personally – chosen not for their skills and independent judgment but for their willingness to go along. They might depend on the board fee as a material portion of their income, creating an economic incentive to avoid rocking the boat. They might simply prefer the collegial atmosphere of a board that does not challenge management, finding it more comfortable than the confrontation that effective oversight sometimes requires.

Shapiro's prescription for co-opted directors was characteristically blunt: they do not need education – "they just need to be shown that there's a sword out there and it's going to go into their heart if they don't do what's right and they know what's right." The activist's role with co-opted directors is not to teach them what good governance looks like. It is to demonstrate that the consequences of continued complicity are worse than the discomfort of doing their jobs.

This is why activist campaigns so often focus on individual directors rather than the board as a whole. The activist is not trying to replace everyone – they are trying to shift the balance of power on the board by removing the most captured directors and replacing them with genuinely independent ones. When the co-opted directors see their most compromised colleagues being voted out, the incentive structure changes: going along with the CEO is no longer the safe option.

## Self-Dealing and Complicit Directors

At the far end of the spectrum are directors who are not merely passive or captured but who actively participate in governance failures. These directors benefit personally from the status quo – through related-party transactions, excessive compensation arrangements, or the preservation of a power structure that serves their interests at the expense of shareholders.

Self-dealing directors are the activist's primary targets, because they will not reform voluntarily. No amount of engagement, no number of shareholder letters, no quiet diplomatic pressure will change the behavior of a director who is profiting from the governance failures that the activist has identified. The only remedy is replacement – and that means a proxy fight or a settlement that includes their departure.

For directors reading this book, the range of culpability framework demands honest self-assessment. Where do you fall on the spectrum? Are you genuinely independent, or have you been co-opted by comfort, compensation, or relationship? Would your contributions to the board withstand scrutiny from a sophisticated activist with access to your attendance records, your voting history, your committee work, and your financial relationships with the company?

These are uncomfortable questions. They are also the questions that activists ask before filing a 13D.

# Seeing Your Company Through the Activist's Lens

When we ran Flowers Foods through these screens during our tabletop simulation, the findings were sobering – and they illustrate exactly how this framework works in practice.

Our team identified a consumer packaged goods company with fresh bread consumption declining, GLP-1 drug adoption threatening further erosion, and a net margin of 4.9 percent that provided mini-

mal buffer. We found recent acquisitions – Papa Pita and other spe-
cialty brands – that had not been fully integrated, and $1.5 billion
in debt limits constraining financial flexibility. Roosevelt Giles, our
program leader, was blunt in his assessment: "One of the issues that
Flowers Foods have is on the capital allocation. That's where they
will get dinged on."

But it was the governance analysis that produced the most striking
moment. Abby, one of my cohort members serving on the board
defense team, was trying to reconcile the company's reported margins with its actual financial statements – and couldn't. "I'm struggling to understand how they're coming up with the margins that
they quote," she said, "because from their cash flow and their income
statement, if you divide one number by the other, I'm not getting the
same percentages they get." Giles paused. "That's a great observation," he said. Here was a member of the defense team – the people
assigned to protect the company – who couldn't find evidence to support management's own numbers.

Even more telling was Abby's broader conclusion: "If they have a
secret sauce on how they're going to transform the company, they've
talked about transformation in one of the meetings publicly, but it's
not obvious to me from all the studying that I have done how this
company is going to be transformed... it feels like they've painted
themselves into a corner."

When even the board's defenders cannot articulate the strategy, the
transparency problem is real.

The self-assessment framework that follows is not theoretical. It is
the analytical process that activists use to evaluate potential targets
– and it is what we applied to Flowers Foods. Every director should
conduct this assessment annually – not because an activist might be
coming, but because the discipline of conducting it is the discipline
of effective governance.

## Financial Screens

**Total shareholder return (TSR) vs. peers.** Compare your
company's one-year, three-year, and five-year TSR against your
disclosed peer group. If you are underperforming on all three time
horizons, you are generating the most visible signal that activists

screen for. If you are underperforming on the three-year and five-year but outperforming on the one-year, the improvement trend may be enough to deter a campaign – but only if you are communicating that trajectory effectively.

**Return on assets (ROA) vs. industry.** Are your assets generating returns that are competitive with peers? If your ROA is in the bottom quartile, an activist will immediately begin examining your asset base for the problems described in Problem 1 – excess cash, money-losing divisions, underutilized real estate.

**Return on equity (ROE) vs. industry.** Compare your ROE to peers, and if it lags, decompose it using the DuPont analysis (margin, turnover, leverage) to identify the specific driver of underperformance. If the problem is leverage – if your ROA is competitive but your ROE is not – an activist will focus on your capital structure.

**Capital allocation track record.** How has the company deployed capital over the past five years? What was the return on acquisitions? On capital expenditure programs? On R&D? A track record of value-destroying acquisitions or capital spending that does not generate adequate returns is a bright red flag.

## Governance Screens

**Board independence.** Calculate true independence – not just technical compliance with listing standards, but substantive independence. How many directors were recruited by the CEO? How many have material financial relationships with the company beyond their board fees? How many have served for more than 10 years?

**CEO-Chair separation.** If the CEO and Chair roles are combined, how effective is the lead independent director? Does the lead director control the board agenda, lead executive sessions, and serve as a genuine counterweight to management?

**Director tenure analysis.** Map the tenure of every director. If the average tenure exceeds ten years and there has been no meaningful refreshment in the past three to five years, the board may appear stale and insular to outside observers.

**Compensation alignment.** Does the executive compensation

structure tie a meaningful portion of pay to long-term shareholder returns?  Or does it provide generous payouts regardless of performance?  Activists scrutinize compensation structures for evidence that management is being rewarded for showing up rather than for creating value.

## Communication Assessment

**Investor engagement quality.**  Does the company hold regular investor days?  Do independent directors participate in shareholder meetings?   Does management engage substantively with shareholder concerns, or does it manage communications to minimize accountability?

**Proxy statement quality.**  Is the proxy statement a substantive governance document, or is it boilerplate?   Does it explain the board's reasoning on key governance decisions – board composition, CEO compensation, strategic direction – or does it simply comply with minimum disclosure requirements?

**Analyst and shareholder sentiment.**  What are sell-side analysts saying about the company's governance and strategy?  What questions are shareholders asking?  Are there shareholder proposals receiving significant support that the board has not addressed?

# The Activist's Decision Point

After conducting this analysis, the activist arrives at a decision point: is the underperformance improvable, and is the board likely to make the improvements voluntarily?

If the answer to both questions is yes – the problems are fixable, and the board appears willing and able to fix them – the activist may decide that the investment is not worth the campaign costs. The board is doing its job, and the market will eventually recognize the improvements.

If the underperformance is improvable but the board is unlikely to act – because it is captured, disengaged, or entrenched – then the activist has identified a target. The value gap between where the company is and where it could be, combined with the governance failure that prevents the company from closing that gap on its own, creates the economic justification for a campaign.

For directors, the question is not whether to fear this process but whether to embrace it. Every element of the activist's analytical framework – the financial screens, the governance assessment, the communication evaluation – is something that effective boards should be doing themselves. The boards that conduct rigorous, honest self-assessments are the boards that close the value gaps before an activist identifies them. The boards that do not are the boards that learn about their vulnerabilities from a 13D filing.

Shapiro captured this principle with a question that every director should ask at least once a year: "Good boards take action. Are they taking actions to deal with it, and are they articulating and communicating that they're taking actions to deal with it?"

If the answer is yes, you have built the first line of defense against activism – not a wall, but a practice. If the answer is no, then the four improvable problems are not just an analytical framework for activists. They are a to-do list for your board.

In Part II, we will step inside the activist's campaign and follow the process from target selection through proxy fight – the complete playbook that activists use to turn analysis into action.

# Chapter 5: Target Selection and Research – How Activists Choose Their Battles

During our activist investor tabletop exercise, Andrew Shapiro cut through the abstractions with a question that reframed everything our team thought we knew about campaign strategy. We had been debating which financial metrics to emphasize in our presentation – return on assets, total shareholder return, EBITDA margins – when Shapiro redirected us to what actually matters. "The most important thing on Flowers Foods if it's at risk: share ownership – the voting composition of the shares and its valuation. Then you're looking at how soon could a majority of the board be turned over?"

That single comment crystallized months of analysis into a two-part test. Can you win? And can you win fast enough to make the investment worthwhile?

Every activist campaign begins long before the first public filing, the first letter to the board, or the first call to a proxy solicitor. It begins with research – methodical, data-driven, ruthlessly honest research that answers a deceptively simple question: is this company's underperformance fixable, and can I be the one to fix it?

This chapter walks through the activist's target selection process from the inside. Understanding how activists choose their battles is not just useful for aspiring activists. It is essential intelligence for any director or executive who wants to see their company through an activist's eyes – and address vulnerabilities before someone else exploits them.

## The Financial Screen: Where Underperformance Becomes Opportunity

The starting point for every activist campaign is financial underperformance. Not underperformance in the abstract – specific, measurable, peer-relative underperformance that can be documented with publicly available data and presented to institutional investors in a way that demands action.

Here's the reality: activists are not looking for companies that are merely struggling. They are looking for companies that are struggling unnecessarily – companies where the gap between actual performance and achievable performance represents a concrete, quantifiable opportunity to create shareholder value.

The financial screen typically begins with total shareholder return. An activist will compare the target's stock price performance against its disclosed peer group over one-year, three-year, and five-year periods. A company that has underperformed its peers by twenty or thirty percent over three years is not just a statistical curiosity. It is a data point that will appear on the first slide of the activist's investor presentation, rendered in bold red numbers against the peer group's green.

But stock price alone is a symptom. The diagnostic work goes deeper.

The diagnostic metrics should be familiar from the framework discussion in Chapter 4 – **return on assets**, **return on equity**, **capital allocation history**, and **revenue and volume trends** – but the activist applies them with a specificity that most boards never match. In our Flowers Foods analysis, the company's EBITDA margins of 10.6% against a peer average of 14-15% represented what our team calculated as $80-120 million in annual improvement opportunity. That kind of margin gap does not go unnoticed by professional activists who screen hundreds of companies per year.

*Author's note: The financial data and campaign scenarios pre-*

*sented in this chapter and throughout the Flowers Foods tabletop exercise sections of this book were developed as part of the SLGI Board Readiness Program simulation. While the exercise used Flowers Foods as a real, publicly traded company and drew on its actual SEC filings for the foundational analysis, the specific campaign assumptions – including share prices, target valuations, and certain margin calculations – reflect the scenario parameters established for the educational exercise. Readers should not interpret these figures as current investment recommendations or as a commentary on Flowers Foods' present financial condition.*

The capital allocation story was even more damning. Our activist team built an entire section of the campaign around the company's $795 million acquisition of Simple Mills – a deal that was EPS-dilutive, increased leverage to 3.5x at precisely the wrong time, and came when the core business was already declining. The narrative writes itself: management made the largest acquisition in company history while the foundation was cracking.

Revenue and volume trends completed the picture – declining volumes masked by price increases, a dividend payout ratio that exceeded free cash flow, and guidance cuts that eroded management credibility. Each data point became a chapter in the story our team would tell institutional shareholders.

The financial screen is not complicated. It does not require proprietary data or sophisticated modeling. Everything an activist needs is available in the company's own SEC filings – 10-K annual reports, 10-Q quarterly reports, and earnings releases. The question is not whether the data is accessible. It is whether anyone is looking at it honestly.

# The Governance Screen: Structural Vulnerability

Financial underperformance gets the activist's attention. Governance structure determines whether a campaign is feasible.

An activist investor conducting a governance screen is asking a specific set of tactical questions: How quickly can I change the composition of this board? What structural barriers exist? And how will the company's governance profile look to institutional investors and proxy advisory firms when they evaluate my campaign?

**Board election structure** is the first checkpoint. A company with annual elections for all directors gives an activist the opportunity to replace a majority of the board in a single annual meeting cycle. A staggered board – where directors serve three-year terms and only one-third of seats are up for election each year – forces the activist to win at two consecutive annual meetings to gain majority control. That is a fundamentally different campaign calculus. Shapiro noted the paradox that staggered boards remain surprisingly common despite being viewed as poor governance by most institutional investors.

**Advance notice bylaws** determine whether the activist can even get on the ballot. These provisions require that director nominations be submitted months before the annual meeting, typically sixty to ninety days in advance – and some companies draft their provisions to be genuinely punitive. The mechanics and legal challenges around advance notice provisions are examined in detail in Chapters 9 and 10. For now, the key point is this: for an activist, reading the fine print of a target's bylaws is not a legal formality. It is a campaign-critical assessment.

**Combined CEO/Chairman roles** signal potential board capture – a single individual who controls both the management agenda and the governance agenda. An activist will argue that the lack of an independent board chair means the board is not providing genuine oversight but rather ratifying management decisions. In our Flowers Foods analysis, the combined CEO/Chairman role of A. Ryals Mc-Mullian – a seventy-seven-year-old director with twenty-one years of tenure – became a centerpiece of the governance critique. The optics alone were powerful: two decades of entrenchment while shareholder value eroded.

**Director tenure and qualifications** undergo granular examination. The activist is looking for directors who have served so long that their independence is questionable – regardless of what the proxy statement's independence standards say. They are looking for directors who sit on too many boards (overboarded directors who cannot give adequate attention to any single company). They are looking for directors whose professional backgrounds have no obvious relevance to the company's strategic challenges. Each of these findings becomes a data point supporting the argument that the board needs refreshment.

**Dual-class share structures** can make a campaign mathematically impossible. When founders or insiders hold super-voting shares that give them majority voting control regardless of their economic ownership, the activist's path to board change is effectively blocked. If the governance screen reveals dual-class control, most activists walk away. The math simply does not work.

# Ownership Analysis: Reading the Shareholder Register

A governance campaign is ultimately a voting contest. The activist needs to understand who owns the shares and how they are likely to vote.

The primary tool for this analysis is the company's proxy statement (DEF 14A), which discloses institutional ownership, insider holdings, and the results of recent shareholder votes. The activist supplements this with 13F filings – quarterly reports filed by institutional investors managing more than $100 million – to build a detailed picture of the shareholder base.

The critical question is deceptively simple: how will the top five shareholders vote?

In a typical public company, the five largest institutional shareholders collectively own thirty to fifty percent of the outstanding shares. If the activist can persuade even a fraction of these holders to support the campaign, the outcome is largely determined. BlackRock, Vanguard, and State Street – the three largest asset managers in the world – maintain investment stewardship teams that independently evaluate governance at the companies they own. These teams have published voting guidelines, and they take governance seriously. An activist who understands these guidelines can tailor a campaign to align with the criteria these stewardship teams use to make voting decisions.

Insider ownership presents a different challenge. A company where management and the board collectively own twenty percent or more of the shares is significantly harder to campaign against. Those insider shares will almost certainly vote with management, which means the activist needs to win a higher percentage of the institutional vote to prevail. Conversely, a company with minimal insider ownership – which describes most large-cap public companies – is more accessible to an activist campaign because the vote is determined entirely by external shareholders.

The ownership analysis also reveals potential allies. Are there other institutional investors who have been vocal about governance concerns? Have any large holders filed 13D or 13G filings that might signal activist intent? Have mutual funds or pension funds with strong governance mandates increased their positions recently? The activist is not just counting votes. They are identifying potential coalition partners.

Recent voting results provide another crucial signal. If thirty percent or more of shares were voted against a management say-on-pay proposal, that tells the activist something important about investor sentiment. If a shareholder proposal on governance reform received forty percent support despite management opposition, that suggests a receptive shareholder base. These voting patterns are publicly disclosed in the company's 8-K filing after each annual meeting, and they are some of the most valuable intelligence an activist can gather.

# Defensibility Analysis: Mapping the Obstacles

Before committing capital and reputation to a campaign, a sophisticated activist maps every structural defense the target company has in place.

**Shareholder rights plans** – poison pills – are designed to prevent hostile acquisitions by diluting any investor who crosses a specified ownership threshold, typically ten to twenty percent. While poison pills are not specifically designed to prevent governance-focused activist campaigns, they do cap the size of the activist's position and limit their ability to accumulate shares quickly. Delaware courts have upheld poison pills when adopted for legitimate corporate purposes, but they have also imposed limits on their duration and scope. An activist evaluating a company with a poison pill in place will factor the ownership cap into their position-sizing and campaign strategy.

**Supermajority voting requirements** can make certain governance changes prohibitively difficult. If the company's charter requires a seventy-five percent vote to amend bylaws or remove directors, the activist faces a much higher bar than a simple majority. These provisions are increasingly viewed as entrenchment mechanisms by proxy advisory firms, but they remain effective as defensive tools.

**Forum selection provisions** that require governance litigation to be filed in a specific jurisdiction – typically Delaware – affect the activist's legal options. While Delaware's courts are experienced and efficient in governance disputes, the forum selection clause removes the option of filing in a potentially more favorable jurisdiction.

The defensibility analysis is not a binary assessment. It is a map of the terrain the activist will need to navigate. A company with annual elections, no poison pill, and a dispersed shareholder base presents a very different campaign landscape than a company with a classified board, a rights plan, and concentrated insider ownership. The activist's strategy – how much capital to deploy, what timeline to plan for, what demands to make – flows directly from this analysis.

# Building the Investment Thesis

The investment thesis is where all the research converges into a single, compelling narrative: here is what is wrong, here is how to fix it, and here is what the stock is worth when the problems are addressed.

A well-constructed activist investment thesis has several essential elements.

**The diagnosis** must be specific and data-driven. Not "the company is underperforming" but "the company's EBITDA margins trail peer average by 350-400 basis points, representing $180-200 million in annual opportunity." Not "governance is weak" but "three of eight directors have served more than fifteen years, the CEO also serves as Chairman, and CEO compensation increased twenty-five percent while the stock declined forty-five percent." The diagnosis must be built entirely on publicly verifiable data – SEC filings, earnings reports, proxy statements – because institutional investors will check every claim.

**The prescription** must be actionable and specific. Separate the CEO and Chairman roles. Replace three identified directors with independent candidates who bring turnaround and digital expertise. Conduct a strategic review of the portfolio. Implement a capital return program. Reduce operating costs by $80-120 million through identified initiatives. Each recommendation must connect directly to the diagnosis – this is the problem, and this is the specific action that addresses it.

**The valuation** must show what success looks like in financial terms. In our Flowers Foods exercise, the activist team's investment thesis projected that the stock could reach $22-25 per share within twenty-four months – representing seventy to ninety percent upside from the campaign's launch price of approximately $13. That valuation was built on specific assumptions: margin improvement to peer levels, portfolio optimization, disciplined capital allocation. The upside case gives institutional investors a reason to support the campaign beyond governance principles – it gives them a financial incentive.

**The catalyst** must explain what will trigger the value creation. Without a catalyst, the thesis is just an observation about underperformance. The catalyst might be a strategic review that leads to asset sales. It might be a management change that brings operational discipline. It might be a recapitalization that optimizes the balance sheet. The activist must articulate not just what should change but what specific action will cause the stock to rerate.

# The Go/No-Go Decision

Not every campaign proceeds. The research phase often reveals that a target is less attractive than initial screening suggested – or that the obstacles to success are too formidable to justify the cost and risk.

The go/no-go decision is one of the most disciplined moments in the activist's process. It requires honest assessment of several factors: Is the financial upside large enough to justify the campaign costs? Is the governance thesis strong enough to win institutional support? Is the shareholder base receptive? Can the campaign be won within a reasonable timeline?

Starboard Value's experience with Pfizer illustrates this discipline. Starboard took a significant position in Pfizer in late 2024 and began pushing for operational improvements. But as Pfizer's financial performance improved through 2025 – partly driven by the attention Starboard's involvement generated – the improvement destroyed Starboard's own thesis. The company was no longer underperforming badly enough to justify an aggressive campaign. Starboard exited its position entirely. This is the sign of a disciplined activist: the willingness to walk away when the facts no longer support the thesis, even after significant capital has been invested in research and position-building.

Other factors can trigger a no-go decision. Concentrated insider ownership that makes the vote unwinnable. A classified board that extends the campaign timeline beyond what investors will tolerate. Defensive provisions that give the company too many tools to delay and deflect. A shareholder base that is too passive or too aligned with management. An industry environment that makes it difficult to find qualified independent director candidates.

The question is not whether the company has problems – most do. The question is whether those problems are fixable through the mechanisms available to an activist investor, within a timeline and at a cost that makes the campaign a sound investment.

## Seeing Your Company Through Activist Eyes

Here is the uncomfortable truth that every director and executive needs to internalize: everything described in this chapter uses publicly available information. The financial data comes from your own SEC filings. The governance analysis comes from your own proxy statement. The ownership data comes from 13F filings and voting results you are required to disclose.

An activist is not working with secret intelligence. They are working with your company's own disclosures – but reading them with an investor's eye rather than a management lens. The gap between how management sees the company and how an activist sees the company is almost always the same gap between internal narrative and external reality.

The most valuable exercise any board can undertake is to conduct this analysis on itself. Pull the 10-K and benchmark your financial performance against peers. Read your own proxy statement as an activist would – looking for tenure, overboarding, combined CEO/Chair roles, compensation misalignment. Map your shareholder base and assess how institutional investors would vote if challenged. Review your defensive provisions and ask whether they signal confidence or entrenchment.

I can tell you from experience that this exercise is uncomfortable. When our team ran the Flowers Foods analysis, I watched those in the board director role in the exercise – seasoned executives and others who had served in various board and board advisory roles for years – see their own governance assumptions challenged by data they could have accessed anytime. One colleague looked at the combined CEO/Chairman tenure figure and said, simply, "I would never have caught that on my own board." The problem was not a lack of intelligence or diligence. It was a lack of the adversarial perspective that forces honest assessment.

If the results of that analysis make you uncomfortable, that discomfort is itself valuable information. It means an activist would find the same ammunition – and they would know how to use it.

The directors who serve their shareholders best are those who can hold the activist's magnifying glass up to their own company and act on what they see. The ones who wait for someone else to do it rarely enjoy the experience.

# Chapter 6: Quiet Accumulation – Building the Position

On July 19, 2024, reports surfaced that Elliott Investment Management had accumulated a stake of approximately $1.9 billion in Starbucks. The market reacted immediately. The stock jumped. Analysts scrambled to assess what Elliott wanted. Media coverage was instantaneous and extensive.

But the filing itself was not the beginning of the campaign. It was the end of a phase that had been underway for months – a phase of quiet, methodical accumulation during which Elliott had been purchasing Starbucks shares, conducting research, assembling campaign materials, and building its investment thesis entirely out of public view. By the time the market learned about Elliott's involvement, the activist had already done most of its work.

This invisible phase – the period between the decision to target a company and the first public disclosure – is where activist campaigns are truly built. Understanding how it works is essential for any board member or executive who wants to detect activist interest before the 13D lands on their doorstep.

When we began our Flowers Foods tabletop exercise, we started the campaign from this exact point – an activist team with a target, with conviction, and with no obligation to tell anyone what we were doing. The exercise compressed months of work into weeks, but the experience of building a case in silence while the company continued business as usual was itself instructive. You begin to understand why boards are so often surprised.

## The Sub-5% Accumulation Phase

Under current SEC rules, an investor has no obligation to publicly disclose a position in a company's stock until they cross the five percent ownership threshold with the intent to influence the company's management or policies. Below five percent, the activist is invisible.

This regulatory structure creates an asymmetric information advantage that is fundamental to how activist campaigns work. While the company goes about its business, the activist is simultaneously building a meaningful economic position and conducting the deep research that will form the foundation of the campaign. The company's management and board have no idea they are being studied – let alone targeted.

During this accumulation phase, the activist is doing several things simultaneously. They are purchasing shares, typically through multiple brokers to avoid creating patterns that might alert the market or the company's investor relations team. They are conducting the financial and governance analysis described in the previous chapter. They are identifying potential director candidates. They are beginning to draft campaign materials – the letter to the board, the investor presentation, the press release that will accompany the public launch.

The pace of accumulation depends on the activist's strategy and the target's trading dynamics. A large-cap company with high daily trading volume – like Starbucks, which trades millions of shares per day – allows for rapid accumulation without moving the stock price. A smaller company with thinner trading volume requires more patience. Aggressive buying that pushes the stock price up before the campaign launches reduces the activist's potential return and increases the cost of the position.

Here's the reality: the accumulation phase is not just about buying shares. It is about building conviction. As the activist deepens its research, it is constantly stress-testing its own thesis. Can the underperformance really be improved? Are the governance weaknesses as significant as they appeared in initial screening? Is the shareholder base receptive? Every share purchased represents a bet that the answers to these questions will hold up under the scrutiny that a public campaign will invite.

# Institutional Breadcrumbs: 13F Filings

While the activist operates below the 13D threshold, their accumulation is not entirely invisible to those who know where to look.

Institutional investors managing more than $100 million in qualifying securities are required to file Form 13F with the SEC on a quarterly basis, disclosing their equity holdings as of the end of each calendar quarter. These filings are public, searchable, and – for anyone paying attention – a potential early warning system.

If an activist hedge fund appears in a company's 13F filings for the first time, or if an existing position increases significantly quarter over quarter, that may signal accumulation activity. The limitation is timing: 13F filings are due forty-five days after the end of each quarter, which means the data is always at least six weeks old by the time it becomes public. An activist who begins accumulating in January might not appear in a 13F filing until mid-May, disclosing a position that reflects ownership as of March 31.

Sophisticated investor relations teams and corporate governance advisors monitor 13F filings for exactly this reason. They track changes in institutional ownership quarter by quarter, flagging any new positions by known activist funds. Services like WhaleWisdom aggregate 13F data and make it searchable by fund name, which allows companies to set up alerts when specific activist investors report new positions.

But 13F monitoring has significant blind spots, and this was one of the most eye-opening lessons from our SGLI program. Not all activist vehicles are required to file 13F reports. Some activists use structures that fall below the reporting threshold or operate through entities that are not classified as institutional investment managers. And even when 13F filings do reveal accumulation, they provide no information about the activist's intent. A new position could represent a passive investment, a sector allocation decision, or the opening moves of a campaign. Without additional signals, the 13F data alone is ambiguous. I asked our instructor how many board members actually monitor 13F filings proactively. The answer – very few – was both surprising and unsurprising.

## Derivatives and Synthetic Positions

The most sophisticated activists have tools available that go beyond simple share purchases – tools that can create economic exposure to a company's stock without triggering traditional ownership disclosure requirements.

**Total return swaps** allow an activist to receive the economic return on shares without actually owning them – the counterparty bank holds the shares and the disclosure obligation. **Options strategies** provide another avenue, giving economic exposure during the research phase that converts to actual ownership when the activist is ready to go public. **Short-dated equity swaps** offer still more flexibility, structured to provide economic exposure without conferring voting rights or triggering beneficial ownership reporting.

The SEC has periodically proposed reforms to close what many governance advocates consider disclosure loopholes in the derivatives space. The regulatory landscape remains in flux. But for directors and executives, the practical implication is clear: a company's true exposure to activist accumulation may be significantly larger than what traditional ownership filings reveal. The absence of a 13D or 13G filing does not mean the absence of activist interest.

## The Crossing Point: When 13D Filing Is Triggered

The moment an investor crosses the five percent beneficial ownership threshold and has the intent to influence the company's management, policies, or control, they are required to file a Schedule 13D with the SEC within ten calendar days. This filing is the first unambiguous public signal that an activist campaign is underway.

The distinction between Schedule 13D and Schedule 13G is critical – the key differentiator is intent. A 13G filing signals passive investment. A 13D signals engagement. The conversion from 13G to 13D is one of the most significant signals in activist monitoring, frequently triggering a stock price reaction as the market prices in the likelihood of a campaign.

The ten-day filing window between crossing the threshold and the required disclosure is itself a strategic element – one that the next chapter examines in detail alongside the anatomy of the 13D filing itself. Some activists use this window aggressively, accumulating additional shares at pre-disclosure prices before the market reacts.

## Strategic Timing: When to Launch

The timing of an activist campaign – specifically, when to cross the 13D threshold and go public – is a strategic decision that experienced activists think about with the same rigor they apply to the investment thesis itself.

**Earnings cycles** create natural launch windows. Filing a 13D shortly before a weak earnings report amplifies the activist's narrative. If the activist can predict – based on channel checks, industry data, or management's own guidance trajectory – that the next quarter will disappoint, launching just before the earnings release ensures that the company's own results validate the activist's thesis in real time. Conversely, launching before a strong quarter risks having the company's results undermine the urgency of the campaign.

**Annual meeting calendars** impose hard deadlines that work backward through the campaign timeline. If the activist wants to nominate directors at the next annual meeting, they must submit nominations by the advance notice deadline specified in the company's bylaws – typically sixty to ninety days before the meeting. This means the 13D filing, the initial letter to the board, and the private engagement phase must all occur with enough lead time to meet nomination deadlines if private engagement fails. An activist who files a 13D in January targeting a company with a May annual meeting has a very different timeline pressure than one who files in August.

**Market conditions** affect both the activist's cost of entry and the receptiveness of the institutional shareholder base. In a bear market, institutional investors may be more sympathetic to calls for change – they are watching their portfolios decline and looking for catalysts. In a bull market, the status quo bias is stronger – boards can point to rising stock prices as evidence that current strategy is working, even if the company is underperforming relative to peers or indices.

**Regulatory and political cycles** can also influence timing. Changes in SEC leadership or policy emphasis may affect the regulatory environment for activism. Major macroeconomic events – rate decisions, trade policy changes, geopolitical crises – can either create opportunities or generate noise that drowns out the activist's message.

## Building the War Chest

Activist campaigns are expensive. The cost of a full proxy contest can range from $5 million for a smaller company to $25 million or more for a large-cap target – the economics are examined in detail in Chapter 9. But the scale of capital commitment varies enormously. Elliott Management committed approximately $11 billion across activist positions in Q2 2024 alone. Engine No. 1, as we saw in Chapter 2, won three board seats at ExxonMobil while managing roughly $250 million.

This dynamic is important for directors to understand. A small activist with a compelling thesis and strong institutional support can be more dangerous than a large activist with a weak case. The war chest matters – campaigns cost money, and an underfunded activist may lack the resources to sustain a prolonged fight. But the decisive resource in most campaigns is not capital. It is credibility with the institutional shareholders who will ultimately cast the deciding votes.

## The Accumulation Phase from the Company's Perspective

For directors and executives, the quiet accumulation phase represents a period of maximum vulnerability and minimum awareness.

The activist is studying your company with an intensity that most boards never match. They are reading your SEC filings more carefully than your own audit committee. They are talking to your sell-side analysts, your competitors' management teams, your former employees. They are building a case – and you do not know it is happening.

The question is not whether you can prevent accumulation – under current rules, you cannot. The question is whether you can detect it early enough to prepare a thoughtful response rather than a panicked one.

Practical early warning measures include monitoring 13F filings for new positions by known activist funds, tracking unusual trading volume or patterns in the company's stock, maintaining relationships with your transfer agent to watch for changes in the shareholder register, and engaging proactively with governance-focused institutional investors who may be approached by the activist during the coalition-building phase.

But the most effective preparation for the accumulation phase is the work described in the previous chapter: seeing your company through the activist's eyes before the activist does. If your financial performance is lagging peers, if your governance structure invites criticism, if your capital allocation decisions are difficult to defend – these are not problems that begin when a 13D is filed. They are problems that have been building for quarters or years. The 13D filing is just the moment when someone else decides to make them public.

The activist's quiet accumulation phase is your preparation phase – whether you know it or not.

# Chapter 7: The Opening Move – From 13D Filing to First Contact

Andrew Shapiro has a term for what he writes in Item 4 of his Schedule 13D filings – the section where SEC rules require the activist to describe the purpose of their transaction and their plans for the company. He calls them "entertaining love letters."

The phrase is characteristically Shapiro: disarming, a little irreverent, and precisely accurate. The 13D filing is the activist's first public communication with the company and its shareholders. It is simultaneously a legal disclosure, a statement of intent, a strategic document, and – if the activist is any good at this – a compelling piece of persuasive writing that will be read by the company's board, its institutional investors, the proxy advisory firms, the financial press, and anyone else trying to understand what is about to happen.

This chapter examines the critical transition from private research to public campaign – the opening moves that set the tone, define the narrative, and often determine whether the campaign ends in early resolution or escalates to a prolonged public fight.

## The Schedule 13D Filing: The First Public Signal

The Schedule 13D filing is a structured SEC disclosure, but within its regulatory framework lies considerable room for strategic communication. The filing requires disclosure of the filer's identity, the amount and source of funds used to acquire the position, the purpose of the transaction, and any plans or proposals the filer has with respect to the target company.

Item 4 – Purpose of Transaction – is where the activist's strategy becomes visible for the first time. A filing that simply states the shares were acquired for investment purposes, with the possibility of future engagement with management and the board regarding shareholder value, is a moderate opening. It signals intent without committing to specific demands. A filing that lays out a detailed critique of the company's governance and strategy, names specific directors for replacement, and outlines a comprehensive value creation plan is an aggressive opening that compresses the timeline and narrows the space for private negotiation.

Amendments to the 13D – filed as 13D/A – are equally important signals. Each amendment indicates that the campaign is intensifying. The activist may be increasing their position, adding new demands, or disclosing that private engagement has failed. A 13D that goes through multiple amendments over several months tells the market that the activist is escalating, not walking away. For board members monitoring an activist's approach, the cadence and content of 13D amendments are among the most reliable indicators of the activist's commitment level.

The filing itself creates immediate market effects. The stock price typically moves on the day the 13D is disclosed – usually upward, as the market prices in the possibility that the activist's campaign will unlock value. This price movement creates a dynamic tension. The activist's position is now worth more, which validates their thesis. But the higher stock price also raises the bar for the campaign's value creation targets and makes it more expensive for the activist to accumulate additional shares.

## The Activist Letter: Anatomy of a First Strike

The letter to the board is the activist's primary communication vehicle. It is typically filed as an exhibit to the 13D or sent privately to the board – sometimes both, with a private delivery followed by a public filing after the company has had time to read and respond.

An effective activist letter has a structure that is now well-established across the industry, though the best practitioners bring their own voice and emphasis. Having built one during our Flowers Foods tabletop exercise – a letter that we drafted, debated, revised, and ultimately presented as if we were a real activist team approaching a real board – I can describe the anatomy from the inside.

**The opening** establishes standing and tone. The activist identifies themselves as significant shareholders – in our Flowers Foods exercise, holding approximately 6.5% of outstanding shares – and states that they are writing to express concerns and present a plan. The opening sets the emotional register for everything that follows. "We are writing as significant shareholders of Flowers Foods, Inc., to express our deep concern regarding the company's persistent under-performance and to present a comprehensive value creation plan" is direct without being hostile. It positions the activist as a constructive investor, not a corporate raider.

**The bottom line up front** distills the entire campaign into a single, memorable thesis. In our exercise, the opening summary framed Flowers Foods as "a fundamentally sound business trapped in operational mediocrity and strategic drift." That sentence does an enormous amount of work. It validates the company's underlying assets (fundamentally sound) while indicting its management (operational mediocrity) and strategic direction (strategic drift). Every institutional investor who reads the letter will remember that framing.

**The evidence section** presents the case for change with data. This is the longest section of the letter and the one that institutional investors will scrutinize most carefully. It must be exhaustive, specific, and verifiable. Stock performance versus peers. Revenue and volume trends. Margin comparisons with industry benchmarks. Capital allocation decisions and their outcomes. Governance metrics – director tenure, board composition, compensation alignment. Each claim must be sourced from the company's own public filings so that it is impossible to dispute the data, only the interpretation.

**The value creation plan** transitions from diagnosis to prescription. Having documented what is wrong, the activist must articulate what should be done about it – and what the results will be. The plan must include specific, measurable actions: achieve peer-average EBITDA margins through identified operational improvements. Separate the CEO and Chairman roles. Add directors with turnaround and digital expertise. Conduct a strategic portfolio review. Implement a defined capital return program. Vague recommendations – "improve governance" or "enhance shareholder value" – will not persuade institutional investors who are accustomed to evaluating specific, actionable proposals.

**The proposed directors** section presents the activist's board candidates with detailed biographies and a clear explanation of why their skills address identified board gaps. This section is often filed separately but referenced in the letter. The quality of the activist's director nominees is one of the most important factors in how institutional investors and proxy advisory firms evaluate the campaign.

**The closing** typically invites constructive engagement while implicitly reserving the right to escalate. The activist wants to signal willingness to work collaboratively, because institutional investors prefer resolution over confrontation. But the closing also needs to convey that the activist is prepared to take the campaign public if the board refuses to engage.

## The Tone Spectrum

The tone of an activist's opening communication falls on a spectrum from collaborative to confrontational, and the choice of tone is itself a strategic decision.

At the collaborative end, the activist positions themselves as a partner who wants to work with the board to create value. The language is respectful, the demands are framed as suggestions, and the emphasis is on shared goals. ValueAct Capital has historically operated at this end of the spectrum – building relationships with management, requesting board representation through private channels, and avoiding public confrontation whenever possible. This approach works best when the activist has a long-term orientation, the company's problems are operational rather than governance-related, and the board is composed of reasonable people who might genuinely listen.

At the confrontational end, the activist leads with public pressure.

The letter is filed publicly on the same day it is sent to the board. The language is blunt about governance failures and management incompetence. The demands are non-negotiable. The implicit message is: engage on our terms, or face a proxy fight. Carl Icahn has historically operated closer to this end – though even Icahn has become more nuanced over time.

Most effective activists operate somewhere in the middle, and many begin at the collaborative end with a clear willingness to escalate. Elliott Management exemplifies this approach – professional and constructive in tone, but with a depth and specificity that carries an unmistakable implicit message: implement these changes or we will find people who will.

The tone the activist selects reflects their assessment of the board. A board with experienced, independent directors may respond to collaboration. A board captured by management or that has already rejected private outreach may require confrontation to force engagement.

## Private Engagement: The Preferred Path

Despite the public spectacle that proxy fights generate, most experienced activists prefer to resolve campaigns privately. Public confrontation is expensive, uncertain, distracting, and – critically – it puts the activist's thesis and judgment on public display in a way that makes retreat difficult. Private engagement preserves flexibility for both sides.

The private engagement phase typically begins with a request for a meeting – specifically, a meeting with the board's independent directors without management present. This request is itself significant. The activist is signaling that they view the governance problem as a board-level issue, not an operational one that management can address. They want to speak to the directors who are supposed to be exercising independent oversight – not to the executives who may be part of the problem.

What happens in these meetings varies enormously. The best outcomes occur when the board approaches the meeting with genuine curiosity and intellectual honesty. The activist presents their analysis. The directors ask probing questions. There is a substantive exchange about the company's strategy, governance, and capital allocation. The directors may push back on specific points – and a good activist expects and welcomes this, because it signals that the board is actually engaging with the substance.

The worst outcomes occur when the board treats the meeting as a formality – showing up with lawyers and communication advisors, reading from prepared talking points, and refusing to engage with the substance of the activist's concerns. Shapiro was blunt about this dynamic: if the company goes into "bunker" mode – stopping disclosure, becoming less transparent, blocking information – the activist has no choice but to assume the worst and escalate.

Here's the reality: the private engagement phase is where most campaigns should end. If the activist has legitimate concerns – and as we discussed in Chapter 4, they usually do – a board that engages honestly can often find common ground. Maybe the activist's proposed directors are genuinely qualified and would strengthen the board. Maybe the capital allocation critique has merit. Maybe the governance reforms the activist is requesting – separating the CEO and Chair roles, adding director term limits, improving shareholder engagement – are things the board should have done years ago.

The boards that handle activism well are not the ones with the strongest defensive provisions. They are the ones with the intellectual honesty to ask: is the activist right about anything?

## Building the Coalition

While private engagement unfolds between the activist and the board, the activist is simultaneously building support among the company's broader shareholder base. This coalition-building effort is one of the most important and least visible aspects of the opening phase.

The activist's team reaches out to the company's largest institutional investors – the BlackRocks, Vanguards, and State Streets – to share their thesis and gauge receptiveness. These conversations are carefully choreographed. The activist wants to understand whether the institutional investor has governance concerns about the company, how they would evaluate the activist's proposals, and whether they would be inclined to support the campaign if it goes to a vote.

The Salesforce experience in 2023 illustrates the power of coalition dynamics taken to an extreme. Five major activist investors – Elliott, Starboard Value, ValueAct Capital, Third Point, and Inclusive Capital – simultaneously targeted the company. While each had their own position and their own thesis, the combined weight of five credible activists pushing for change at the same company created overwhelming pressure. Salesforce implemented significant governance and operational reforms, including board changes, cost reductions, and margin improvement commitments, without any of the activists ever going to a proxy vote. The coalition itself was sufficient leverage.

Sell-side analysts are another crucial audience during the coalition-building phase. These analysts cover the company for investment banks and publish research that institutional investors read. An activist who can convince a sell-side analyst that their thesis has merit gains a powerful amplification channel. Shapiro was candid about this dynamic: sell-side analysts will often tell an activist things in private that they would not put in a public research report – particularly candid assessments of management effectiveness and strategic direction.

## The Initial Media Strategy

The decision of when and how to engage the media is one of the most consequential strategic choices in the opening phase. Going public amplifies pressure but eliminates the privacy that makes negotiated resolution easier.

Most activists maintain a staged approach. The 13D filing is technically public, but it is typically not accompanied by press outreach. If the board engages constructively, the media strategy may remain muted. If the board refuses to engage, the activist escalates. The full media and communications arsenal – press releases, investor presentations, campaign websites, analyst briefings – is examined in detail in the next chapter.

# Case Study: Elliott's Starbucks Campaign

Elliott Management's approach to Starbucks in 2024 illustrates how a masterful opening move can compress an entire campaign timeline.

In July 2024, Elliott disclosed its $1.9 billion stake via a 13D filing. The filing was accompanied by a detailed operational improvement plan that covered virtually every aspect of Starbucks' business – store operations, labor management, supply chain, digital strategy, capital allocation. The specificity was striking. This was not a generic call for "shareholder value enhancement." It was a granular business plan that demonstrated Elliott's team had spent months analyzing Starbucks' operations at a level of detail that rivaled – or exceeded – the company's own strategic planning.

What made Elliott's opening move particularly effective was its combination of operational depth and governance restraint. Elliott did not demand the CEO's head in its initial communication. It did not publicly name specific directors for replacement. It presented a detailed plan and invited the board to engage. The implicit message was unmistakable – implement these changes or we will find people who will – but the explicit communication was constructive and professional.

The result was remarkable in its speed. Within two months of Elliott's disclosure, Starbucks replaced its CEO. Brian Niccol, the CEO of Chipotle who had led one of the most successful restaurant turnarounds in recent history, was appointed in a move that was widely seen as a direct response to Elliott's campaign. The activist did not need a proxy fight. It did not need a public campaign. The quality of its analysis and the credibility of its thesis – combined with the implicit threat of escalation – produced a CEO change at one of the world's most visible consumer brands in approximately sixty days.

This is the power of a well-executed opening move. When the activist's research is deep enough, the thesis is compelling enough, and the proposed changes are specific enough, the opening move can also be the closing move. The boards that respond effectively – that evaluate the activist's proposals on their merits and act decisively – can resolve campaigns before they ever become public battles.

The boards that do not respond effectively tend to find themselves in the situation described in the next chapter: facing a full campaign arsenal designed to build public pressure and force change from the outside.

# Chapter 8: The Campaign Arsenal – Materials, Media, and Messaging

When our activist team in the Flowers Foods tabletop exercise was told we had eight weeks to build a complete campaign, I assumed the hardest part would be the financial analysis. I was wrong. The hardest part – the work that consumed the most time and demanded the most strategic thinking – was building the campaign materials that would translate our analysis into a persuasive narrative for institutional investors, media, and the broader shareholder base.

By the time we presented our capstone, our team had produced an eighteen-page investor letter, a comprehensive twenty-page presentation deck, a condensed fifteen-slide version for institutional calls, a complete press release, an FAQ document addressing thirty anticipated questions, a campaign website content structure with design specifications, proposed independent director candidate profiles, and a data quality validation report verifying every financial claim. We had also produced three different versions of the investor presentation – varying in length and emphasis – for different audiences and engagement contexts.

That volume of material is not unusual. It is standard. And every piece of it serves a specific strategic purpose in the campaign's communication architecture.

This chapter breaks down the activist's campaign arsenal – what each component does, how it is structured, and why it matters. Understanding these materials from the inside is essential for any board member or executive who will need to evaluate, respond to, or counter them.

# The Investor Presentation: Telling the Story of Underperformance

The investor presentation is the centerpiece of the activist's public campaign. It is the document that institutional investors will study most carefully, that proxy advisory firms will reference in their analyses, and that the financial press will mine for quotable data points.

A well-constructed activist presentation tells a story in four acts.

**Act One: The Problem.** The opening slides establish the financial case for change with peer-relative benchmarking that makes underperformance impossible to deny. Total shareholder return versus the peer group and relevant indices. Revenue and volume trends. Margin comparisons. Valuation multiples. Each metric is presented with the company in red and its peers in green – a visual grammar that every institutional investor recognizes instantly. In our Flowers Foods presentation, the opening section documented a forty-five percent stock price decline while the S&P 500 gained sixteen percent over the same period. (As noted in Chapter 5, the financial data in the Flowers Foods tabletop sections reflects the scenario parameters of the SLGI simulation exercise, which drew on the company's actual SEC filings but incorporated campaign-specific assumptions for educational purposes.) The visual impact of that divergence on a single slide was more powerful than any paragraph of written analysis could achieve.

**Act Two: The Root Causes.** Having established the financial symptoms, the presentation diagnoses the underlying problems. This is where the activist connects governance failures to financial underperformance – arguing that the company's stock price is not the victim of industry headwinds or macroeconomic forces but of specific, identifiable management and board decisions. Our Flowers Foods analysis identified five root causes: catastrophic shareholder value destruction, volume collapse and market share erosion, the

ill-timed Simple Mills acquisition, operational mediocrity reflected
in the margin gap, and board and management failures including
a combined CEO/Chairman with twenty-one years of tenure. Each
root cause was documented with data from the company's own SEC
filings.

**Act Three: The Plan.** The prescriptive section lays out specific,
measurable, time-bound actions that the activist believes will create
shareholder value. This must be concrete, not aspirational. In
our exercise, the value creation plan identified $80-120 million
in annual savings through five specific operational categories –
ingredient procurement optimization, manufacturing efficiency,
distribution and logistics improvements, overhead reduction, and
energy efficiency – each with identified dollar ranges and specific
initiatives. The plan also included governance reforms (separate
CEO/Chair, board refreshment, performance-based compensation)
and strategic actions (portfolio review, capital allocation discipline). Every recommendation connected directly to a documented
problem.

**Act Four: The Valuation.** The closing section shows what the
stock is worth if the plan is executed. This is the economic incentive for institutional investors to support the campaign. Our Flowers
Foods presentation projected a target share price of $22-25 within
twenty-four months, representing seventy to ninety percent upside
from the approximately $13 share price at the time of the hypothet-
ical campaign launch. That valuation was built on specific assumptions – closing the margin gap to peer average, realizing identified
cost savings, optimizing the capital structure – that institutional investors could independently evaluate.

The activist team typically produces multiple versions of the presentation for different contexts. A comprehensive version running
twenty or more slides provides the full analysis for investors who
want to dig deep. A condensed version of twelve to fifteen slides
serves as the basis for institutional investor calls where time is limited. Both versions tell the same story, but the condensed version
focuses on the highest-impact data points and the most compelling
elements of the value creation plan.

# The Press Release: Shaping the Public Narrative

The press release serves a fundamentally different purpose than the investor presentation. Where the presentation is designed for sophisticated institutional investors who will evaluate the financial analysis in detail, the press release is designed for the financial media and the broader investment community – audiences that need the story distilled into its essential elements.

An effective activist press release follows a tight architecture: headline capturing the core message, opening paragraph identifying who, what, and why, data-heavy middle paragraphs with the highest-impact metrics, and a closing that outlines the solution and invites constructive engagement.

In our Flowers Foods exercise, the press release distilled an eighteen-page letter and a twenty-page presentation into three pages of tightly written copy. Every sentence was evaluated against a single criterion: would a financial journalist at the Wall Street Journal find this quotable? The data points were selected for maximum impact – the forty-five percent stock decline, the EBITDA margin gap representing $80-120 million in annual opportunity, the CEO compensation increase of twenty-five percent while the stock collapsed. These are the numbers that become headlines.

The press release also serves a legal function. It establishes the public record of what the activist demanded and when. If the campaign escalates to a proxy fight, the press release – along with the 13D filing and the letter to the board – becomes part of the proxy solicitation materials that the SEC reviews.

# The Campaign Website: Creating a Credible Public Presence

Many activist campaigns now include a dedicated campaign website – a standalone online presence that consolidates the activist's materials, thesis, and proposed directors in an accessible, professionally designed format.

The Flowers Foods exercise included a complete website content structure and design specification. The site was organized around a clear information architecture: an executive summary landing page, a detailed investment thesis section, the proposed director candidates with biographies, an FAQ addressing shareholder and media questions, a document library containing all campaign materials for download, and a news and updates section for press releases and campaign developments.

The campaign website serves several purposes. It provides a single, controlled destination where anyone – institutional investors, retail shareholders, reporters, employees, customers – can access the activist's complete case. It signals professionalism and commitment. It creates an alternative information channel that is not filtered through the company's investor relations function. And it provides a platform for ongoing campaign communication as events develop.

The website design itself sends a message. Professional typography, clean layout, and polished production values signal a serious, well-funded campaign. A poorly designed website – or the absence of a website altogether – can undermine the perception of sophistication that institutional investors expect from a credible activist. Even the naming convention matters – names like "RestoreValueAtFlowersfoods.com" frame the campaign as constructive value creation rather than hostile attack.

## The FAQ Document: Anticipating the Hard Questions

The FAQ document is one of the most strategically important and least appreciated components of the campaign arsenal. It represents the activist's attempt to control the narrative by anticipating every question – from shareholders, from the media, from the company's own response – and framing the answers on the activist's terms.

Our Flowers Foods FAQ addressed approximately thirty questions organized around several themes. There were questions about the activist's motives and track record. Questions about the financial analysis and whether the value creation plan was realistic. Questions about the proposed director candidates – their qualifications, their independence, their compensation expectations. Questions about the campaign timeline and what would happen at each stage. And, critically, questions about the scenarios the company's defense team would likely raise: "Isn't the activist just in this for short-term profits?" "Won't this campaign distract management from running the business?" "Aren't you cherry-picking financial metrics?"

The most valuable questions in the FAQ are the ones that address the activist's weaknesses head-on. A sophisticated institutional investor will not be persuaded by a document that only addresses easy questions. They want to see that the activist has thought about the hardest parts of the thesis – the potential counterarguments, the execution risks, the scenarios where the plan does not work. An FAQ that acknowledges uncertainty and provides honest assessments of risk is paradoxically more persuasive than one that presents an unrealistically optimistic view.

The FAQ also functions as an internal alignment document for the activist's team. During a campaign, the activist will field hundreds of questions from investors, media, and other stakeholders. Having a pre-approved set of answers ensures that everyone on the team – the portfolio managers, the proxy solicitors, the communications advisors, the legal counsel – is delivering a consistent message. Inconsistency is the enemy of credibility in an activist campaign.

## Proposed Director Candidates: Presenting Credible Alternatives

When an activist proposes to replace directors, the quality of the alternative candidates is often the single most important factor in whether institutional investors and proxy advisory firms support the campaign. A compelling financial thesis paired with weak director nominees will lose. A strong thesis paired with exceptional nominees can be unstoppable.

The activist's director candidates must satisfy several criteria simultaneously. They must have professional qualifications that are obviously relevant to the company's strategic challenges – not just generic business experience, but specific expertise in the areas where the activist has identified board gaps. If the activist's thesis centers on operational underperformance, the nominees should include executives with demonstrated turnaround experience. If the thesis focuses on digital transformation, the nominees should include technologists who have led successful transformations.

The candidates must be genuinely independent. Any material relationship with the activist fund – past employment, consulting arrangements, co-investment history – will be scrutinized and used by the company's defense team to argue that the nominees are not truly independent but are the activist's proxies on the board. Proxy advisory firms evaluate nominee independence carefully, and a finding of non-independence can be campaign-ending.

The candidates must also be willing to serve. Running for a contested board seat is a significant personal commitment. The nominee will face public scrutiny of their professional record, potential opposition research by the company's defense team, and the uncertainty of a contested election. Not every qualified executive is willing to subject themselves to this process.

In our Flowers Foods exercise, the proposed director candidates were presented with complete professional biographies that specifically tied each candidate's experience to identified board gaps. The presentation was designed to make the contrast between the proposed nominees and the incumbent directors as stark as possible – fresh expertise versus long tenure, relevant skills versus generic backgrounds, independence versus entrenchment.

## Research Validation: Ensuring Bulletproof Data

One component of the campaign arsenal that receives less attention than it deserves is the research validation process. Before any campaign materials are released publicly, a responsible activist team conducts a rigorous verification of every financial claim, every data point, and every peer comparison in the campaign materials.

Our Flowers Foods exercise included a formal data quality validation document that verified all financial figures against source SEC filings, confirmed the accuracy of peer comparisons, and documented the methodology behind calculated metrics like margin gaps and implied cost savings. This validation process was not academic. It was essential.

Here's the reality: a single factual error in an activist's campaign materials can be devastating. The company's defense team will seize on any inaccuracy – however minor – to undermine the activist's credibility with institutional investors. "If they got this number wrong, what else did they get wrong?" is a devastating line of defense when delivered to a portfolio manager who is deciding how to vote millions of shares.

The validation process serves both an offensive and a defensive purpose. Offensively, it gives the activist's team confidence that their analysis will withstand scrutiny from the company, from proxy advisory firms, and from institutional investors' own analysts. Defensively, it creates a documented record showing that the activist took reasonable care to ensure accuracy – a record that may become relevant if the company alleges that the activist's materials are misleading.

## Media Engagement: Amplifying the Message

The activist's media strategy operates on two timelines. The first is the initial burst of coverage when the campaign goes public – the 13D filing, the letter to the board, and the accompanying press release generate immediate media attention. The second is the sustained communication effort over the weeks and months that follow, during which the activist needs to keep the campaign visible and the pressure on the board consistent.

For the initial launch, the activist's communications team – typically an external public relations firm with expertise in activist situations – conducts targeted outreach to financial journalists who cover activism. This is not a mass distribution exercise. The goal is to place detailed stories with reporters who will take the time to understand the thesis and write substantive coverage that reaches the institutional investors who control the vote.

Analyst briefings supplement the media strategy. The activist's team arranges calls with sell-side analysts who cover the target company, presenting the investment thesis and answering questions. These conversations serve dual purposes: they educate the analyst community about the activist's case, and they generate research coverage that reaches institutional investor clients. A sell-side analyst who writes favorably about the activist's thesis – or who downgrades the company's stock in response to the governance concerns the activist has raised – becomes a powerful amplification channel.

The sustained media effort requires discipline. The activist needs to generate a steady cadence of news and commentary that keeps the campaign in the financial press without overexposing the message. Campaign updates, additional analysis, responses to the company's defense arguments, announcements of institutional investor support – each becomes an opportunity for media engagement. The goal is to maintain narrative momentum while avoiding the appearance of desperation.

## Third-Party Validation

The most sophisticated campaigns supplement the activist's own materials with independent analysis from credible third parties. This may include commissioned white papers from governance advisory firms, industry benchmarking studies from consulting firms, or expert assessments of the company's strategy from former industry executives.

Third-party validation addresses the credibility challenge inherent in activist communication. Everything the activist says is, by definition, self-interested. When an independent expert reaches the same conclusions – that the company is underperforming, that the governance structure is problematic, that the proposed changes would create value – the activist's thesis gains the weight of independent corroboration.

The effectiveness of third-party validation depends on the credibility of the source. A white paper from a recognized governance advisory firm carries significant weight. An analysis from a former CEO in the target's industry carries even more. The company's defense team will attempt to discredit any third-party analysis as paid advocacy – which is why the independence and reputation of the source matters as much as the content of the analysis.

## The Campaign Timeline: Orchestrating the Escalation

All of these materials do not arrive simultaneously. The campaign unfolds according to a timeline that the activist has planned months in advance – a choreographed escalation designed to build pressure incrementally while preserving the option of resolution at each stage.

The Flowers Foods campaign flow document – one of the tabletop exercise's planning tools – mapped this timeline explicitly across seven phases. Phase 1 (Days -90 to 0) covers pre-campaign preparation: research, position building, team assembly, and materials development. Phase 2 (Day 0) is the initial public launch: the 13D filing, the private letter, and the public campaign announcement. Phase 3 (Days 1-30) covers private engagement with the board. Phase 4 (Days 30-90) escalates to public campaign activities if private engagement fails. Phase 5 (Days 90-180) involves the proxy contest mechanics if needed. Phase 6 (Days 180+) covers post-campaign implementation. Phase 7 addresses long-term preparedness.

Each phase has defined objectives, required materials, and decision points. At each transition, the activist evaluates whether to escalate or settle. The materials described in this chapter – the presentations, the letters, the press releases, the website, the FAQ, the director nominees – are deployed at specific points in this timeline according to the campaign's strategic logic.

Understanding this timeline is as important for the company's defense team as it is for the activist. The board that recognizes where the activist is in the campaign sequence can anticipate the next move and respond accordingly. The board that reacts to each new development in isolation – without understanding the overall campaign architecture – will always be one step behind.

The campaign arsenal is not just a collection of documents. It is a carefully orchestrated communication system designed to build institutional investor support, shape the public narrative, and demonstrate that the activist has done the work to earn the right to propose changes. The companies that take these materials seriously – that evaluate the analysis honestly and engage with the substance rather than dismissing the source – are the ones most likely to resolve the situation before it reaches the phase described in the next chapter: the proxy contest.

# Chapter 9: The Proxy Contest – When Engagement Becomes a Fight

In late 2023, Nelson Peltz's Trian Partners launched what would become one of the most expensive and closely watched proxy fights in corporate history. The target was The Walt Disney Company. The prize was two board seats. The combined cost – for both the activist's campaign and the company's defense – reportedly approached $65 million. Disney spent approximately $40 million defending itself. Trian spent roughly $25 million on the attack.

Peltz lost, and he lost decisively. Shareholders voted against both Trian nominees by approximately a two-to-one margin. Disney's defense – led by a reinvigorated Bob Iger and a board that aggressively countered Trian's narrative – proved overwhelmingly persuasive.

And yet. During the campaign period itself, Disney's stock price rose approximately fifty percent as the company announced cost cuts, restructured its streaming business, and implemented many of the operational improvements that activists had been advocating. Whether or not Peltz won the vote, the campaign itself appeared to create significant shareholder value – raising a question that haunts every proxy contest: does the activist need to win the election to win the campaign?

I remember discussing this paradox with my SGLI cohort. Shapiro had a term for it – the "subatomic particle" effect. The act of observation changes the behavior of what is being observed. The moment an activist targets a company, the company begins to change, regardless of whether the activist ever wins a vote. That insight reframes everything about how proxy contests should be evaluated.

The proxy contest is the nuclear option of shareholder activism. It is expensive, uncertain, public, and irreversible. But it is also the mechanism that gives everything else in the activist's playbook its credibility. Without the credible threat of a proxy fight, private engagement becomes a conversation the board can politely ignore. This chapter examines how proxy contests work – the mechanics, the economics, the strategy, and the outcomes that shape modern corporate governance.

## The Decision to Launch

No activist takes the decision to launch a proxy fight lightly. It is the single most consequential decision in any campaign – the moment when the activist commits substantial capital, puts their professional reputation on the line, and creates a public confrontation that neither side can walk away from without consequence.

The decision to launch typically follows a failed private engagement process. The activist has filed their 13D, sent their letter, requested meetings with independent directors, and presented their thesis. The board has either refused to engage, engaged but rejected the activist's proposals, or offered concessions that the activist considers inadequate. The question becomes: do we accept the board's position and move on, or do we escalate to the ballot box?

The calculus is brutal. Proxy fights are expensive – legal fees, proxy solicitation, investment banking advisory, public relations, printing and mailing costs, and the enormous opportunity cost of management and activist team time. A campaign against a mid-cap company might cost $5-10 million. A campaign against a large-cap target can cost $20-25 million or more. And there is no guarantee of winning. The activist is asking shareholders to vote against a slate of directors that the company's nominating committee has selected, that the company's proxy statement has endorsed, and that in many cases the company's management team is actively campaigning to support.

The decision framework typically weighs four factors. First, is the financial upside large enough that winning the proxy fight will generate returns that justify the campaign costs? Second, is the governance thesis strong enough to win support from proxy advisory firms and institutional investors? Third, does the ownership analysis suggest that enough shareholders will vote for the activist's nominees? And fourth, are the activist's director candidates strong enough to withstand the scrutiny that a contested election will invite?

If the answer to any of these questions is no, a disciplined activist will settle for the best available negotiated outcome – or walk away entirely. The decision to launch a proxy fight that you are likely to lose is the hallmark of an undisciplined campaign.

# Director Nominations:  Navigating the Bylaws

The proxy contest begins formally when the activist submits director nominations to the company, triggering the advance notice provisions in the company's bylaws. This is a procedural step that carries outsized strategic importance, because a nomination that fails to comply with the bylaws can be rejected outright – ending the proxy contest before it starts.

Advance notice bylaws typically require that nominations be submitted sixty to ninety days before the annual meeting. The notice must include detailed information about the nominee – professional background, board affiliations, relationships with the activist, ownership of the company's securities, and responses to a questionnaire specified in the bylaws. The company reviews the nomination for compliance and, if it finds any deficiency – even a minor one – may reject the nomination as non-compliant.

In 2023, approximately ten percent of activist nomination notices were rejected for non-compliance with advance notice provisions. That statistic should be sobering for any activist contemplating a proxy contest. The bylaws are a minefield, and the company's legal team will scrutinize every word of the nomination notice looking for grounds to reject it. A misstatement in the nominee questionnaire, a missed deadline, an incomplete disclosure – any of these can be fatal.

The practical implication is that bylaw compliance is not a task for the activist's general counsel alone. It requires specialized proxy contest counsel who understand the specific requirements of the target company's bylaws and the interpretive standards that Delaware courts have applied when nomination rejections are challenged. Getting the nomination right is not optional. It is the prerequisite for everything that follows.

Some companies have adopted advance notice bylaws that governance advocates consider genuinely punitive – provisions designed not to ensure orderly elections but to discourage or prevent activist nominations entirely. These may include extraordinarily detailed disclosure requirements for nominees, short nomination windows, requirements that nominees submit to extensive background checks, or provisions that allow the board to request additional information on an open-ended basis. When activists challenge these provisions in court, the outcomes depend on whether the court views the provisions as reasonable governance measures or as entrenchment devices designed to prevent shareholder input.

# The Universal Proxy Card: Making It Personal

As discussed in Chapter 2, the SEC's universal proxy card rule – effective September 1, 2022 – changed the fundamental dynamics of contested elections. Shareholders can now mix and match nominees from both sides, voting for any combination of company and activist candidates.

The consequences have been the opposite of what many predicted. Instead of a surge in contested proxy fights, the universal proxy card has accelerated settlements – reaching ninety-two percent of board seats obtained through settlement rather than contested election by early 2025. The reason is straightforward: companies can no longer be confident that shareholders will vote for the entire management slate simply because the alternative was voting for the entire activist slate. The ability of shareholders to pick off individual directors has made companies far more willing to settle.

For individual directors, the implications are significant and personal. Before the universal proxy card, a contested election was a referendum on the board as a whole. Now it can become a referendum on specific directors. A director who has served for twenty years, who sits on four other boards, or whose compensation exceeds governance guidelines faces a different kind of risk than they did before 2022. The universal proxy card has made director accountability more granular – and more personal.

## Proxy Solicitation Mechanics

Once the activist has filed their nominations and launched their proxy contest, the campaign enters the solicitation phase – the period during which both sides are actively seeking shareholder votes.

Both the company and the activist file proxy statements with the SEC, each reviewed by SEC staff for deficiencies. The voting mechanics are more complex than most people realize. The **record date** – set four to six weeks before the annual meeting – determines who votes; only investors who owned shares on that date can cast votes, regardless of subsequent trading.

**Proxy solicitation firms** – Innisfree, Morrow Sodali, D.F. King – manage the logistics on both sides, maintaining shareholder databases, managing voting platforms, and tracking incoming votes in real time. The ongoing vote count becomes a closely guarded strategic asset.

**Institutional investor engagement** during solicitation is intensive. Both sides conduct one-on-one meetings with the largest shareholders, presenting their case. For major index fund managers – BlackRock, Vanguard, State Street – these meetings follow structured evaluation processes, with investment stewardship teams meeting both sides, evaluating arguments, and making voting recommendations to internal committees. In the final days before the deadline, both sides monitor the count obsessively, making last-minute calls to undecided investors in what campaign operatives describe as the most intense period of the entire contest.

# Proxy Advisory Firms: ISS, Glass Lewis, and Their Influence

The recommendations of proxy advisory firms – primarily Institutional Shareholder Services (ISS) and Glass Lewis – significantly influence voting outcomes in contested elections. While the extent of their influence is debated, their role in the process is undeniable.

Both firms publish detailed reports analyzing contested elections. These reports evaluate the activist's thesis, the company's response, the qualifications of competing director nominees, and the governance context. The reports conclude with a voting recommendation – support the activist's nominees, support the company's slate, or a split recommendation supporting some nominees from each side.

Many institutional investors use proxy advisory firm recommendations as a starting point for their own analysis. Some smaller institutional investors follow the recommendations more or less automatically. Larger asset managers – particularly the firms with dedicated investment stewardship teams – conduct their own analysis but give significant weight to the advisory firm reports.

A split recommendation – where ISS recommends supporting the activist's nominees but Glass Lewis recommends supporting the company's slate, or vice versa – creates uncertainty that can cut either way. The Disney/Trian proxy fight saw exactly this dynamic. ISS recommended against all of Trian's nominees. Glass Lewis recommended withholding support from one Disney director. The split gave both sides a talking point, but Disney's decisive victory suggested that ISS's recommendation carried the heavier weight in that particular contest.

For activists, the proxy advisory firm engagement is a campaign within the campaign. Both ISS and Glass Lewis conduct their own meetings with the activist and the company, review the campaign materials, and ask detailed questions about strategy, director qualifications, and governance commitments. The activist's team prepares for these meetings with the same intensity they bring to meetings with the largest institutional shareholders – because an unfavorable recommendation from ISS or Glass Lewis can effectively end a campaign.

The proxy advisory landscape is undergoing the most dramatic structural transformation in its history – and it will fundamentally change how proxy fights are waged and won.

In October 2025, Glass Lewis announced that beginning with the 2027 proxy season, it will no longer issue voting recommendations based on a single "benchmark" or "house" policy. The 2026 proxy season will be the final year for the one-size-fits-all approach that has defined Glass Lewis's business model for decades. In its place, Glass Lewis will offer four separate research perspectives – management-aligned, governance fundamentals, sustainability, and active owner – and clients will select which perspective or combination of perspectives to apply. Instead of one recommendation per company per issue, there will be multiple.

The implications for proxy fights are profound and still unfolding. Under the old model, if an activist secured a favorable ISS recommendation, it could predict a meaningful vote swing from institutional investors who followed benchmark policies. That mechanical relationship between recommendation and votes is breaking down. When Glass Lewis's four-perspective model goes live in 2027, a contested election report could theoretically produce different recommendations depending on which perspective an investor has selected. The "Active Owner" perspective may favor the activist's nominees while the "Management-Aligned" perspective supports the incumbent slate – from the same advisory firm.

ISS has taken a different path. It maintains its benchmark voting policy but has introduced new products – including Gov360, which delivers research reports without voting recommendations, and Custom Lens, which provides tailored analysis based on each investor's proprietary voting policies. ISS also made a significant shift in its 2026 benchmark: environmental and social shareholder proposals that previously received a presumption of support are now evaluated on a case-by-case basis. This change alone will alter the calculus for activists who have historically counted on ISS support for ESG-related proposals.

The forces driving these changes are not subtle. In December 2025, the White House issued an executive order titled "Protecting American Investors from Foreign-Owned and Politically-Motivated Proxy Advisors," targeting ISS and Glass Lewis by name and directing the

SEC, FTC, and Department of Labor to review the firms' practices. Texas enacted SB 2337, the first state law imposing significant obligations on proxy advisors – including requiring specific financial analysis for any recommendation opposing management. The FTC opened an antitrust investigation into whether the duopoly's combined ninety-plus percent market share constitutes anticompetitive concentration. State attorneys general in Missouri and Florida filed their own enforcement actions.

The institutional investors are responding in kind. In January 2026, JPMorgan Asset Management – managing over seven trillion dollars in client assets – announced it was severing all ties with proxy advisory firms, replacing them with Proxy IQ, an AI-powered internal platform. JPMorgan CEO Jamie Dimon publicly characterized ISS and Glass Lewis as a "cancer" on corporate governance. BlackRock split its stewardship function into separate teams for index and active funds. Vanguard is splitting into two distinct entities with separate stewardship functions. State Street created a parallel sustainability stewardship service. The practical effect: a single company may now face multiple different voting teams at the same asset manager, each operating under distinct mandates and reaching different conclusions.

For anyone trying to predict the outcome of a proxy fight, this fragmentation is the most significant development since the introduction of the universal proxy card. The old playbook – secure ISS support, engage Glass Lewis, model the institutional vote based on known policies – is becoming obsolete. Both activists and corporate defenders must now map which investors use which advisory frameworks, customize their messaging for governance-focused, sustainability-focused, and financially-focused audiences separately, and invest in far more granular vote projection models. The party that invests more in direct shareholder engagement and relationship-building – rather than relying on proxy advisor recommendations as a shortcut – will have the advantage in this new landscape.

# The Institutional Investor Vote: The Decisive Variable

When all the materials have been filed, all the presentations have been made, and all the advisory firm reports have been published, the outcome of a proxy contest comes down to a single question: how will the institutional investors vote?

In a typical public company, the five largest shareholders collectively own thirty to fifty percent or more of the outstanding shares. These institutional investors – BlackRock, Vanguard, State Street, Fidelity, Capital Group, and their peers – are the decisive voters in any contested election. The activist's own shareholding, while meaningful, is rarely sufficient to win without institutional support.

Institutional investors evaluate proxy contests through governance frameworks that have become increasingly formalized. BlackRock's Investment Stewardship team, for example, publishes detailed voting guidelines and engagement priorities. Vanguard's Investment Stewardship program operates with similar transparency. These frameworks typically emphasize board quality and composition, alignment of compensation with performance, capital allocation discipline, and responsiveness to shareholder concerns.

The activist who understands these frameworks – and who tailors their campaign to align with the criteria institutional investors use to make voting decisions – has a significant advantage over the activist who approaches the proxy contest as a purely financial argument. Institutional investors care about financial returns, of course. But they also care about governance process, about the credibility and independence of director nominees, and about whether the activist's proposals represent genuine long-term value creation or short-term financial engineering.

## Campaign Economics: The Cost of a Proxy Fight

The economic burden of a proxy contest falls on both sides – and the costs have been rising. For the activist, a fully contested proxy fight at a large-cap company can cost $15-25 million: legal counsel ($1.5-

2 million), proxy solicitation ($1-1.5 million), investment banking advisory ($1.5-2.5 million), public relations ($0.5-1 million), plus research, printing, and communication costs. Smaller campaigns may run $5-10 million.

For the company, costs are comparable or higher – and management distraction adds an incalculable burden. The CEO, CFO, and general counsel spend weeks focused on the proxy fight rather than running the business. This economic calculation creates a natural incentive for settlement: a negotiated resolution – one or two board seats in exchange for a standstill agreement – allows both sides to avoid millions in costs while addressing governance concerns.

## Win Conditions and Recent Trends

The data on proxy contest outcomes tells a story of evolving dynamics. Activist win rates in contested proxy fights have fluctuated significantly in recent years. In 2023, activists won some form of board representation in approximately fifty-six percent of contests that went to a vote. In 2024, that rate declined to approximately thirty-eight percent – driven partly by a series of high-profile losses (Disney/Trian, ExxonMobil's successful defense against climate-focused activists) and partly by the increasing sophistication of corporate defense strategies.

But these headline numbers obscure a more important trend: the proxy contest is becoming the exception rather than the rule. As of early 2025, ninety-two percent of activist board seats were obtained through settlement rather than contested election. The universal proxy card, the professionalization of both activist campaigns and corporate defense, and the high costs of proxy fights have all pushed both sides toward negotiated outcomes.

This does not mean the proxy contest is irrelevant. Quite the opposite. The credible threat of a proxy fight is what gives the settlement process its urgency. A company that knows the activist is capable of and willing to run a proxy contest will take settlement negotiations far more seriously than one that believes the activist is bluffing. The proxy contest, even when it does not occur, shapes every interaction between activists and boards.

# Case Studies: The Spectrum of Outcomes

The proxy contest landscape is best understood through specific cases that illustrate the range of possible outcomes.

**Disney/Trian (2024): The activist loses but the company changes.** Trian's $25 million campaign was decisively defeated, with shareholders voting approximately two-to-one against both Trian nominees. But Disney's stock rose nearly fifty percent in the following year as the company accelerated the operational improvements that both the activist and management acknowledged were necessary. The campaign appears to have served as a catalyst for change even without producing a favorable vote – raising the question of whether proxy fights create value through the pressure they apply regardless of the electoral outcome.

**Phillips 66/Elliott (2024): The split decision.** Elliott's campaign against Phillips 66 produced a rare split result – the activist won two of the four seats it sought. This outcome, unusual in an era of all-or-nothing results, reflected the universal proxy card's ability to allow shareholders to make granular director-level judgments. Some of Elliott's nominees were seen as clearly superior to the incumbents they challenged. Others were not. Shareholders voted accordingly.

**Gildan Activewear/Browning West (2023-2024): Total board replacement.** In one of the most dramatic proxy contest outcomes in recent years, activist Browning West succeeded in replacing virtually the entire board of Gildan Activewear after the board had fired the company's founding CEO, Glenn Chamandy. Shareholders voted to reinstall Chamandy and replace the directors who had removed him – a nearly unprecedented repudiation of a sitting board. The Gildan case demonstrated that in extreme circumstances, shareholders will take dramatic action when they believe the board has lost its way.

**Southwest Airlines/Elliott (2024): Winning without a vote.** Elliott's campaign against Southwest Airlines targeted the company's long-tenured board and its resistance to operational modernization. Facing the prospect of a proxy fight, Southwest agreed to add five Elliott-nominated directors to its board and replaced its CEO – all through negotiated settlement. The outcome illustrates the pattern that has become dominant: the credible threat of a proxy fight producing governance change without a shareholder vote.

Each of these cases teaches a different lesson, but a common thread runs through all of them. The proxy contest – whether it occurs or merely threatens to occur – is the mechanism that gives shareholder activism its ultimate credibility. Without the ballot box as a final resort, everything else in the activist's playbook is a request that the board can choose to ignore. The proxy contest makes the request enforceable.

The question for directors is not whether your company will face a proxy fight. The question is whether your governance, your strategy, and your communication with shareholders are strong enough that you would win one – because the activist is asking that question, too.

# Chapter 10: Litigation as a Campaign Tool

In January 2024, ExxonMobil did something that no major public company had done before. It sued its own shareholders.

The target was not a hostile hedge fund seeking to dismantle the company. It was Arjuna Capital and Follow This – activist shareholders who had submitted proposals requesting that Exxon accelerate its greenhouse gas emissions reduction targets. These were non-binding shareholder proposals of the kind that companies receive and respond to every proxy season. Exxon's response was to file a federal lawsuit in a Texas court seeking a ruling that the proposals could be excluded from the company's proxy statement.

Both Arjuna Capital and Follow This withdrew their proposals rather than face the cost and burden of litigation. The lawsuit achieved its tactical objective. But the strategic consequences were severe. CalPERS – the California Public Employees' Retirement System and one of the world's largest institutional investors – voted against all Exxon directors at the next annual meeting in protest. Governance advocates condemned the lawsuit as a chilling attack on shareholder rights. The episode became a cautionary tale about litigation as a weapon in governance disputes – a tool that can be wielded by either side, but one that carries risks far beyond the courtroom.

Litigation is a distinctive and increasingly important element of the activist investor landscape. It serves purposes that other campaign tools cannot: forcing the production of documents that reveal what happened inside the boardroom, challenging defensive measures that prevent shareholders from exercising their rights, and creating leverage that shifts the calculus of settlement negotiations.

I will confess that the legal dimensions of activism were the area I understood least when I entered the SGLI program. I came from a cybersecurity and technology leadership background – I understood boardroom dynamics, risk management, and strategic decision-making, but Delaware corporate law was new territory. What surprised me was how much the litigation tools described in this chapter function as governance mechanisms rather than purely legal ones. They exist to answer a fundamental question: when the board's door is closed, what actually happened inside?

## Section 220 Demands: The Activist's Discovery Tool

Before an activist can sue a board for breach of fiduciary duty, they need evidence. Section 220 of the Delaware General Corporation Law provides the mechanism for obtaining it.

Section 220 allows any stockholder of a Delaware corporation to demand inspection of the company's books and records – provided the stockholder states a "proper purpose" for the inspection and the demand is reasonably related to that purpose. This right has become one of the most powerful tools in the activist's litigation arsenal.

A Section 220 demand is not a fishing expedition – at least not in theory. Delaware courts require that the stockholder articulate a credible basis for suspecting wrongdoing or mismanagement. The stockholder does not need to prove that wrongdoing occurred. They need to demonstrate that there are reasonable grounds to believe that something worth investigating may have happened – a standard that Delaware courts have described as the lowest burden of proof in law.

In practice, activists use Section 220 demands to obtain board minutes, committee materials, management presentations, and internal communications that reveal how the board actually made specific decisions – materials that are not available through public SEC filings. If the parties cannot agree on scope, the activist petitions the Delaware Court of Chancery, which resolves these disputes on an expedited basis, often within weeks.

For directors, the practical implication goes beyond the specific documents at issue. Every board minute, every committee presentation,
every email between directors becomes a potential exhibit in a future
proceeding. As governance counsel frequently advise: assume that
everything the board produces will eventually be read by someone
outside the boardroom.


# Books and Records: What Activists Can and Cannot Obtain

The scope of a Section 220 inspection is not unlimited. Delaware
courts have developed a substantial body of case law defining what
activists can and cannot obtain – and the boundaries matter.

**Board minutes and committee reports** are almost always producible when the activist has a credible basis for investigation. **Internal communications** – emails between directors and management – are more contested; courts order production of directly relevant emails but resist broad requests. **Attorney-client privileged
materials** are generally protected, though the privilege is not absolute if the company is routing business documents through counsel
to manufacture a privilege claim. **Third-party communications**
with investment bankers and consultants occupy a middle ground,
generally producible if they were considered by the board in its deliberations.

The practical effect of Section 220 is that it creates an asymmetry
that favors the activist. The company knows what is in its own board
materials. The activist does not – but they have a legal mechanism
to find out. A board that has consistently documented its deliberations, that has shown evidence of thoughtful decision-making in its
minutes, and that has relied on independent advice from qualified
advisors has little to fear from a Section 220 inspection. A board
that has been careless about documentation, that has made decisions
without adequate analysis, or that has relied on conflicted advisors
may find that its own records become the activist's most powerful
weapon.

# Caremark Claims: Suing for Failure of Oversight

The Caremark doctrine – named for the 1996 Delaware Court of Chancery decision in *In re Caremark International Inc. Derivative Litigation* – establishes that directors have a fiduciary duty to implement and monitor systems designed to ensure that the corporation complies with applicable laws and regulations. A failure to exercise this oversight duty can expose directors to personal liability.

For decades, Caremark claims were considered nearly impossible to win. The standard required the plaintiff to demonstrate that the directors either completely failed to implement any oversight system (a "prong one" claim) or that having implemented such a system, they consciously ignored red flags that required attention (a "prong two" claim). Both prongs required a showing of bad faith – a standard that most courts interpreted as requiring virtually willful blindness.

The Boeing 737 MAX disasters – two fatal crashes that killed 346 people – changed this landscape. The Delaware Court of Chancery allowed Caremark claims against Boeing's directors to proceed, finding that the board had failed to establish any board-level system for monitoring airplane safety. The Boeing decision signaled that Caremark claims, while still difficult, are no longer the dead letter that many practitioners had assumed.

For activists, Caremark claims serve a dual purpose. On the litigation track, they provide a basis for suing directors who the activist believes failed in their oversight responsibilities. On the campaign track, the threat of Caremark liability adds pressure to the activist's governance critique. An activist who can plausibly argue that the board's failure to oversee a specific risk – cybersecurity, environmental compliance, product safety, financial reporting – constitutes a Caremark violation is making a claim that has implications beyond the proxy contest. Directors facing potential personal liability have a different motivation to engage with the activist's concerns than directors who view the dispute as purely a disagreement about strategy.

The practical standard remains demanding. The activist must show not just that the board made a bad decision, but that the board was not adequately informed – that it lacked the systems, the information flows, or the engagement necessary to fulfill its oversight role. This is where Section 220 demands become strategically interconnected with Caremark claims. The documents obtained through a books and records inspection may reveal whether the board actually had oversight systems in place and whether directors were actually paying attention to the information those systems generated.

## Challenging Defensive Measures

Activists frequently use litigation to challenge the defensive mechanisms that companies deploy to resist shareholder engagement. These challenges have produced some of the most important governance precedents in Delaware corporate law.

**Poison pill challenges.** When a company adopts a shareholder rights plan that the activist believes is designed primarily to entrench the board rather than to protect shareholder interests, the activist may challenge the plan in court. Delaware courts evaluate poison pills under the *Unocal* standard – asking whether the board identified a legitimate threat to the corporation and whether the defensive measure adopted was proportionate to that threat. Courts have generally upheld poison pills with reasonable thresholds and limited durations. But they have struck down pills with very low triggers (designed to prevent activists from accumulating meaningful positions), pills adopted in the face of no identifiable threat, and pills with excessively long durations.

**Advance notice bylaw challenges.** As discussed in the previous chapter, advance notice bylaws set the procedural requirements for director nominations. When these provisions go beyond ensuring orderly elections and become tools designed to prevent nominations altogether, activists can challenge them in court. The Delaware courts distinguish between reasonable advance notice requirements – which serve legitimate governance purposes – and punitive provisions that effectively disenfranchise shareholders. The analysis is fact-specific, but the trend line favors shareholders: courts have increasingly scrutinized bylaws that impose requirements that no reasonable shareholder could comply with.

**Board entrenchment challenges.** In some cases, activists challenge board actions that they argue are designed to perpetuate the incumbent directors' control rather than to serve shareholder interests. These challenges may involve the board's decision to delay an annual meeting, to change the record date for voting, to expand the board and fill the new seats with management-aligned directors, or to adopt a rights plan specifically in response to the activist's campaign.

# The Moelis Decision: A Landmark Ruling

In February 2024, the Delaware Court of Chancery issued a decision in *West Palm Beach Firefighters' Pension Fund v. Moelis & Company* that sent shockwaves through the governance community. The court invalidated a stockholder agreement between Moelis & Company and its founder and CEO, Kenneth Moelis, that gave Moelis veto power over a wide range of board decisions – including the approval of equity compensation, the incurrence of debt, and changes to the company's business strategy.

The court ruled that the agreement violated a fundamental principle of Delaware corporate law: that the business and affairs of a corporation are managed by or under the direction of its board of directors. By giving a single stockholder – even a controlling stockholder – veto power over decisions that the law assigns to the board's independent judgment, the agreement impermissibly constrained the board's authority.

The implications extend well beyond Moelis & Company. The ruling has prompted companies across the corporate landscape to review stockholder agreements, pre-IPO governance arrangements, and standstill agreements for provisions that might be vulnerable to challenge. For activists, it provides a framework to attack arrangements that entrench insiders at the expense of the board's independent authority. For companies, it is a reminder that creative governance arrangements – however well-intentioned – must respect the board's fundamental authority to manage the corporation's affairs.

# The Delaware Advantage

The overwhelming majority of major activist litigation occurs in the courts of Delaware, for reasons that go beyond the fact that most public companies are incorporated there.

Delaware's Court of Chancery – the specialized equity court that handles corporate governance disputes – offers several advantages for governance litigation. The judges are experts in corporate law. The procedures are designed for speed. The precedent is extensive and well-developed. And the court's decisions carry national significance because they define the fiduciary duties that govern directors at the majority of America's public companies.

The Court of Chancery's expertise matters because governance disputes are complex. They involve intersecting questions of fiduciary duty, securities regulation, corporate procedure, and strategic judgment. A generalist court might take months to understand the issues. The Court of Chancery understands them on day one.

The court's speed matters because governance disputes are time-sensitive. An activist challenging a poison pill adoption or an advance notice bylaw interpretation needs resolution before the annual meeting – not two years later. The Court of Chancery routinely handles governance disputes on expedited schedules, with hearings and decisions within weeks of filing.

For activists planning litigation strategy, Delaware's courts represent a sophisticated and generally predictable forum. The legal standards are well-established. The judges are experienced. The outcomes, while never certain, can be assessed with reasonable confidence based on existing precedent. This predictability itself has strategic value – both for the activist evaluating whether to file a claim and for the company evaluating whether to settle.

# Exxon's Counter-Attack:  When Companies Sue Activists

The ExxonMobil lawsuit against Arjuna Capital and Follow This in early 2024 introduced a new dynamic into the litigation landscape: the company suing its own activist shareholders.

Exxon's legal theory was that the shareholder proposals submitted by Arjuna and Follow This were improper and could be excluded from the company's proxy statement.  Rather than seeking a no-action letter from the SEC – the traditional mechanism for excluding shareholder proposals – Exxon filed a lawsuit in federal court in Texas seeking a declaratory judgment that the proposals were excludable.

The tactical objective was straightforward:  force the activists to choose between withdrawing their proposals and bearing the cost of defending a lawsuit. Both activists chose to withdraw – a rational economic decision for organizations with limited litigation budgets. Exxon's lawsuit cost the company relatively little in legal fees but achieved the goal of removing the proposals from the ballot.

The strategic consequences, however, were substantial and largely negative for Exxon. CalPERS – one of Exxon's largest shareholders – voted against all of the company's directors at the subsequent annual meeting, explicitly citing the lawsuit as the reason. Other institutional investors expressed concern that Exxon's approach would have a chilling effect on shareholder engagement – deterring shareholders from filing proposals for fear of litigation retaliation.

The Exxon episode illustrates a broader truth about litigation in governance disputes:  the courtroom is not an isolated arena.  Every legal decision has governance implications, and every governance decision has potential legal consequences.  An aggressive litigation strategy that wins in court can lose catastrophically in the court of institutional investor opinion.  Directors contemplating litigation – whether offensive or defensive – must evaluate not just the legal merits but the governance optics.  How will the company's largest institutional shareholders view this action?  Will it be seen as a reasonable defense of corporate authority, or as an attempt to silence shareholder engagement?

# Litigation as Leverage Versus Litigation as Endpoint

Most activist litigation does not result in large damage awards. Unlike securities fraud class actions or merger objection lawsuits, activist governance litigation is primarily about two things: information access and leverage.

Information access – through Section 220 demands and books and records inspections – allows the activist to see inside the boardroom. This information may reveal governance failures that strengthen the activist's campaign narrative. It may identify specific director conduct that supports Caremark claims. Or it may reveal that the board's decision-making was more thoughtful than the activist assumed – in which case the information actually helps the company.

Leverage – through the threat of fiduciary duty claims, defensive measure challenges, or bylaw litigation – shifts the calculus of settlement negotiations. A company facing a credible litigation threat has additional incentive to negotiate seriously. The cost of defending a lawsuit, the risk of an unfavorable ruling, the distraction of litigation discovery, and the reputational impact of having governance failures aired in court proceedings all push toward settlement.

The cost-benefit analysis for activists contemplating litigation is straightforward but fact-specific. Section 220 demands are relatively inexpensive – typically tens of thousands of dollars in legal fees – and the information obtained can be enormously valuable for the campaign. Challenging defensive measures involves moderate costs and can produce results quickly in the Delaware Court of Chancery. Full Caremark claims are expensive, uncertain, and time-consuming – but the threat of such claims can be leveraged without actually filing them.

For most activists, litigation is a complement to the proxy campaign, not a substitute for it. The documents obtained through a Section 220 demand strengthen the activist's investor presentation. The challenge to a punitive advance notice bylaw clears the procedural path for a director nomination. The threat of a Caremark claim adds urgency to settlement negotiations. Each legal tool serves the broader campaign strategy.

The companies that navigate litigation risk most effectively are those that maintain the kind of governance practices that make litigation claims difficult to sustain – thorough board documentation, independent advisory relationships, rigorous oversight processes, and transparent communication with shareholders. Good governance is not just good policy. In an era of increasing activist litigation, it is the most effective form of legal risk management a board can implement.

# Chapter 11: When the Letter Arrives – The First 72 Hours

The room went quiet in a way I had not experienced before in a professional setting. It was December 9, 2025 – the capstone day of our activist investor tabletop simulation at the SLGI Board Readiness Program – and the management and board teams had just received the activist demand letter from Sterling Capital Partners. The document was crisp, well-researched, and pointed. It laid out a case for underperformance at Flowers Foods with a precision that made even the simulated board members uncomfortable. I watched the body language change in real time. Crossed arms. Tight jaws. Someone muttered, "Can they actually do this?"

They could. And the way those teams responded in the next thirty minutes told me more about corporate governance under pressure than months of classroom instruction ever had.

Here is the reality: most boards are unprepared for the moment an activist investor letter arrives. Not because they lack intelligence or experience, but because the experience of being challenged – directly, publicly, and with data – triggers a set of reflexive responses that almost always make things worse. The first 72 hours after an activist's letter arrives are the most consequential of the entire campaign. What happens in those hours determines whether the board will navigate the situation from a position of strength or spend the next six months playing defense.

This chapter is about getting those hours right.

# The Initial Shock: What Most Boards Get Wrong

The reflexive response of most boards to an activist demand letter follows a predictable pattern: call the lawyers, circle the wagons, and refuse to engage. The general counsel calls outside counsel. Outside counsel recommends hiring a proxy solicitor and a crisis communications firm. The CEO drafts a defensive press release. The board goes into lockdown mode. No one talks to the activist. No one talks to the media. No one talks to anyone.

Andrew Shapiro, who has filed thirteen Schedule 13D campaigns over a career spanning more than three decades, was blunt in his assessment of this approach: it is often the worst possible strategy.

The problem is not that boards seek legal counsel – they absolutely should. The problem is that the defensive crouch becomes the entire strategy. When a board's first and only move is to hire lawyers and lock the doors, it sends a signal to the activist, to institutional investors, and to the market that the board views shareholder engagement as a threat rather than a responsibility. That signal has consequences.

In our Flowers Foods simulation, the management team's first instinct was exactly this. They wanted to know what legal mechanisms they could deploy. They wanted to know about the advance notice bylaws. They wanted to know whether a poison pill was already in place. These are not unreasonable questions. But they are not the right first questions. The right first question – the one that separates boards that navigate activist campaigns successfully from those that do not – is simpler and harder: Is the activist right about anything?

We will get to that question. But first, the mechanics.

# The Response Team: Who Should Be in the Room

Within the first 24 hours of receiving an activist demand letter, the board needs to assemble its response team. The composition of this team matters enormously – not just for the expertise it brings, but for the signal it sends about how the board intends to approach the situation.

**General counsel** is the natural starting point. The GC should be the first call and the coordinator of the initial response. Their role is not to dictate strategy but to ensure that every action the board takes is legally sound and properly documented. Board deliberations during an activist campaign are likely to be scrutinized later – in litigation, in regulatory filings, and in the court of public opinion. The GC's job is to make sure the record reflects a board that acted thoughtfully and in good faith.

**Outside counsel with governance expertise** is essential, and the emphasis on governance is deliberate. A board facing an activist campaign does not need a general corporate litigator. It needs a lawyer who understands proxy contests, SEC filing requirements, advance notice bylaws, and the evolving case law around defensive measures. The difference between competent advice and expert advice in this area can be measured in millions of dollars and board seats.

**An investment banker with proxy fight experience** brings a different perspective. Bankers who have worked proxy contests understand the financial arguments that activists make, the peer group analyses they construct, and the valuation frameworks they deploy. More importantly, they understand how institutional investors evaluate these arguments. A banker who has only done M&A work will not have the right lens.

**A proxy solicitor** is the team member most boards overlook until it is too late. Proxy solicitors understand the mechanics of shareholder voting – who owns the shares, how those owners make voting decisions, and what it takes to win a contested election. They can provide a real-time assessment of the board's likely support among institutional investors, which is the single most important data point in the entire campaign.

**A crisis communications firm** with experience in shareholder activism – not just general crisis management – rounds out the team. Activist campaigns are fought in the media and in investor presentations as much as they are fought in proxy statements. The communications strategy needs to be integrated with the legal and financial strategy from day one.

Now, who should NOT be in the room? Anyone who will make it personal rather than analytical. The CEO who views the activist as a personal attack. The director who was recruited by the CEO and cannot evaluate the demands objectively. The board member who wants to "send a message" rather than solve a problem. Activist campaigns become destructive when they become personal. The response team needs people who can look at the activist's demands with the dispassion of a surgeon evaluating an X-ray.

## Engaging Advisors: Timing Matters

Here is something that surprises most directors when they first encounter it: the companies that respond most effectively to activist campaigns are not the ones that hire the best advisors. They are the ones that hired their advisors before the campaign began.

Companies that have governance counsel, an investment banker, and a proxy solicitor on retainer can begin their response within hours of receiving the activist's letter. They already have relationships. They already have context. The proxy solicitor already has an ownership analysis. The investment banker already has a financial model. The lawyers already know the company's governance structure, its bylaws, and its defensive provisions.

Companies that scramble to hire advisors after the letter arrives waste critical days – sometimes weeks – getting new advisors up to speed. During that time, the activist is building support among institutional investors, refining their messaging, and establishing the narrative. Every day the board is silent is a day the activist's narrative goes unchallenged.

Sheryl Palmer, who provided the board and management perspective during our program, was emphatic about this. Corporate preparedness is not something you develop during a crisis. It is something you build before the crisis arrives. The companies that have done the work – that have run vulnerability assessments, that have engaged their top shareholders, that have thought through their response framework – are the companies that respond from a position of strength rather than panic.

The practical implication is straightforward: if you serve on a board that does not have at least a governance counsel and a proxy solicitor identified and briefed, you are unprepared. Not unprepared in the abstract. Unprepared in the specific sense that when the letter arrives – and for many companies, it is a matter of when, not if – you will lose days or weeks that you cannot afford to lose.

# The Critical First Decision: Engage or Entrench?

Every activist campaign reaches a fork in the road in its first 72 hours. The board must decide whether to engage with the activist or entrench behind its defenses. This decision shapes everything that follows.

The question is not whether engagement carries risks – it does. The activist may use information from early conversations to sharpen their campaign. They may interpret engagement as a sign of weakness. They may publicize the fact that the board agreed to meet, positioning it as validation of their concerns.

But the risks of entrenchment are almost always greater. An economic activist with legitimate governance concerns who is treated as a hostile raider will escalate – and when they do, they will have a compelling narrative about a board that refuses to listen to its own shareholders. Institutional investors – the people whose votes actually determine the outcome – pay close attention to whether the board engaged constructively. A board that refused to take the activist's call, that issued a dismissive press release without addressing the substance of the activist's concerns, that adopted defensive measures rather than engaging with the critique – that board has handed the activist its most powerful argument.

Shapiro's observation on this point was among the most important things I heard during the entire program. When an activist with a credible investment thesis and legitimate governance concerns is treated as a hostile actor, the escalation that follows is predictable and often devastating. The activist's narrative shifts from "this company is underperforming" to "this company is underperforming AND the board refuses to listen." The second narrative is far more damaging than the first, because it goes to the heart of what institutional investors care about most: whether the board is fulfilling its fiduciary duty to shareholders.

The data supports this. Companies that engage early tend to reach settlements faster and on more favorable terms. Companies that entrench tend to face longer, more expensive, and more public campaigns – often ending with worse outcomes than they would have achieved through early engagement. Starbucks provides a compelling illustration: when Elliott Management took a position in 2024, the board acted preemptively – replacing the CEO before Elliott explicitly demanded it – which resolved the campaign faster than anyone expected. The board's willingness to engage with the underlying issue rather than fighting the activist saved the company months of distraction and millions of dollars in proxy fight costs.

Southwest Airlines offers another instructive example. Elliott's campaign moved from initial stake disclosure to a six-seat settlement – the largest in U.S. history – relatively quickly, in part because both sides recognized that protracted warfare would serve neither the company nor its shareholders.

## Reading the Activist's Filing: What Their Demands Actually Mean

The activist's letter and SEC filings are the opening moves in a negotiation, not a final position. Reading them correctly requires looking past the rhetoric to the substance – and understanding that every demand serves a strategic purpose.

Start with the Schedule 13D filing, specifically Item 4, which describes the activist's purpose and plans. Shapiro called these his "entertaining love letters" – and the description is apt. The 13D filing is simultaneously a legal document, a public relations tool, and a negotiating position. It is crafted to achieve multiple objectives at once: to comply with SEC requirements, to establish credibility with institutional investors, to put the board on notice, and to create a public record of the activist's concerns.

When you read the activist's demands, sort them into categories:

**Specific governance changes** – requests to separate the CEO
and Chair roles, to add independent directors, to refresh the board,
to eliminate staggered board terms. These demands are typically
the easiest to evaluate because governance best practices are well-
established. If the activist is requesting changes that ISS, Glass
Lewis, and institutional investors would also support, the board
needs to take them seriously regardless of the source.

**Financial and strategic demands** – requests for capital returns,
divestitures, changes to dividend policy, or strategic reviews. These
require more careful analysis because they involve business judgments. But they also tend to be grounded in financial data that can
be independently verified.

**Board composition demands** – specific requests to add the activist's nominees or remove existing directors. These are the most
sensitive demands because they go to the heart of board control. But
they are also the demands most likely to end up in a settlement, because board seats are the currency of activist campaigns.

**Operational demands** – requests for specific cost reductions, operational improvements, or management changes. These are often
the most detailed and the most difficult to evaluate quickly, because
they require operational expertise.

The question to ask about each demand is not "Is this something
we would have done on our own?" It is "Is this something our shareholders would want us to consider?" The distinction matters because
boards that filter activist demands through the lens of their own preferences miss the point. The relevant audience is not the board – it
is the broader shareholder base whose votes will determine the outcome if the campaign escalates.

In the Flowers Foods simulation, our activist team – led by Taylor
Price – structured our demands exactly this way. We led with governance concerns that had broad institutional support: CEO-Chair
separation, board refreshment, independent director additions. We
followed with financial and operational demands that were supported by detailed analysis. And we reserved our most aggressive
demands – director removals, compensation reform – for later in
the negotiation, where they served as leverage rather than opening
positions.

## Assessing the Substance: Is the Activist Right About Anything?

This is the hardest question in the entire chapter. It is also the most important.

Shapiro's assessment of this question was characteristically uncomfortable. His view – explored in depth in the next chapter – is that when an activist targets a company, more often than not, the activist has identified something real. That observation challenges the assumption that boards are generally competent and that activists are generally disruptive. But the data supports it. Academic research consistently shows that companies targeted by activists tend to experience governance improvements and improved financial performance in the years following a campaign. The pattern demands intellectual honesty.

The hardest version of this question arises when the activist's diagnosis is correct but their prescription is wrong. The company may genuinely be underperforming. The board may genuinely have governance weaknesses. The capital allocation may genuinely be suboptimal. But the activist's proposed solution – replace three directors, divest a division, return capital through a special dividend – may not be the right answer. Boards that can distinguish between "the activist has identified a real problem" and "the activist's solution is the right one" are boards that can negotiate from a position of intellectual integrity.

The practical exercise for any board in the first 72 hours is this: take the activist's letter and evaluate every factual claim independently. Is the underperformance data accurate? Is the peer group methodology reasonable? Are the governance criticisms supported by the proxy statement? Are the financial projections defensible? Not every claim will be accurate. But some of them will be. And the board needs to know which ones before it responds publicly.

In our simulation, the activist team and the management team disputed the peer group – both had valid arguments. The activist team used a narrower peer group that made the underperformance look more dramatic. The management team used a broader peer group that softened the comparison. The board had to evaluate which analysis was more credible. This is exactly the kind of judgment call that real boards face, and the boards that get it right are the ones that evaluate the data honestly rather than defaulting to whatever analysis supports their preferred conclusion.

# Communication Protocols: Who Needs to Know What, and When

Information management during the first 72 hours is both a governance responsibility and a strategic imperative. The wrong information reaching the wrong audience at the wrong time can escalate a manageable situation into a crisis.

**The full board** needs the activist's filing and an objective summary of the demands – emphasis on objective. The summary should not editorialize. It should not characterize the activist's demands as "unreasonable" or "hostile." It should present the demands as they are and identify which ones require immediate board-level discussion. Every director needs enough information to participate meaningfully in the strategic discussion that will follow.

**Management** needs a response framework – a clear understanding of who is authorized to communicate with the activist, what can and cannot be discussed, and what the timeline for the board's response will be. Management also needs to understand that the board, not management, owns the response strategy. This is a fiduciary obligation of the directors, and management's role is to support the board's decision-making, not to drive it.

**Employees** need reassurance. Activist campaigns generate anxiety, rumors, and distraction. A brief, factual communication to employees – acknowledging the situation, emphasizing business continuity, and redirecting focus to operations – is far better than silence, which allows rumors to fill the vacuum.

**Shareholders** need to know that the board is engaged and taking the situation seriously. The initial communication to shareholders does not need to respond to every demand. It needs to convey that the board has received the activist's concerns, is evaluating them thoughtfully, and will respond in a manner that serves all shareholders' interests.

**Regulators and analysts** may need to be notified depending on the specifics of the situation. The GC and outside counsel should advise on disclosure obligations.

The key principle across all of these audiences is the same: the board controls the narrative by being proactive, factual, and measured. The moment the board loses control of the narrative – through silence, through defensiveness, or through leaked disagreements – the activist gains leverage.

## The Worst First Moves

After observing and participating in the Flowers Foods simulation, and after absorbing Shapiro's three decades of campaign experience, I can identify five first moves that almost always make things worse. These are not theoretical risks. They are patterns that repeat themselves in campaign after campaign.

**Issuing a defensive press release that dismisses the activist without addressing substance.** This is the most common mistake. The board issues a statement saying something like "We are confident in our strategy and believe our current board has the right skills and experience to deliver long-term value for all shareholders." This statement says nothing. It addresses nothing. And it tells institutional investors that the board has not engaged with the activist's arguments on their merits. It is worse than silence because it is dismissive.

**Adopting a poison pill immediately.** Shareholder rights plans have legitimate uses, but adopting one in direct response to a 13D filing signals panic. It tells the market that the board's first instinct is to protect itself rather than to engage with shareholder concerns. Proxy advisory firms take note. Institutional investors take note. And the activist takes note – and uses it as evidence that the board prioritizes entrenchment over accountability.

**Refusing to take the activist's call.** This is the entrenchment decision in its starkest form. The activist has requested a meeting. The board declines. The activist then tells every institutional investor, every proxy advisory analyst, and every journalist who will listen that the board refused to engage. The narrative writes itself: this board will not even listen to its own shareholders.

**Launching a personal attack on the activist.** Some boards respond to activist campaigns by questioning the activist's motives, track record, or character. This is almost always counterproductive. Institutional investors do not care about the personal history between the board and the activist. They care about whether the activist's arguments have merit and whether the board's response is credible. A personal attack shifts the conversation from substance to personality – exactly the terrain where the activist wants the fight to happen, because it allows them to position the board as defensive and insecure.

**Going silent.** The board receives the letter and says nothing for weeks. No public statement. No communication to shareholders. No response to the activist. The silence is interpreted as confusion, dysfunction, or fear – none of which inspire confidence. Every day of silence is a day the activist's narrative goes unchallenged.

## Setting the Tone for What Comes Next

The first 72 hours set the tone for the entire campaign. A board that responds with professionalism, intellectual honesty, and a genuine willingness to engage with the substance of the activist's concerns establishes a foundation for a constructive resolution. A board that responds with defensiveness, personal attacks, or silence establishes a foundation for an expensive, distracting, and often losing proxy fight.

The distinction is not about being soft or accommodating. It is about being strategic. The board that engages early, that evaluates the activist's claims honestly, that communicates proactively with shareholders, and that assembles the right team is the board that retains control of the process. The board that entrenches, deflects, and delays is the board that cedes control to the activist – and to the proxy advisory firms and institutional investors who will ultimately decide the outcome.

In the chapters that follow, we will examine how to evaluate the activist's demands on their merits, what defense mechanisms actually work, and how to negotiate a settlement that serves shareholders.

But none of that matters if the first 72 hours go wrong. The opening moves define the range of possible outcomes. Get them right, and you have options. Get them wrong, and you are playing defense for the rest of the campaign.

As I watched the management team in our Flowers Foods simulation process the activist letter, I saw something that I believe happens in real boardrooms every week: capable, experienced people defaulting to reflexive defense rather than reflective analysis. The teams that ultimately performed best in the simulation were not the ones with the most impressive credentials. They were the ones who paused, read the letter carefully, asked "What here is actually true?" – and then built their strategy around an honest answer to that question.

That is the discipline these first 72 hours demand. Not courage. Not aggression. Honesty.

# Chapter 12: Evaluating the Activist's Demands – Substance Over Reflexive Defense

There is a moment in every activist campaign where the board must stop reacting and start thinking. The lawyers have been called. The advisors have been briefed. The communications team has drafted a holding statement. The adrenaline of the first 72 hours has begun to fade. And now the board faces the question it has been avoiding since the letter arrived: Is the activist right about anything?

This question is harder than it sounds. Not intellectually – any competent director can evaluate a financial analysis or a governance critique. It is hard because it requires the board to examine itself honestly, in real time, under pressure, and in public. It requires directors to consider the possibility that the company they have been overseeing – the strategy they approved, the CEO they hired, the capital allocation they endorsed – may have genuinely underperformed. And it requires them to do this while an adversary is actively exploiting every weakness they acknowledge.

The boards that get through this exercise with their credibility intact are the ones that approach it with intellectual honesty. The boards that do not are the ones that confuse defending the company with defending themselves.

# The Intellectual Honesty Imperative

Andrew Shapiro's observation haunts this chapter: "In many instances, if a company's been targeted by an activist, more likely than not, I'm probably going to agree with the activist – that the board deserves it."

That is not the observation of a hostile outsider. It is the observation of someone who has spent more than three decades evaluating the same companies that boards are overseeing. And the implication is uncomfortable but unavoidable: if an activist has committed the capital, the time, and the reputational risk to launch a campaign against your company, there is a meaningful probability that their analysis has merit.

This does not mean the activist is always right. It does not mean their proposed remedies are appropriate. It does not mean the board should capitulate to every demand. But it does mean that the board's evaluation of the activist's demands must begin with a genuine willingness to find truth in the critique – not just ammunition for the defense.

The intellectual honesty imperative is not a soft concept. It is a strategic one. Institutional investors – the shareholders whose votes actually determine the outcome of proxy contests – can tell the difference between a board that has genuinely evaluated an activist's demands and one that has simply hired lawyers to construct a rebuttal. When ISS and Glass Lewis analysts read the board's response, they are looking for evidence of substantive engagement, not legal boilerplate. A board that can acknowledge where the activist has identified genuine issues while disagreeing credibly on the proposed solutions is far more persuasive than a board that dismisses everything the activist says.

The boards that lose proxy fights are almost never the boards that engaged too much with the activist's arguments. They are the boards that engaged too little.

# A Framework for Evaluation

Not every activist demand carries the same weight, the same credibility, or the same strategic implication. The board needs a systematic framework for sorting demands into categories that drive different responses. Here is the framework I developed through the Flowers Foods simulation and refined through months of studying real campaigns:

**Category 1: Valid governance concerns that should be addressed regardless of the activist.** These are demands that align with established governance best practices and that proxy advisory firms, institutional investors, and governance rating agencies would support. Separating the CEO and Chair roles when the same person holds both. Adding genuinely independent directors to replace long-tenured insiders. Eliminating classified board structures. Enhancing shareholder engagement. If the activist is demanding changes that ISS would recommend in a routine governance assessment, the board gains nothing by resisting them – and loses credibility by appearing to fight best practices simply because an activist recommended them.

**Category 2: Legitimate strategic questions that deserve board-level review.** These are demands that involve genuine business judgment – divestitures, capital returns, changes to growth strategy, operational restructuring. They may or may not be good ideas. They require careful financial analysis, competitive assessment, and consideration of long-term consequences. But they deserve the same rigorous evaluation the board would give to any strategic proposal that came from management. The fact that the idea came from an activist does not make it wrong. The fact that it came from an activist does not make it right. It makes it worth evaluating.

**Category 3: Self-serving demands that primarily benefit the activist's short-term interests.** These are demands where the activist's economic incentives diverge from the interests of long-term shareholders. Forced sale of the company at a premium that enriches the activist but undervalues the company's long-term potential. Capital returns that boost the stock price in the near term but undermine the company's ability to invest in growth. Board seats for the activist's own principals – not independent directors, but the activist fund's employees – where the purpose is information access and control rather than governance improvement. These demands should be scrutinized with particular care, because the activist's interests and the company's interests may genuinely conflict.

**Category 4: Unreasonable demands that would harm the company.** These are demands that, on the merits, would destroy value, undermine the company's competitive position, or violate the board's fiduciary obligations. They may be included in the activist's letter as negotiating leverage – extreme positions designed to make more moderate demands seem reasonable by comparison. The board should identify these demands clearly but should not make the mistake of treating the entire campaign as unreasonable because some demands are.

The discipline of this framework is in the sorting, not in the conclusions. Most boards skip directly to the rebuttal – constructing arguments against the activist's position on every point. The framework demands that the board first identify what is actually legitimate. Only after that honest assessment can the board credibly argue against the demands that are not.

# Financial Analysis: Is the Underperformance Claim Supported?

Activists build their campaigns on a foundation of financial data. The underperformance narrative – this company has destroyed shareholder value relative to its peers – is the centerpiece of virtually every economic activist campaign. The board's first analytical task is to determine whether that narrative is true.

This sounds straightforward. It is not. I learned this firsthand during our Flowers Foods tabletop exercise. Our activist team spent weeks constructing a financial case that we believed was airtight – and it was, within our chosen analytical framework. When the management team responded with a different peer group, a different time horizon, and a different set of metrics, their numbers were equally accurate. Both analyses were honest. They simply told different stories. That experience taught me that the board's job is not to deter-

mine which set of numbers is "right." It is to determine which analytical framework is more reasonable – a judgment call that requires
intellectual honesty rather than mathematical precision.

The question is not whether the activist's numbers are accurate –
they almost always are, because competent activists know that a factual error in their financial analysis destroys their credibility. The
question is whether the activist's analytical framework is reasonable.
Check these elements:

**Peer group composition.** Who is the activist comparing the company to? Are the peers genuinely comparable in terms of size, business model, end markets, and geographic exposure? In the Flowers
Foods simulation, the activist team and the management team disputed the peer group – both had valid arguments. The activist team
used a narrower set of direct competitors that highlighted Flowers
Foods' relative underperformance. The management team used a
broader set that included companies with different business characteristics, softening the comparison. The board had to evaluate which
peer group was more analytically honest – not which one produced
a more flattering result for either side.

**Time period selection.** Is the activist measuring performance
over one year, three years, five years, ten years? Short time periods can be distorted by one-time events. Long time periods may include leadership or strategic changes that make historical comparisons less relevant. The most credible analyses look at multiple time
periods and identify consistent patterns rather than cherry-picking
the period that best supports the thesis.

**Metric selection.** Total shareholder return is the most common
metric, but it can be supplemented with return on invested capital,
return on equity, revenue growth, margin trends, and free cash flow
generation. An activist who leads with TSR but ignores operational
metrics may be telling an incomplete story. A management team that
highlights operational improvements but ignores stock price underperformance is telling an equally incomplete story.

**Attribution.** Even if the underperformance is real, the board
needs to understand its causes. Is the underperformance driven
by company-specific factors that the board can address? Or is it
driven by industry-wide headwinds, macroeconomic conditions, or

one-time events? An activist will attribute all underperformance to governance and management failures. The truth is usually more nuanced.

The board should commission an independent financial analysis – not from the activist's advisors and not from management – that evaluates the underperformance claim objectively. This analysis is the foundation of every subsequent decision the board makes. If the underperformance is real and attributable to factors the board can influence, the response needs to include a credible plan for improvement. If the underperformance is exaggerated or attributable to factors outside the board's control, the response needs to make that case with data, not rhetoric.

# Governance Assessment: Are the Board Composition Criticisms Legitimate?

Activist campaigns almost always include critiques of board composition. These critiques follow predictable patterns because governance weaknesses follow predictable patterns:

**Long-tenured directors.** Directors who have served for fifteen, twenty, or twenty-five years are a standard activist target. The argument is that extended tenure compromises independence – directors who have served alongside the same CEO for decades lose the ability to evaluate management objectively. ISS generally flags directors with tenure exceeding twelve to fifteen years. Glass Lewis examines tenure in the context of overall board refreshment. If your board has multiple directors with twenty-plus years of service, an activist will identify this as a governance weakness – and proxy advisory firms are likely to agree.

**Former CEO still on the board.** This is one of the clearest signals of governance concern. When a former CEO remains on the board after their successor takes over, it raises legitimate questions about whether the new CEO can truly lead independently. In the Flowers Foods exercise, the continued presence of the company's former CEO on the board was one of the governance red flags that made the company an attractive activist target. The former CEO's relationships, history, and influence can dominate board dynamics in ways that formal independence definitions do not capture.

**Combined CEO and Chair.** The separation of the CEO and Chair roles is one of the most common activist demands – and one of the most frequently debated governance questions. The argument for separation is straightforward: the Chair manages the board, and the board manages the CEO. When the same person holds both roles, the board's ability to provide independent oversight is compromised. The counter-argument – that a strong lead independent director provides adequate oversight – is increasingly viewed as insufficient by institutional investors and proxy advisory firms.

**Overboarded directors.** Directors serving on too many boards – beyond the ISS and Glass Lewis thresholds discussed in Chapter 9 – may lack the time or attention to provide effective oversight.

**Lack of relevant expertise.** Activists frequently argue that the board lacks directors with the specific expertise needed to oversee the company's strategy – a technology company without technologists, a financial services company without capital markets experience. These critiques can be devastating when they are accurate, because they go to the heart of the board's ability to provide informed oversight.

The honest assessment requires the board to evaluate each of these criticisms against its own governance practices – not against what it wishes were true, but against what is actually true. A board that dismisses every governance critique as unfounded will not be credible with the institutional investors whose votes determine the outcome.

# Strategic Review: Does the Activist's Alternative Strategy Have Merit?

Beyond governance, many activists propose specific strategic changes: divestitures, capital returns, operational restructuring, management changes, or fundamental shifts in business strategy. Evaluating these proposals requires the board to engage with the substance of the activist's business case – something many boards are reluctant to do because it implicitly acknowledges that the current strategy may be flawed.

The question is not whether the activist's strategy is perfect. No strategy is. The question is whether it is more likely to create value for shareholders than the current approach. This requires the board to be honest about the trajectory of its own strategy.

Consider Honeywell's response to Elliott Management's $5 billion-plus stake in early 2025. Elliott proposed splitting Honeywell into three separate companies – an aerospace company, an automation company, and an advanced materials company. Elliott's thesis was that the conglomerate structure was creating a valuation discount and that the individual businesses would be worth more as standalone entities. Honeywell's board agreed to a breakup plan. The board's willingness to evaluate the activist's strategic thesis on its merits – rather than reflexively defending the status quo – allowed it to maintain control of the process while addressing the legitimate concern that the conglomerate structure was not serving shareholders.

The counter-example is equally instructive. Pfizer's response to Starboard Value's campaign in 2024 was not to accept Starboard's strategic prescriptions but to deliver financial results that made those prescriptions irrelevant. Pfizer's Q3 2024 results showed revenue more than thirty percent above the prior year, with meaningful progress on the operational improvements that Starboard had criticized. Starboard's $1 billion campaign effectively collapsed – not because Pfizer dismissed the activist's concerns, but because Pfizer addressed them through performance.

The lesson is that the best defense against an activist's strategic critique is a credible strategic alternative. If the board's current strategy is working, the evidence will speak for itself. If it is not, no amount of defensive positioning will obscure that reality from institutional investors.

## The Uncomfortable Truth: When the Activist Is Right

Academic research on activist campaigns consistently finds a pattern that boards prefer not to acknowledge: companies targeted by activists tend to experience governance improvements and, in many cases, improved financial performance in the years following a campaign. The activists are not always right about the remedy. But they are often right about the diagnosis.

This creates an uncomfortable dynamic for directors. If you accept that the activist's identification of problems is frequently legitimate, you must also accept that your board – the board you serve on, the board whose decisions you approved – may have genuinely failed to address those problems. That is not a comfortable admission for anyone, let alone for experienced professionals with significant reputations.

But intellectual honesty demands it. And strategic necessity demands it. Because the alternative – pretending that the activist has identified no legitimate issues when they clearly have – is a recipe for losing the proxy fight, losing the confidence of institutional investors, and losing the board seats that the settlement negotiation might have preserved.

Gildan Activewear provides a cautionary example. In 2023, the board fired the company's founder-CEO without adequately considering shareholder sentiment. When an activist rallied shareholders around the founder's reinstatement, the entire board was replaced. The board's failure was not in making a difficult decision – replacing a CEO can be a legitimate exercise of fiduciary duty. The failure was in not recognizing that shareholders might see the situation differently. The board's self-assurance – its conviction that it knew best, without testing that conviction against shareholder views – led to its complete removal.

Norfolk Southern's delayed response to the East Palestine, Ohio, derailment in 2023 provides another illustration. The company's handling of the crisis – not just the crisis itself, but the governance and operational failures that contributed to it – created the opening for Ancora Holdings to mount a successful campaign that ultimately won three board seats (with a fourth added later) and led to the CEO's departure. The board had ample opportunity to address the operational concerns proactively. It did not. And when the activist arrived, the board's prior inaction became Ancora's most powerful argument.

# Building the Board's Honest Self-Assessment

The framework for evaluating the activist's demands should not be a one-time exercise conducted under crisis conditions. It should be a standing practice – something the board does annually, before the activist arrives.

The Four Improvable Problems framework from Chapter 4 provides the diagnostic structure: low return on assets, suboptimal capital structure, governance and management failures, and transparency deficiencies. Every year, the board should evaluate the company against these four criteria – the same criteria that activists use to identify targets.

If the board conducts this assessment honestly – and acts on what it finds – it accomplishes two things. First, it addresses the vulnerabilities that attract activists, reducing the probability of a campaign. Second, it builds a record of proactive governance that strengthens the board's position if a campaign does materialize. A board that can demonstrate that it identified and addressed governance weaknesses before the activist arrived is a board that institutional investors are likely to support.

The question for every director reading this chapter is not whether your company will face an activist campaign. It is whether you have the intellectual honesty to conduct the assessment that the activist would conduct – and the courage to act on what you find, even when the findings are uncomfortable.

The boards that emerge from activist campaigns with their credibility intact, their positions preserved, and their companies stronger are not the boards that fought the hardest. They are the boards that listened the most honestly. That is the paradox at the heart of activist defense: the strongest position is not defensiveness. It is a genuine, demonstrable commitment to the same shareholder value creation that the activist claims to be pursuing.

The question is not whether the activist is your friend or your enemy. The question is whether the activist has identified something real – and whether you have the integrity to find it before they do.

# Chapter 13: Defense Mechanisms – What Works, What Doesn't, and What Backfires

Every board facing an activist campaign wants to know the same thing: What can we do to protect ourselves? It is a natural question, and the corporate governance industry has spent decades developing an arsenal of defensive mechanisms to answer it. Shareholder rights plans. Classified boards. Advance notice bylaws. Dual-class shares. Board packing. The list is long, the legal frameworks are complex, and the history of their deployment is instructive.

I remember asking this exact question during our SGLI program. After weeks of studying activism from the activist's perspective – building the campaign, constructing the thesis, preparing the materials – I wanted to understand what the defense looked like from the inside. Shapiro's response was characteristically direct: most of the mechanisms that boards rely on were designed for a different era and a different kind of threat. The defense that actually works, he told us, is the one that most boards find hardest to implement – because it requires changing themselves rather than changing the rules.

But here is the reality that most defense advisors are reluctant to state plainly: the defensive mechanisms that work against hostile takeovers are largely ineffective against modern activist campaigns. The activist who wants three board seats and a strategic review is playing a fundamentally different game than the acquirer who wants to buy the company at a discount. The tools designed to stop the second are often irrelevant – or actively counterproductive – against the first.

This chapter examines every major defense mechanism available to boards, evaluates what actually works, identifies what does not, and highlights what actively backfires. The goal is not to discourage boards from using their legal authority. It is to ensure they use it strategically rather than reflexively.

## Shareholder Rights Plans: The Poison Pill

The shareholder rights plan – universally known as the "poison pill" – is the most recognized defensive mechanism in corporate governance. Its mechanics are straightforward: when an investor acquires a specified percentage of the company's shares (typically ten to twenty percent), the plan is triggered, and all other shareholders receive the right to purchase additional shares at a significant discount. The effect is to massively dilute the triggering investor's position, making a hostile acquisition prohibitively expensive.

Poison pills were designed to combat hostile takeovers, and in that context, they work. Delaware courts have generally upheld poison pills when adopted for legitimate corporate purposes – specifically, to give the board time to evaluate an unsolicited acquisition offer and negotiate from a position of strength rather than being forced into a premature sale. The landmark Moran v. Household International decision in 1985 established the legal foundation, and subsequent decisions have refined the boundaries.

But here is the critical distinction: activist campaigns that seek board representation are not hostile takeovers. An activist seeking three board seats is not trying to acquire control of the company. They are exercising their rights as shareholders to influence governance. A poison pill does nothing to prevent this. The activist can accumulate shares below the trigger threshold, nominate directors, solicit proxies, and win board seats without ever triggering the rights plan.

The real danger of the poison pill in an activist context is not that it fails to work. It is that adopting one sends exactly the wrong signal. When a board adopts a poison pill in direct response to an activist's

13D filing, the market interprets it as panic. Proxy advisory firms interpret it as entrenchment. Institutional investors interpret it as a board that is more concerned with protecting its own positions than with engaging with shareholder concerns.

This does not mean poison pills have no role in activist situations. A narrowly tailored, limited-duration pill adopted in response to a specific accumulation threat – where there is evidence that the activist or another party is attempting to gain effective control without paying a premium – can be defensible. But a broad, indefinite pill adopted as a general response to activist attention is almost always counterproductive.

Delaware courts have increasingly scrutinized the use of poison pills in activist contexts. The courts will examine whether the pill was adopted in response to a genuine threat to the company – not a threat to the incumbent board – and whether its terms are proportionate to that threat. A pill with an unusually low trigger, an extended duration, or terms that appear designed to entrench the board rather than protect shareholders is vulnerable to legal challenge and, even if it survives litigation, to the devastating narrative that the board is using its legal authority to insulate itself from accountability.

## Staggered Boards: The Most Effective Structural Defense

If the poison pill is the most recognized defense mechanism, the staggered board is the most effective one. In a classified board structure, directors serve three-year terms with only one-third of the board elected each year. This means an activist who wins the current year's election still controls only one-third of the board. To gain a majority, the activist would need to win elections in two consecutive years – a timeframe that tests the patience and capital of even the most committed activist.

The math is powerful. In a company with a nine-member board and staggered three-year terms, an activist needs to win at least five seats for a majority. Even if they sweep all three seats in Year 1, they need to win at least two more in Year 2. That is two consecutive years of campaign costs, proxy solicitation, media engagement, and share-holder outreach. Most activists – even well-funded ones – find this prospect unappealing. The classified board does not make activism impossible, but it dramatically changes the economics.

And yet the staggered board is in decline. Institutional investors and proxy advisory firms have increasingly pushed for annual elections, viewing classified boards as an entrenchment mechanism that re-duces director accountability. ISS recommends voting against direc-tors on classified boards in many circumstances. Glass Lewis takes a similar view. The result is that many large-cap companies have de-classified their boards under shareholder pressure – ironically mak-ing themselves more vulnerable to the same activists whose cam-paigns the classified structure would have prevented.

Andrew Shapiro identified the paradox with characteristic direct-ness: more and more companies are going public with staggered boards, and worse, with dual-class shares, whereby staggered boards are not even needed. The implication is clear: companies that have the option to maintain a classified board structure should think carefully before giving it up under generalized governance pressure. The companies that have declassified may have traded a significant defensive advantage for a modest improvement in their governance ratings.

This is not an argument for classified boards in every circumstance. There are legitimate governance concerns about directors who face elections only every three years. But boards facing activist attention should understand what they are giving up if they declassify – and what they have already given up if they did so in the past.

# Advance Notice Bylaws: Standard Provisions vs. Punitive Provisions

Advance notice bylaws require shareholders to submit director nomi-nations within a specified window before the annual meeting – typi-cally sixty to ninety days. These provisions serve a legitimate pur-pose: they give the company time to evaluate nominees, prepare proxy materials, and ensure an orderly election process. Standard advance notice provisions are universal and uncontroversial.

The controversy arises when advance notice provisions cross the line from reasonable procedural requirements to punitive barriers designed to discourage nominations entirely. Some companies have adopted provisions requiring nominees to provide extraordinary levels of personal and financial disclosure, to commit to specific governance positions, or to meet qualifications that the company's own directors do not meet. These provisions are designed not to inform the election process but to create procedural grounds for rejecting nominations.

As noted in Chapter 9, companies rejected a record ten percent of activist nomination notices for non-compliance with advance notice provisions in 2023 – reflecting a growing trend of companies using procedural bylaws as a first line of defense.

This tactic has limits. Delaware courts have increasingly scrutinized advance notice provisions that appear designed to entrench the incumbent board rather than to protect the integrity of the election process. The Chancery Court's willingness to examine the purpose behind bylaw provisions – not just their facial validity – means that punitive advance notice bylaws carry legal risk as well as reputational risk.

The practical guidance for boards is this: maintain reasonable advance notice provisions that serve the legitimate purpose of orderly elections. Do not adopt provisions that a reasonable observer would view as designed to prevent shareholder nominations. The reputational cost of being seen as a company that uses procedural tricks to avoid shareholder input far exceeds any tactical advantage those tricks provide.

## Dual-Class Share Structures: The Ultimate Defense

Dual-class share structures concentrate voting control in the hands of founders, insiders, or a specific class of shareholders. A founder who holds shares with ten votes per share controls the company's governance regardless of how many single-vote shares outside investors own. This makes activist campaigns mathematically impossible. The activist can accumulate shares, write letters, nominate directors, and launch media campaigns – none of it matters if the controlling shareholder holds a majority of the voting power.

From a defensive standpoint, dual-class structures are absolute. No activist has ever won a proxy fight against a company where the controlling shareholder held a majority of the votes and chose to vote against the activist. The math simply does not work.

But the cost is significant. Dual-class structures insulate the controlling shareholder from all accountability – not just from activists, but from institutional investors, proxy advisory firms, and the market itself. The same structure that prevents an activist from forcing governance improvements prevents anyone from forcing governance improvements. When the controlling shareholder is a visionary founder executing a compelling strategy, this can be tolerable. When the controlling shareholder is an entrenched manager resisting accountability, it is a governance disaster.

The trend is growing. More companies are going public with dual-class structures, and some are pairing them with classified boards for an almost impregnable defense. Shapiro noted this trend with obvious concern. Institutional investors have pushed back – some index providers exclude dual-class companies from their indices, and some institutional investors refuse to invest in them – but the trend continues.

For boards considering dual-class structures, the trade-off is clear: absolute protection against activist campaigns in exchange for absolute insulation from shareholder accountability. For boards that already have dual-class structures, the question is whether the controlling shareholder's governance practices justify the extraordinary power that the structure confers.

## Board Packing: The Aggressive Response

Board packing – adding new directors to dilute the representation of activist nominees – is the most aggressive defensive tactic available to boards. If an activist wins two board seats in an election, the board can respond by adding three, four, or five new directors, ensuring that the activist's nominees remain a small minority.

This tactic is legal in most circumstances. Boards generally have the authority to set the size of the board within the limits specified in the bylaws or charter. But the fact that something is legal does not make it wise.

Board packing signals desperation. It tells institutional investors that the board is willing to manipulate its own composition rather than work constructively with new directors elected by shareholders. It invites litigation – Delaware courts have examined board-packing decisions for evidence of entrenchment, and courts are likely to scrutinize whether the new directors were added for legitimate governance purposes or solely to dilute shareholder-elected nominees. And it almost guarantees that the activist will escalate, because the activist now has a powerful narrative: the board is so committed to maintaining control that it will override the will of its own shareholders.

The practical reality is that board packing rarely achieves its intended purpose. Even if it temporarily dilutes the activist's representation, it accelerates the campaign rather than resolving it. The next annual meeting becomes a referendum on the board's decision to pack itself, and the institutional investor backlash is often severe.

## What Does Not Work: The Failure of Passive Defense

Beyond structural defenses, many boards deploy passive tactics – stonewalling, generic press releases, personal attacks on the activist, or hiding behind advisors. Chapter 11 examined these in detail as "worst first moves." The common thread is that each of these approaches avoids engagement rather than addressing the activist's concerns – and each one hands the activist a narrative about board entrenchment that is more damaging than the original governance critique.

The distinction is worth emphasizing: structural defenses (poison pills, classified boards) are mechanisms designed into the governance architecture. Passive defenses are behavioral choices that reflect the board's mindset. And it is the behavioral choices – the decision to stonewall rather than engage, to attack the activist's character rather than address their arguments, to delegate all communication to advisors rather than having directors speak for themselves – that most reliably predict whether a board will lose a proxy fight.

## What Actively Backfires: Creating the Narrative of Entrenchment

The most dangerous outcome for a board facing an activist campaign is not losing a proxy fight. It is giving the activist the narrative that the board is entrenched – that it is more interested in protecting its own positions than in serving shareholders. Once the activist can credibly make that argument, the campaign dynamics shift decisively against the board.

Phillips 66 provides a recent and instructive example. When the company's chairman succession proceeded against Elliott Management's stated preference in late 2024, the situation escalated from what might have been a negotiated settlement to a full proxy fight. The board's apparent unwillingness to engage with Elliott's concerns about the succession – the appearance that the board had already made its decision and was not interested in shareholder input – gave Elliott a powerful narrative about board entrenchment. Whether the board's succession decision was substantively correct became almost irrelevant. The process by which it was made – or the perception of that process – became the issue.

The pattern repeats across campaigns. When a board takes an action that a reasonable observer would interpret as prioritizing board continuity over shareholder interests, the activist's job becomes dramatically easier. The activist no longer needs to prove that the company is underperforming or that the governance is flawed. They simply need to point to the board's own behavior as evidence that the directors are not acting in shareholders' best interests.

This is why the most dangerous defensive measures are not the ones that fail – they are the ones that succeed in the short term but destroy the board's credibility in the long term. A board that successfully blocks an activist's nominees through procedural technicalities, packs itself with friendly directors, or adopts a poison pill to prevent engagement may "win" the immediate battle. But it will likely lose the war, because institutional investors have long memories and proxy advisory firms document everything.

## Proactive Defense: What Actually Works

The defense mechanisms that actually work in modern activist campaigns are not defensive mechanisms at all. They are offensive ones – proactive actions that address the vulnerabilities the activist would exploit.

**Proactive strategic transformation.** Disney's response to Trian Partners' campaign in 2023-2024 is the gold standard. Before the proxy vote, Disney announced cost cuts, a path to streaming profitability, and a comprehensive ESPN strategy that addressed the core elements of Trian's critique. Disney did not adopt the activist's plan – it developed its own plan that addressed the same concerns. The result was that Trian's proxy fight failed because Disney's proactive response persuaded institutional investors that the board was already doing what needed to be done.

**Demonstrable performance improvement.** Pfizer's response to Starboard Value's campaign demonstrated that the best defense is results. Pfizer's strong Q3 2024 earnings – revenue more than thirty percent above the prior year – destroyed Starboard's underperformance narrative. No defensive mechanism, no press release, no legal maneuvering could have been as effective as the simple fact of improved financial performance.

**Board refreshment ahead of campaigns.** Boards that proactively refresh themselves – adding directors with relevant expertise, retiring long-tenured members, bringing in fresh perspectives – eliminate one of the activist's most common arguments before it can be made. A board that has recently added qualified independent directors with relevant industry experience is a much harder target than a board that has not changed in a decade.

**Strong positioning with ISS and Glass Lewis.** Proxy advisory firms are not the enemy. They are the referees. Boards that maintain strong governance practices, engage constructively with proxy advisory firm feedback, and ensure their proxy disclosures are comprehensive and transparent build a reservoir of credibility that pays dividends when an activist campaign materializes. A board with favorable ISS and Glass Lewis governance scores enters a proxy fight with significant built-in advantage.

**Retail shareholder engagement.** While institutional investors are the most important audience in a proxy fight, retail shareholders can matter in close contests. Companies that maintain active investor relations programs, communicate clearly about strategy and performance, and make it easy for retail shareholders to vote can benefit from a base of individual investors who are less susceptible to the activist's institutional campaign.

## The Evolving Legal Landscape

The legal framework governing defensive measures is not static. As Chapter 10 examined in detail, the Moelis decision in 2024 limited the enforceability of stockholder agreements that constrained board authority, and Delaware courts continue to apply the Unocal standard with increasing scrutiny – asking whether defensive measures respond to genuine corporate threats or merely to threats to incumbent directors' positions.

The broader trend is unmistakable. Institutional investors are penalizing companies with excessive defensive provisions. Governance rating agencies factor defensive measures into their assessments. Proxy advisory firms recommend against directors who adopt aggressive defensive measures. The range of acceptable defensive behavior is narrowing, and boards that rely on structural defenses rather than on the quality of their governance are swimming against the current.

## The Defense That Cannot Be Taken Away

After studying activist campaigns for months, participating in the Flowers Foods simulation, and absorbing the perspectives of both activists and defenders, I have reached a conclusion that is both simple and difficult:

The only defense that truly works – the only one that cannot be overcome by a determined activist with a credible argument – is genuine performance. A board that delivers returns, maintains strong governance, communicates transparently, and engages constructively with its shareholders has a defense that no activist can breach. Not because the activist cannot file a 13D. Not because the activist cannot nominate directors. Not because structural defenses prevent it. But because the institutional investors whose votes determine the outcome will not support an activist campaign against a board that is clearly doing its job.

Every other defense is a substitute for this one. Poison pills buy time. Classified boards slow the process. Advance notice bylaws create procedural hurdles. But none of them change the fundamental dynamic: if the board is not performing, if the governance is not strong, if the transparency is not there, no defensive mechanism will save it. And if the board is performing, if the governance is strong, if the transparency is exemplary – then no defensive mechanism is necessary.

That is the uncomfortable truth about activist defense: the companies that need defensive mechanisms the most are the companies for which they work the least. And the companies that have earned the right not to worry about activists are the companies that never needed the defenses in the first place.

# Chapter 14: The Settlement Negotiation – Finding a Deal Both Sides Can Live With

The conference room on December 9, 2025, was set up like a courtroom drama. The activist team on one side. The management and board team on the other. Andrew Shapiro in the middle – not as a participant, but as the experienced practitioner who would intervene when the negotiation went off the rails or when both sides needed a dose of reality.

Our activist team – Sterling Capital Partners, the fictional firm we had built over the eight weeks of the Flowers Foods tabletop exercise – had spent weeks preparing. We had the letter. We had the investor deck. We had our demands prioritized, our concessions mapped, and our walk-away positions defined. The management team had their defensive positions, their counter-arguments, and their own set of priorities. The board team had to navigate between them.

What followed over the next several hours was the most instructive experience of the entire program. Not because it went according to plan – it did not. But because the dynamics of the negotiation revealed truths about activist settlements that no textbook could convey.

The first truth: settlement is not defeat. It is strategy. And the boards that understand this consistently achieve better outcomes than the boards that treat every negotiation as an existential threat.

# Why Most Campaigns End in Settlement

The statistics tell the story. As documented in Chapters 1 and 9, ninety-two percent of activist board seats in 2025 were won through settlement, and the average time to settlement has compressed from seventy-seven days in 2022 to just sixteen and a half days. The contested proxy fight – for all its drama – is the exception. Settlement is the rule.

Several structural factors drive this dominance. The costs are prohibitive – as the Disney-Trian campaign demonstrated, a large-cap proxy fight can cost both sides a combined $65 million or more. The outcomes are uncertain, with activist win rates fluctuating between thirty-eight and fifty-six percent in recent years. The process is publicly damaging – every aspect of governance, strategy, and performance is scrutinized by proxy advisory firms, media, and analysts. And institutional investors prefer settlement, having repeatedly signaled that constructive engagement serves shareholders better than proxy warfare.

For all of these reasons, the settlement calculus is usually straightforward. The question is not whether to settle. It is how to negotiate a settlement that addresses legitimate concerns, preserves the board's essential governance authority, and positions the company for success after the agreement is signed.

# The Settlement Calculus: Fight vs. Deal

Every board facing an activist campaign must conduct a rigorous analysis of its options. The fight-or-deal decision should be based on data, not emotion. Here is the framework:

**Probability of winning a proxy fight.** This requires an honest assessment – not a hopeful one – of the board's likely support among institutional investors. The proxy solicitor's analysis is essential here. What percentage of shares are held by institutions that are likely to support the board? What percentage are held by institutions with governance policies that align with the activist's demands? What are the ISS and Glass Lewis governance ratings? If the proxy solicitor's analysis suggests that the board's support is marginal, a proxy fight is a gamble that the board is likely to lose.

**Cost of fighting.** Legal fees, proxy solicitor fees, investment banking fees, crisis communications fees, printing and mailing costs, and the internal costs of management distraction. For large-cap companies, these costs routinely exceed $30 million. For mid-cap companies, they can represent a material impact on earnings.

**Cost of losing.** If the board fights and loses, the outcome is almost always worse than the settlement the board could have negotiated before the fight began. A board that loses a proxy fight loses not just the specific seats contested but the credibility and leverage to negotiate favorable terms for the remaining governance issues. The activist, emboldened by victory, will push harder on every demand.

**Cost of settling.** Settlement involves concessions – board seats for activist nominees, governance reforms, potentially a strategic review or capital return commitment. These concessions have costs, but they also have benefits. New directors may genuinely improve the board. Governance reforms may strengthen the company. A strategic review may identify value-creation opportunities. The question is whether the concessions the activist is demanding are net positive or net negative for shareholders.

**Time horizon.** How long will the dispute consume board and management attention if it escalates to a proxy fight? Weeks of preparation. Months of campaigning. The annual meeting itself. And then the aftermath – integrating new directors, managing media coverage, reassuring employees and customers. Settlement compresses this timeline dramatically, allowing the board to return its attention to the business.

Shapiro's guidance on this calculus was unambiguous: the company should negotiate a mutually acceptable settlement rather than having a scorched earth proxy contest that will result in that being your last board. The implied warning is clear. A board that fights and loses often does not get a second chance. A board that settles on reasonable terms lives to govern another day.

# Standstill Agreements: Structure and Standard Terms

The standstill agreement is the primary legal instrument for settling activist campaigns. It establishes the terms of the deal – what each side gets, what each side gives up, and how long the agreement lasts. Understanding the anatomy of a standstill agreement is essential for any director who may participate in negotiating one.

**Board seats for activist nominees.** This is the centerpiece of most settlements. The activist agrees to support the company's governance in exchange for a specified number of board seats filled by the activist's nominees. The number of seats varies widely. Elliott Management won six seats at Southwest Airlines in 2024 – the largest settlement in U.S. history. Browning West replaced the entire board at Gildan Activewear. More typical settlements involve one to three seats.

An important trend: in 2024, seventy-eight percent of board seats won through settlements were filled with independent directors, not activist fund principals. The days when activists routinely placed their own employees on boards are fading. Instead, activists nominate genuinely independent directors with relevant expertise – directors who can credibly claim to represent all shareholders, not just the activist. The notable exception was Starboard Value's Jeff Smith, who personally joined Kenvue's board as part of a three-seat settlement – one of the few recent cases where an activist fund principal took a seat directly.

**Governance reforms.** Settlements frequently include governance commitments beyond board seats. Common provisions include:

- CEO and Chair role separation, either immediately or within a specified timeframe
- Board refreshment commitments – agreement to retire a specified number of long-tenured directors over a defined period
- Committee restructuring – changes to audit, compensation, or nominating committee composition
- Compensation reform – alignment of executive pay with performance metrics, clawback provisions, or stock ownership re-

quirements
- Strategic review commitments – agreement to evaluate specific strategic alternatives, such as divestitures, capital returns, or operational restructuring

**Activist obligations.** In exchange for board representation and governance reforms, the activist typically agrees to:

- Support the company's full board slate at the next annual meeting
- Refrain from acquiring additional shares beyond a specified ownership threshold (typically the current level or a modest increase)
- Maintain confidentiality regarding board deliberations and non-public information
- Refrain from public criticism of the company or its management during the standstill period
- Refrain from launching or supporting additional proxy contests during the standstill period

**Duration and termination.** Most standstill agreements have a duration of twelve to twenty-four months, though some extend to thirty-six months. The termination provisions are critically important. Standard exceptions that allow the activist to exit the standstill include:

- A merger or acquisition proposal from a third party that the activist wishes to evaluate independently
- A material decline in the company's financial performance below specified thresholds
- The company's failure to comply with its obligations under the agreement
- The expiration of the standstill period

These termination provisions are the subject of some of the most intense negotiation in any settlement. The activist wants broad exceptions that preserve their ability to act if circumstances change. The board wants narrow exceptions that provide genuine standstill protection. The final terms typically reflect the relative leverage each side brings to the negotiation.

# Board Seats: How Many, and for Whom?

The negotiation over board seats is the heart of virtually every settlement discussion. The number of seats, the identity of the nominees, and the committee assignments all involve complex strategic considerations.

**How many seats?** The number depends on the activist's leverage, the strength of their campaign, the size of the board, and the board's willingness to engage. A single seat may be appropriate when the activist's demands are narrow and the campaign is early. Three seats – the number won by Kenvue's Starboard settlement, Carl Icahn's Illumina campaign, and Ancora's Norfolk Southern campaign – is the most common outcome in significant campaigns. Six seats, as in the Southwest Airlines settlement, represents extraordinary leverage and an exceptional situation.

The board's goal should be to concede the minimum number of seats needed to achieve a settlement while ensuring that the seats go to directors who will genuinely contribute. A common mistake is to view seats as pure losses – territory surrendered to the enemy. In reality, well-chosen activist nominees can improve the board. They bring fresh perspectives, financial expertise, and a shareholder-oriented mindset that may have been lacking. The question is not whether to add new directors but whether the new directors will make the board more effective.

**Independent directors vs. activist principals.** As noted above, the trend is overwhelmingly toward independent nominees rather than activist fund employees. This is generally positive for the board, because independent nominees owe their loyalty to shareholders broadly rather than to the activist fund specifically. However, the board should conduct its own due diligence on activist nominees – reviewing their qualifications, checking references, and ensuring they bring the skills and experience the board needs.

**Committee assignments.** Activist nominees frequently request – and often receive – seats on key committees: audit, compensation, or nominating and governance. These committee assignments give the activist's nominees influence over the areas that are typically the focus of activist campaigns: financial oversight, executive pay, and board composition. The board should negotiate committee assign-

ments carefully, ensuring that the nominees' expertise is matched to
the committee's responsibilities.

## Negotiation Dynamics: Lessons from the Flowers Foods Simulation

The December 9 capstone negotiation covered the full range of issues
that real activist settlements address. Our activist team presented
demands across six categories: CEO and Chair separation, board
member removal and replacement, succession planning, capital allocation, compensation reform, and operational improvements. The
management and board teams had to evaluate each demand, assess
its merit, and construct counter-proposals in real time.

Several dynamics emerged that I believe reflect the reality of actual
settlement negotiations:

**Opening positions are not final positions.** Our activist team
led with aggressive demands – not because we expected to get everything, but because we needed negotiating room. We demanded
two specific director removals knowing we would likely settle for one.
We demanded immediate CEO-Chair separation knowing we would
likely accept a phased transition. Boards that react to the activist's
opening position as though it were a final demand miss the opportunity to negotiate. Every demand is an opening bid.

**Prioritization matters more than breadth.** Our team had a
long list of demands, but we had internally ranked them by priority.
The CEO-Chair separation and the addition of independent directors
were non-negotiable. The specific director removals were strongly
preferred but tradable. The operational improvements were aspirational – we wanted them, but we would accept a commitment to
a strategic review rather than specific operational changes. Knowing our priorities allowed us to make concessions on lower-priority
items in exchange for wins on higher-priority ones.

**The board's credibility is its most valuable asset.** When the
management team presented a credible plan for addressing the concerns we had raised – not a plan to fight us, but a plan to improve
the company – the negotiation dynamic shifted. We were no longer
fighting against an entrenched board. We were negotiating with a

board that shared our goal of improving shareholder value. The disagreement was about means, not ends. That shift made settlement dramatically easier.

**Andrew Shapiro's interventions were revealing.** Throughout the negotiation, Shapiro offered observations that reflected decades of real-world experience. His most important intervention was reminding both sides that the alternative to settlement was a proxy fight that would cost both sides dearly – in money, in time, and in reputation. The company should negotiate a mutually acceptable settlement rather than having a scorched earth proxy contest that will result in that being your last board. That warning – directed at both teams – reframed the negotiation from a zero-sum contest to a problem-solving exercise.

**The chairman question dominated the negotiation.** The separation of CEO and Chair roles consumed more negotiation time than any other issue. The management team argued that the current structure worked, that the lead independent director provided adequate oversight, and that forcing a separation would be destabilizing. Our activist team argued that combining the roles concentrated too much power in one person and compromised the board's independence. The compromise – elevating an existing independent director to the Chair role over a defined transition period – required extensive discussion of which director, what timeline, and what authority the new Chair would have.

**Personal dynamics matter.** Despite the structured format of the simulation, personal dynamics influenced the negotiation significantly. The trust – or lack of trust – between the lead negotiators on each side affected the pace and tone of the discussions. The simulation taught me that settlement negotiations are not purely analytical exercises. They are human interactions between people with professional reputations, personal pride, and genuine convictions. Boards that acknowledge this human dimension – that treat the activist's representatives with respect even while disagreeing with their positions – tend to negotiate more effectively than boards that treat the negotiation as a battlefield.

# The Standstill's Fine Print

The headline terms of a standstill agreement get most of the attention. But four areas of fine print often determine whether the agreement achieves its intended purpose.

**Voting commitments** – the scope and duration of the activist's obligation to support the company's slate – range from narrow (next annual meeting only) to broad (full standstill period). The difference is the difference between limited and genuine stability.

**Standstill exceptions** – the circumstances under which the activist can exit – are among the most intensely negotiated terms. Standard exceptions include merger proposals, material performance declines, and company non-compliance. But the definitions matter enormously: What constitutes a "material" decline? Who determines compliance? Can the activist unilaterally declare the standstill terminated? These questions determine whether the standstill provides genuine protection or merely an illusion of it.

**Information rights** require careful management. Activist nominees on the board will have access to confidential company information, and the standstill must include Chinese wall provisions, confidentiality obligations, and trading restrictions to protect the company and ensure securities law compliance.

**Termination mechanics** determine the transition from the structured standstill relationship to whatever comes next – a renewed campaign, peaceful coexistence, or full exit. The wind-down provisions, extension rights, and post-termination restrictions all merit careful negotiation.

# The Scorched Earth Warning

Shapiro's most sobering observation about settlement negotiations was his description of the alternative. A scorched earth proxy contest – where both sides spend tens of millions of dollars, governance is dissected in public, and the business suffers months of distraction – benefits no one except the advisory firms billing for the engagement. The economics of proxy fights, examined in detail in Chapter 9, make the case clearly: even a winning board emerges with diminished credibility and strained institutional relationships.

Settlement avoids all of this. It preserves the board's essential authority while addressing the activist's legitimate concerns. It allows both sides to claim a measure of victory. And it allows the company to return its attention to the business, which is ultimately what shareholders care about most. The boards that understand this calculus settle earlier, on better terms, with less damage to the company and its governance.

## Case Studies: Settlements That Shaped the Landscape

Several recent settlements illustrate the range of outcomes and the dynamics that produce them.

**Southwest Airlines and Elliott Management (2024).** Elliott's campaign against Southwest Airlines resulted in a six-seat settlement – the largest in U.S. history. The settlement included the departure of the CEO, the appointment of an independent Chair, and a comprehensive governance overhaul. The scale of the settlement reflected Elliott's leverage: the company's stock had significantly underperformed, the governance concerns were well-documented, and institutional investor support for the activist was strong. The settlement allowed Southwest to begin its transformation without the distraction and expense of a proxy fight.

**Kenvue and Starboard Value (2024).** Starboard won three board seats at Kenvue, the consumer health company spun off from Johnson & Johnson. One of those seats went to Starboard's founder, Jeff Smith – one of the few recent cases of an activist fund principal taking a board seat directly rather than nominating an independent director. The settlement reflected Kenvue's early struggles as an independent public company and the need for fresh governance perspectives.

**Norfolk Southern and Ancora Holdings (2024).** Ancora's campaign against Norfolk Southern focused on operational performance following the East Palestine derailment and the broader question of management accountability. The settlement gave Ancora three board seats initially, with a fourth added later. The

CEO departed as part of the resolution. The campaign illustrated how operational failures can create governance vulnerabilities that activists exploit – and how settlement can provide the mechanism for accountability that the board failed to provide on its own.

# After the Deal: Making Settlement Work

A settlement agreement is not the end of an activist campaign. It is the beginning of a new phase. The activist's nominees are now on the board. The governance reforms must be implemented. The strategic commitments must be executed. And the relationship between the incumbent directors and the new arrivals must be managed constructively.

This phase is often the most challenging, because it requires people who have been adversaries to become colleagues. The incumbent directors may resent the new arrivals. The new directors may arrive with a mandate to challenge the status quo. The CEO may feel undermined. The culture of the boardroom may be disrupted.

The boards that manage this transition successfully share common characteristics. They treat the new directors as full members of the board from day one. They provide comprehensive onboarding. They assign the new directors to committees where their expertise can be leveraged. They maintain open communication about the implementation of settlement terms. And they recognize that the new directors, whatever their origin, owe the same fiduciary duty to all shareholders that every director owes.

The boards that mismanage this transition – that treat the new directors as adversaries, that limit their information access, that exclude them from meaningful deliberations – create the conditions for the next campaign. An activist who placed a director on the board and then sees that director marginalized has every incentive to return with a larger demand at the next annual meeting.

Settlement, when done well, is not a compromise. It is a governance mechanism – one that can produce genuinely better outcomes than the status quo that preceded it. The question is not whether the activist should have been at the table. The question is whether the board will use the opportunity that the settlement creates to build something better than what came before.

That is the question our teams grappled with in the Flowers Foods simulation on that December afternoon. And it is the question that every board facing an activist campaign must ultimately answer – not with defensive mechanisms or legal maneuvering, but with the quality of its governance and the honesty of its engagement with the shareholders it serves.

# Chapter 15: The Role of Institutional Investors – The Decisive Variable

In May 2021, a hedge fund managing approximately $250 million in assets took on a company worth more than $250 billion. By every conventional measure, the contest should not have been close. Engine No. 1 owned a rounding error of ExxonMobil's outstanding shares. It had no name recognition among retail investors. It had never run a proxy fight before. And yet, when the votes were counted at ExxonMobil's annual meeting, Engine No. 1 had won three board seats – a result that rewrote the rules of shareholder activism and demonstrated a truth that every director needs to internalize.

The activist's own shares almost never determine the outcome. The institutional investors do.

This chapter examines the most important variable in any activist campaign: the response of the company's institutional investor base. Understanding how these investors think, what they evaluate, and what drives their voting decisions is not optional for directors in the modern governance era. It is the difference between boards that survive activist campaigns and boards that do not.

## The Power of the Top Five

Here is a number that should keep every director honest: in a typical public company, the five largest shareholders collectively own thirty to fifty percent or more of the outstanding shares. In many large-cap companies, the top three alone – BlackRock, Vanguard, and State Street – may control twenty percent or more of the vote.

The arithmetic is simple and merciless. An activist investor who can persuade even a fraction of these institutional holders to support their campaign has essentially won. The company's management team can mount the most polished defense in corporate history, retain the most expensive advisors, and spend tens of millions on proxy solicitation – and none of it matters if the top five shareholders have already decided to vote with the activist.

This concentration of ownership has intensified over the past two decades as passive index investing has grown to dominate the asset management industry. The Big Three index fund managers – BlackRock, Vanguard, and State Street – collectively manage more than $25 trillion in assets. Their ownership positions in publicly traded companies are not discretionary investments. They are mathematical consequences of tracking an index. When a company is included in the S&P 500 or the Russell 1000, the Big Three must hold it. They cannot sell.

That constraint – the inability to exit – creates a paradox that fundamentally shapes the governance landscape.

## The Passive Funds Paradox

Index fund managers are often described as "passive" investors, and in one sense they are. They do not pick stocks. They do not time markets. They do not build concentrated positions based on investment theses. But calling them passive in the governance context is profoundly misleading.

Here is the reality: because index funds cannot sell, voting is their only tool for expressing dissatisfaction with a company's governance or strategy. A traditional active manager who loses confidence in a company's board can simply sell the stock. BlackRock, Vanguard, and State Street cannot. They are locked in for as long as the company remains in the index. Their only lever is governance engagement – meetings with directors, voting on shareholder proposals, and supporting or opposing management in proxy contests.

This makes index fund managers uniquely powerful in activist campaigns. They are permanent shareholders with enormous blocks of votes and no ability to express displeasure by selling. When an activist presents a credible case that the board is failing in its oversight responsibilities, the index fund manager cannot shrug and move on. They must evaluate the claim and vote their shares. And because their stewardship teams answer to their own boards and beneficiaries – not to the company's management – they have both the authority and the obligation to vote against incumbent directors when the evidence warrants it.

The ExxonMobil campaign demonstrated this dynamic with devastating clarity. Engine No. 1 did not win because it convinced retail shareholders to vote against management. It won because BlackRock, Vanguard, and State Street – the three largest passive holders of ExxonMobil shares – each voted in favor of at least some Engine No. 1 nominees. The California Public Employees' Retirement System and other major pension funds joined them. The company's management had the backing of its own proxy solicitation machine, decades of institutional relationships, and the full weight of one of the world's most recognized corporate brands. None of it was enough.

## How Institutional Investors Evaluate Campaigns

Institutional investors do not outsource their governance decisions – at least not entirely. The largest asset managers maintain dedicated investment stewardship teams that independently assess both the company's governance record and the activist's proposals. Understanding what these teams evaluate is essential for any director preparing for – or hoping to avoid – an activist contest.

The evaluation framework varies by institution, but most stewardship teams assess five dimensions.

**Long-term financial performance.** This is the threshold question. Has the company delivered competitive total shareholder return relative to its peers over meaningful time horizons – typically one, three, five, and ten years? A company that has consistently outperformed its peer group starts from a position of strength. A company whose stock has lagged across every time horizon is vulnerable regardless of how eloquently its management defends its strategy. Stewardship teams are sophisticated enough to distinguish between temporary setbacks and structural underperformance, but they are also disciplined enough to recognize when management's explanations for underperformance have become excuses.

**Governance disclosure quality.** How transparent is the company about its governance practices? Does the proxy statement provide meaningful information about board composition, director qualifications, committee activities, and executive compensation? Or does it rely on boilerplate language that reveals nothing of substance? Institutional investors read proxy statements carefully – in some cases more carefully than the directors who approve them. A proxy statement that lacks specificity about why particular directors were nominated, what skills they bring, and how the board's composition addresses the company's strategic needs signals a nominating process that is not rigorous.

**Activist analysis credibility.** Stewardship teams evaluate the quality of the activist's research and the specificity of their demands. An activist who presents vague complaints about "poor governance" without data will not be taken seriously. An activist who presents detailed peer benchmarking, specific financial metrics, and a constructive plan for improvement will get a hearing. The Engine No. 1 campaign succeeded in part because its analysis was meticulous – every claim was supported by data, every nominee had relevant qualifications, and the thesis was grounded in long-term value creation rather than short-term financial engineering.

**Nominee qualifications.** The universal proxy card has made individual director qualifications more important than ever. Shareholders can now pick and choose among nominees from both slates, which means each candidate must stand on their own merits. Institutional investors evaluate activist nominees against the same criteria they would apply to any director candidate: relevant industry experience, governance expertise, independence from both management and the activist, and the ability to contribute constructively to board deliberations.

**Board responsiveness.** Has the board demonstrated a willingness to engage with shareholder concerns – not just during a crisis, but as an ongoing governance practice? Companies that maintain regular dialogue with their largest shareholders, that respond substantively to shareholder proposals, and that demonstrate a track record of governance improvements build credibility that carries weight during a proxy contest. Companies that engage with shareholders only when forced to do so by an activist filing signal exactly the kind of insularity that institutional investors find concerning.

# Building Relationships Before You Need Them

The question is not whether your company has an investor relations function – it is whether your independent directors have genuine relationships with your largest shareholders.

This distinction matters more than most boards realize. An effective IR program manages the flow of financial information to the investment community. That is necessary but insufficient. What activist campaigns test is not the quality of your earnings calls or the polish of your investor day presentations. What they test is whether your largest shareholders trust your board – and trust requires relationships that go beyond management-mediated communications.

The most effective boards maintain a cadence of engagement that includes several elements.

**Investor days with independent director participation.** Many companies host annual or semi-annual investor days where management presents the company's strategy and financial outlook. The boards that build the deepest institutional relationships make sure that independent directors – particularly the board chair, the lead independent director, and committee chairs – participate meaningfully in these events. This sends a signal that the board is engaged and accessible, not isolated behind management.

**One-on-one meetings between directors and major shareholders.** Some boards go further, arranging periodic meetings between independent directors and the company's largest institutional holders. These meetings – which should be carefully structured to comply with Regulation FD – give institutional investors a direct sense of the board's quality, engagement, and independence. They also give directors an unfiltered view of investor sentiment that management's investor relations function may not fully convey.

**Substantive proxy disclosures.** The proxy statement is many institutional investors' primary source of information about your board. A proxy statement that provides detailed information about director qualifications, board evaluation processes, committee activities, and the rationale for executive compensation decisions builds credibility. A proxy statement that reads like it was generated by a compliance department builds nothing.

Andrew Shapiro emphasized this point with characteristic directness during his presentation to our cohort. He told us that in every campaign he had waged, the first thing his team did after filing the 13D was reach out to the company's largest institutional holders. "I know who they are," he said. "And I know which ones have been frustrated with the board." The question he posed to us was uncomfortable: if the activist already knows your largest shareholders and what they think of your governance, what does it mean if your independent directors have never met them?

The relationship between a company and its institutional investors is not something to cultivate only when an activist appears. It is an ongoing governance responsibility. The credibility reservoir you build through years of transparent, substantive engagement is the asset you will draw upon when an activist arrives and asks those same institutional investors to support a change in board composition.

## When Institutions Side with the Activist

Understanding what triggers institutional investor support for an activist campaign is critical for any board conducting an honest vulnerability assessment. The pattern across recent campaigns is remarkably consistent.

**Persistent total shareholder return underperformance.** This is the single strongest predictor. When a company's stock has lagged its peer group over multiple time horizons – particularly three and five years – institutional investors become receptive to arguments for board-level change. Engine No. 1's case against

ExxonMobil was anchored in TSR data showing underperformance over one, three, five, and ten-year periods. The data was devastating not because any single period was catastrophic, but because the consistency of underperformance across every horizon made management's explanations untenable.

**Governance concerns flagged repeatedly.**    Institutional investors track their engagement history with portfolio companies. When stewardship teams have raised the same governance concerns in multiple consecutive years – board independence, director tenure, executive compensation alignment – and the company has failed to respond substantively, the institutional investor's patience erodes.   By the time an activist arrives making the same points, the institution has already concluded that private engagement has failed.

**Management unresponsive to engagement.** Companies that refuse to meet with institutional investors outside of formal investor days, that provide formulaic responses to governance inquiries, or that ignore shareholder proposals that received significant support signal that they are not interested in investor input. When an activist then arrives with a credible plan for improvement, the institutional investor faces a straightforward choice: continue supporting a board that refuses to listen, or support the activist who is saying what they have been saying for years.

**The activist's analysis is more credible than management's defense.** This is the factor that boards most frequently underestimate.   Institutional stewardship teams are experienced evaluators of governance arguments. They can distinguish between a management defense built on substance and one built on deflection. When management responds to an activist's detailed financial analysis with generalities about "long-term strategy" and "transformation in progress" – without specific metrics, timelines, or accountability mechanisms – the stewardship team notices.   And when the activist's presentation includes the specific data and benchmarks that management's defense lacks, the stewardship team draws the obvious conclusion about which party has done its homework.

# The Engine No. 1 Precedent

The Engine No. 1 campaign against ExxonMobil – examined in detail in Chapter 17 – remains the definitive illustration of institutional investor power in activist contests. A fund managing approximately $250 million defeated a company worth more than $250 billion, winning three board seats not through its own shareholding but by assembling an unprecedented institutional coalition. BlackRock, Vanguard, State Street, CalPERS, and numerous other institutional investors voted for at least some Engine No. 1 nominees – not because they were pressured, but because the activist's analysis of sustained underperformance and board composition gaps was more credible than management's defense.

The lesson for this chapter is specific: institutional investors decided the outcome. ExxonMobil's management had every traditional advantage – size, brand recognition, decades of institutional relationships, and unlimited resources for proxy solicitation. None of it mattered because the institutional investors who controlled the votes had independently concluded that the board had failed in its strategic oversight. The campaign demonstrated that institutional investor support is not something to cultivate during a crisis. It is something to earn continuously, through governance practices and shareholder engagement that build credibility long before it is tested.

# The Disney Counter-Example

The Trian Partners campaign against Disney – also profiled in Chapter 17 – demonstrates that institutional investor support for the activist is not automatic. Peltz lost decisively, defeated by a roughly two-to-one margin despite the most expensive proxy fight in history.

The institutional investor lesson from Disney is the mirror image of ExxonMobil. Disney's board retained institutional support because it had done three things: acted proactively before the vote (announcing cost cuts, a streaming profitability path, and board composition changes), delivered improving financial performance (stock up approximately fifty percent during the campaign period), and maintained a shareholder base – including millions of passionate retail investors – that trusted the board's direction.

The contrast is instructive. ExxonMobil's board had been perceived as dismissive of institutional investor engagement and presided over sustained underperformance. Disney's board had been proactive, transparent, and was delivering results. Institutional investors responded accordingly in both cases – supporting change where it was warranted and supporting the incumbent board where it was earning their confidence.

## The Big Three's Stewardship Evolution

The stewardship teams at BlackRock, Vanguard, and State Street have undergone a dramatic transformation over the past decade – a transformation that has direct implications for how boards should approach governance.

A decade ago, these teams were small, under-resourced, and focused primarily on routine proxy voting. Their engagement with portfolio companies was limited and often formulaic. Today, BlackRock's Investment Stewardship team alone employs dozens of governance specialists covering thousands of companies worldwide. Vanguard and State Street have made similar investments. These teams conduct company-by-company governance analysis, meet regularly with directors and management, and make independent voting decisions on contested proxy matters.

The sophistication of these teams has increased in parallel with their size. Stewardship analysts now routinely analyze board skills matrices, evaluate executive compensation structures against peer benchmarks, assess capital allocation track records, and monitor governance improvements over multi-year periods. They maintain engagement histories for individual companies – records of what they discussed with the board, what commitments the board made, and whether those commitments were kept.

For boards, this evolution means that your governance is being evaluated continuously, not just at annual meeting time. The stewardship team that will ultimately determine how BlackRock or Vanguard votes in a proxy contest has been building its assessment of your board for years before the activist arrived. Every meeting you held with them – or did not hold – is part of that assessment. Every proxy statement they read, every governance reform you implemented or failed to implement, every shareholder proposal you responded to or ignored is in their files.

This continuous evaluation creates both risk and opportunity. The risk is that boards accustomed to minimal stewardship scrutiny are now being evaluated with a depth and rigor they may not expect. The opportunity is that boards that engage proactively with stewardship teams – that provide substantive governance information, that respond to feedback, that demonstrate a commitment to continuous improvement – build a relationship that pays dividends when it matters most.

The Big Three have also evolved in their willingness to vote against management. In the 2024-2025 proxy seasons, BlackRock, Vanguard, and State Street generally voted in favor of incumbent director slates in contested elections – providing a buffer for well-prepared boards. But this default is not guaranteed. They voted with Engine No. 1 against ExxonMobil. They supported activist nominees in numerous lower-profile campaigns. And their voting guidelines make clear that they will oppose incumbent directors when the governance case warrants it.

The practical implication for directors is that the Big Three's support must be earned, not assumed. A board that has engaged substantively with stewardship teams, that has a strong governance track record, and that can demonstrate competitive financial performance will likely retain their support. A board that has been opaque, unresponsive, and presiding over sustained underperformance should not count on the Big Three as a backstop.

# The Institutional Investor Relationship as Governance Infrastructure

The pattern across recent campaigns points to a clear conclusion: the institutional investor relationship is not a nice-to-have governance practice. It is governance infrastructure – as fundamental as your audit committee charter or your director nomination process.

Companies that treat institutional investor engagement as a management function – delegating it entirely to the IR department and the CEO – are building their governance on a fault line. When the activist arrives, the CEO's relationship with institutional investors is precisely the asset that is being questioned. The board needs its own credibility with these investors, established through direct engagement over time.

Companies that treat institutional investor engagement as a crisis response – reaching out to their largest holders only after a 13D is filed – are discovering that credibility cannot be manufactured in a crisis. Institutional stewardship teams notice when a company that has never requested a governance meeting suddenly wants to discuss the strength of its board. The contrast with the activist, who has been building relationships with those same stewardship teams for months, is not flattering.

The boards that navigate activist campaigns most effectively are those that have built institutional investor relationships as a standing governance practice. They have engaged regularly. They have been transparent about their governance decisions. They have responded substantively to feedback. And when the activist arrives, they have a reservoir of credibility to draw upon – not because they were preparing for a fight, but because genuine engagement was always part of how they governed.

Shapiro's observation about the activist vaccine applies directly here. Transparency and articulation – the fourth component of the vaccine – is not just about disclosure documents. It is about relationships. The institutional investors who will determine the outcome of any proxy contest need to know your board before they need to evaluate it. The question for every director is whether that relationship exists – and if it does not, what you are doing to build it before you need it.

# Reflection Questions

1. Can you name your company's five largest institutional shareholders and the individuals on their stewardship teams who cover your company? If not, why not?

2. When was the last time an independent director from your board met directly with an institutional investor without

management present? What was discussed?

3. If an activist approached your largest institutional shareholders tomorrow with a detailed analysis of your company's underperformance, what would those shareholders already know about your board's quality, engagement, and strategic vision – independent of management's messaging?

4. Does your proxy statement provide the kind of specific, substantive information about board composition, director qualifications, and governance practices that institutional stewardship teams are looking for? Or does it rely on boilerplate?

5. Has your board ever conducted an honest assessment of how your company would fare in a contested proxy vote – not based on hope, but on an objective analysis of your institutional shareholder base, your governance record, and the strength of your board's individual directors?

# Chapter 16: Proxy Advisory Firms – ISS, Glass Lewis, and the Evolving Landscape

When ISS and Glass Lewis both recommended that shareholders support Browning West's slate of nominees against Gildan Activewear's incumbent board in May 2024, the outcome was effectively sealed before a single vote was cast. Within weeks, the entire board resigned. The CEO the board had fired – founder Glenn Chamandy – was reinstated. Every director who had voted to remove him was gone.

When ISS and Glass Lewis split on Nelson Peltz's campaign against Disney – ISS supporting one Peltz nominee while Glass Lewis opposed both – the result was far less certain. Disney won decisively, with Peltz losing by a two-to-one margin.

These two outcomes, separated by just weeks, illustrate the paradox at the heart of proxy advisory influence: their recommendations matter enormously and yet are not determinative. A board that understands this paradox – that takes proxy advisory firms seriously without treating their recommendations as inevitable verdicts – has a significant advantage in any activist contest.

During our Flowers Foods tabletop simulation, this paradox became tangible. When our activist team was building the campaign strategy, one of the first questions we debated was whether ISS and Glass Lewis would support our slate. Shapiro was blunt: "You build your campaign for the institutions, not for the advisory firms. But if ISS recommends against you, you have a problem." The management team, for its part, spent considerable time discussing how to "manage ISS" – a phrase that Shapiro challenged sharply. You do not manage ISS, he told them. You build governance that ISS has no reason to criticize. The distinction matters more than most directors realize.

## The Two Dominant Firms

ISS and Glass Lewis are the two dominant proxy advisory firms, and together they cover the vast majority of publicly traded companies in the United States and globally. Their business model is straightforward: institutional investors pay for research and voting recommendations on proxy proposals, saving the cost and complexity of conducting their own governance analysis on every company in their portfolio.

The firms' analytical approaches differ in ways that matter for boards.

**ISS** tends to focus heavily on quantitative governance metrics. Its models weight factors like board independence percentages, director tenure distributions, voting results from prior annual meetings, and pay-for-performance alignment. ISS maintains detailed scorecards – including its Governance QualityScore – that reduce complex governance structures to numerical ratings. These scores are widely referenced by institutional investors and can trigger automatic voting policies at some asset managers. When ISS identifies a company with poor governance scores, that company is already at a disadvantage before any activist appears.

**Glass Lewis** has historically placed greater emphasis on disclosure quality and governance structure. Its analysis tends to be more narrative and contextual than ISS's metric-driven approach. Glass Lewis evaluates how well the company explains its governance decisions – the rationale for board composition, the logic behind executive compensation structures, the quality of shareholder engagement disclosures. A company with strong governance practices but poor disclosure may receive a more favorable assessment from ISS than from Glass Lewis, or vice versa.

Both firms issue detailed reports on contested proxy situations, evaluating the merits of both the company's slate and the activist's nominees. These reports are released to subscribing institutional investors weeks before the annual meeting, giving investors time to incorporate the recommendations into their voting decisions.

## The Influence Debate

How much do proxy advisory firms actually affect voting outcomes? This question has generated considerable debate among governance professionals, corporate executives, and regulators. The honest answer is: significantly, but not conclusively.

The evidence for significant influence is substantial. Academic research has consistently found that an adverse ISS recommendation on a say-on-pay proposal, for example, correlates with a fifteen to twenty-five percentage point decline in shareholder support. In contested director elections, ISS and Glass Lewis recommendations appear to shift meaningful blocks of votes – particularly among smaller institutional investors that lack the resources to conduct their own detailed governance analysis.

But the Gildan and Disney cases illustrate the limits of this influence. When both firms align – as they did in the Gildan campaign – the effect is devastating. The signal to institutional investors is unambiguous: two independent analytical frameworks have reached the same conclusion. For an institutional investor deciding how to vote, the path of least resistance and the path of analytical rigor converge on the same answer.

When the firms split – as they did on Disney – the signal is ambiguous. Institutional investors are forced back onto their own judgment. In the Disney case, many large institutions appear to have concluded that Disney's proactive transformation and improving stock performance warranted continued support for the incumbent board, regardless of ISS's partial endorsement of Peltz.

The lesson for boards is nuanced. A negative recommendation from ISS or Glass Lewis is serious and must be addressed, but it is not a death sentence. A negative recommendation from both firms simultaneously is close to one. And neither firm's recommendation can substitute for the board's own relationship with its institutional investor base.

## JPMorgan's Exit – A Bellwether?

In early 2025, JPMorgan Asset Management announced that it would discontinue its relationships with proxy advisory firms, choosing instead to rely entirely on its own internal governance analysis for voting decisions. The move was significant – JPMorgan is one of the world's largest asset managers, and its decision signaled growing discomfort in some corners of the institutional investment community about the proxy advisory model.

JPMorgan's reasoning was straightforward: the firm believed its own stewardship team could conduct governance analysis of sufficient quality to support independent voting decisions. It also reflected a broader concern that proxy advisory firm recommendations – developed under time pressure across thousands of companies – could not capture the nuance of individual governance situations.

The question is whether JPMorgan's move represents a trend or an exception. As of this writing, it has not triggered a mass exodus from proxy advisory services. Most institutional investors – particularly those managing broadly diversified portfolios – continue to rely on ISS and Glass Lewis recommendations, either as primary voting guides or as analytical starting points that their stewardship teams supplement with their own research.

But the direction of travel is worth watching. As more institutional investors build internal stewardship capabilities – driven by regulatory expectations, beneficiary demands, and the growing recognition that governance voting is a fiduciary responsibility – the proxy advisory firms' influence may gradually decrease. For boards, this means that the audience for your proxy statement and governance disclosures is becoming more diverse and more sophisticated. The strategy of "managing ISS" by checking specific governance boxes is becoming less reliable. What is replacing it is the harder but more durable strategy of building governance practices strong enough to withstand scrutiny from any direction.

# What Triggers an "Against" Recommendation

Understanding the specific factors that trigger adverse proxy advisory recommendations is essential for boards conducting governance self-assessments. While the firms' methodologies differ in detail, several red flags consistently draw negative attention.

**Excessive executive compensation.** Both ISS and Glass Lewis evaluate whether executive pay is aligned with company performance. When total CEO compensation increases significantly while total shareholder return declines – or when compensation exceeds peer group medians without corresponding outperformance – the advisory firms will flag the disconnect. ISS's quantitative model is particularly sensitive to pay-for-performance misalignment, and a negative say-on-pay recommendation from ISS reliably reduces shareholder support by double digits.

**Poor board independence.** Both firms scrutinize the percentage of truly independent directors – not just directors who meet the technical listing standards, but directors free from material relationships with management, significant business dealings with the company, or extended tenure that may compromise independence. Boards where the CEO has significant influence over director nominations, where former executives remain as directors, or where a majority of directors have served for more than twelve to fifteen years will attract skepticism.

**Unresponsive governance.** When shareholder proposals receive significant support – typically more than thirty percent of votes cast – and the board fails to respond with meaningful action, proxy advisory firms take notice. ISS in particular tracks the board's response to prior-year shareholder proposals and may recommend against nominating committee members when the board has ignored high-support proposals.

**Governance structure concerns.** Classified boards, dual-class share structures, the absence of a lead independent director when the CEO also chairs the board, and punitive advance notice bylaws all attract negative attention. While these structural features are not automatic grounds for an adverse recommendation, they lower the threshold for supporting an activist's case for board-level change.

**Lack of board refreshment.** Both firms evaluate whether the board is regularly adding new directors with relevant skills and perspectives. A board that has not added a new independent director in several years signals insularity and resistance to fresh thinking – precisely the kind of governance stagnation that attracts activist attention.

# How to Engage with Proxy Advisory Firms

Boards that wait until a proxy advisory firm has issued its report to engage with that firm have already made a strategic error. Effective engagement with ISS and Glass Lewis is a proactive, year-round governance practice.

**Timing matters.** Both firms solicit input from companies well before their proxy analysis period. ISS's policy survey process – which occurs in the fall of each year, months before most annual meetings – is an opportunity for companies to provide context on their governance practices and to flag issues that the firm's quantitative models may not capture. Glass Lewis similarly accepts written submissions from companies before issuing its reports.

**Materials matter.** The most effective engagements with proxy advisory firms are built on detailed governance analysis – not generic talking points about "strong governance" but specific data: how board composition has changed over recent years, what skills matrix guided director nominations, how executive compensation has tracked company performance relative to peers, and what shareholder engagement activities the board has undertaken.

**Meetings matter.** Both firms offer companies the opportunity to meet with the analysts who cover their proxy filings. These meetings – which should include independent directors, not just management – allow the board to provide context that may not be apparent from public filings. A lead independent director who can articulate the rationale for board composition decisions carries more credibility than a general counsel reading prepared remarks.

The point of engagement is not to lobby for a favorable recommendation. It is to ensure that the proxy advisory firm's analysis is based on complete and accurate information. The firms are evaluating your governance on behalf of their clients – institutional investors who own your shares. Providing them with the context they need to make an informed assessment is a governance responsibility, not a public relations exercise.

# Your Proxy Statement as Primary Communication Vehicle

As discussed in the context of institutional investor relationships in Chapter 15, your annual proxy statement may be the most widely read governance document your company produces. ISS analysts read it. Glass Lewis analysts read it. Stewardship teams at every major institutional investor read it. And when an activist campaign materializes, the proxy statement becomes the reference document against which both the activist's claims and management's defense are evaluated.

Yet most proxy statements read as though they were written by a compliance department for a compliance audience. They check the boxes required by SEC rules. They include the disclosures mandated by exchange listing standards. And they reveal almost nothing about the substance of the board's governance – why these particular directors were nominated, what the board's priorities are, how the board evaluates its own effectiveness, and how executive compensation connects to the company's strategic objectives.

The best proxy statements – the ones that build credibility with institutional investors and proxy advisory firms alike – go well beyond compliance. They explain the board's skills matrix and how each director's qualifications address specific strategic needs. They describe the board's evaluation process and what it revealed. They provide detailed narratives about shareholder engagement activities and the board's response to shareholder feedback. They connect executive compensation to specific, measurable performance metrics with clear rationale for why those metrics were chosen.

When an activist campaign materializes, a strong proxy statement provides the foundation for the board's defense. When it does not materialize – as it will not for most companies in any given year –

a strong proxy statement still builds the institutional credibility that makes activism less likely.

## Regulatory Changes and the Shifting Landscape

The regulatory environment surrounding proxy advisory firms has shifted from theoretical debate to active enforcement. The SEC has alternated between tightening oversight of proxy advisory firms – requiring them to share reports with companies before publication and to provide companies an opportunity to respond – and loosening it. But beginning in late 2025, the regulatory pressure intensified dramatically from multiple directions simultaneously.

The White House executive order of December 2025 directed the SEC, FTC, and Department of Labor to review proxy advisory practices – with particular emphasis on the firms' foreign ownership (ISS by Germany's Deutsche Börse, Glass Lewis by Canada's Peloton Capital Management). Texas enacted the first state law regulating proxy advisors, requiring specific financial analysis for recommendations opposing management and classifying ESG considerations as "non-financial factors" requiring heightened disclosure. The FTC opened an antitrust investigation into the duopoly's market concentration. State attorneys general launched independent enforcement actions.

For boards, the practical implication of this regulatory upheaval is not to build governance strategy around any particular regulatory outcome – these enforcement actions and legal challenges will take years to resolve, and the political landscape will continue to shift. The practical implication is that proxy advisory firms are themselves adapting to this pressure in ways that directly affect how your shareholders will vote. Glass Lewis's decision to abandon its benchmark policy and ISS's shift to case-by-case evaluation of ESG proposals are both responses to these political and regulatory forces. Understanding the direction of these changes – toward fragmentation, customization, and reduced advisory firm influence – is more important than tracking any individual regulatory action.

The underlying principle remains constant: strong governance is the only strategy that does not expire with the next election cycle, the next executive order, or the next proxy advisory firm policy revision.

## When Both Firms Align: The Gildan Lesson

The Gildan Activewear proxy fight of 2024 – profiled in detail in Chapter 17 – provides the most dramatic recent demonstration of what happens when both proxy advisory firms align against the board. When ISS and Glass Lewis both recommended in favor of Browning West's full eight-nominee slate, the result was total board replacement.

The proxy advisory lesson is specific: when both firms align against the board, the institutional investor's decision calculus simplifies to the point where supporting the incumbent board requires actively overriding two independent expert recommendations. Most institutional investors – particularly those with limited internal stewardship resources – will not take that step without compelling reason. A negative recommendation from one firm can be survived, as Disney demonstrated. A negative recommendation from both simultaneously places the board in an almost untenable position. Boards should evaluate their governance practices against both firms' analytical frameworks and ensure that no governance decision could provoke simultaneous adverse recommendations.

## The Evolving Ecosystem

As discussed in detail in Chapter 9, the proxy advisory landscape is undergoing a structural transformation that will reshape how boards engage with these firms. Glass Lewis's decision to replace its single benchmark policy with four distinct research perspectives beginning in 2027, ISS's introduction of no-recommendation research products, and the departure of major institutional investors like JPMorgan from the proxy advisory system entirely all point in the same direction: the era of a centralized, predictable proxy advisory system is ending.

For boards, this evolution demands a fundamental shift in engagement strategy. It is no longer sufficient to "manage ISS" or "check the Glass Lewis boxes." When different investors receive different recommendations from the same advisory firm – and when some investors have abandoned advisory firms altogether in favor of internal AI-powered platforms – the only reliable governance strategy is one built on direct relationships with your largest shareholders and governance practices that withstand scrutiny from any analytical framework.

The boards that will navigate this transition successfully are those that treat shareholder engagement as a continuous governance practice rather than a proxy-season exercise. They will invest in understanding which of their institutional holders use which advisory frameworks. They will customize their governance communications for different investor segments. And they will recognize that in a fragmented advisory landscape, the quality of your governance – not the favorability of your proxy advisor recommendation – is the primary determinant of how shareholders vote.

# Reflection Questions

1. Does your board know the current ISS Governance QualityScore for your company? If it is low, has the board analyzed why and developed a plan to address the identified issues?

2. Has your company engaged proactively with ISS and Glass Lewis during their pre-proxy analysis period – providing context, meeting with analysts, and supplying detailed governance materials?

3. Does your proxy statement provide the kind of substantive, specific disclosure about board composition, director qualifications, and governance practices that proxy advisory firms and institutional investors are looking for?

4. If a proxy advisory firm issued an "against" recommendation on any of your directors, would your institutional investor base have enough independent knowledge of your board's quality to override that recommendation? Or would they follow the advisory firm's guidance by default?

5. Is your company prepared for an environment where proxy advisory influence may be declining but institutional investor scrutiny is increasing – requiring stronger underlying governance rather than better advisory firm management?

# Chapter 17: Case Studies – Major Campaigns That Shaped the Landscape

Theory is necessary. Frameworks are useful. But nothing teaches governance judgment like studying what actually happened when billions of dollars, careers, and corporate legacies were on the line.

This chapter examines seven campaigns from 2021 through 2025 that fundamentally shaped the modern activist investor landscape. Each case illustrates different dynamics – the role of institutional investors, the power of credible analysis, the consequences of board entrenchment, the importance of proactive governance, and the limits of activist leverage. Together, they form a practical encyclopedia of how campaigns unfold, why they succeed or fail, and what every director should learn from each outcome.

During our SGLI program, Shapiro and Sheryl Palmer used several of these campaigns as teaching cases – dissecting the decisions, debating the board's response, and asking us to put ourselves in the room when the critical choices were made. What struck me most was how obvious the right decision seemed in hindsight and how difficult it would have been in real time. The boards that failed were not staffed by incompetent people. They were staffed by experienced executives who made understandable mistakes under extraordinary pressure. That is why case studies matter more than frameworks: they teach judgment, not just analysis.

I have selected these campaigns not because they are the only important ones, but because each demonstrates a principle that boards encounter repeatedly. Read them as a director would: not to judge who was right or wrong, but to ask yourself how your board would have performed in the same situation.

The aggregate data framing these cases – campaigns surging from 243 in 2024 to 297 in 2025, settlement rates above ninety percent, time-to-settlement compressing from months to weeks – was presented in Chapters 1 and 2. Two additional data points are worth noting here. First, the technology sector now represents nearly a quarter of all activist targets, up from single digits a decade ago; the seven campaigns below span energy, entertainment, airlines, apparel, railroads, pharmaceuticals, and industrials, reflecting that no sector is immune. Second, first-time activists accounted for forty-seven percent of all activists in 2024 – boards cannot prepare by studying a finite list of known names but must build governance strong enough to withstand scrutiny from any direction.

# Engine No. 1 vs. ExxonMobil (2021): The Campaign That Changed Everything

**The Setup.** Engine No. 1 was a newly formed hedge fund managing approximately $250 million in assets. ExxonMobil was one of the world's largest companies, with a market capitalization exceeding $250 billion. By every conventional measure, the contest was absurd. Engine No. 1 owned a negligible fraction of ExxonMobil's outstanding shares. It had no track record. It had never run a proxy fight.

**The Thesis.** Engine No. 1's argument was strategic, not environmental. The fund argued that ExxonMobil's board had failed to adapt the company's strategy to the energy transition – not because climate change demanded it morally, but because it demanded it financially. The board lacked directors with relevant energy transition expertise. The company's total shareholder return had lagged peers over every meaningful time horizon – one year, three years, five years, ten years. Engine No. 1 presented this as a failure of governance, not a failure of environmentalism.

This framing was essential. By positioning the campaign as a capital allocation and strategy contest rather than a climate activism campaign, Engine No. 1 made it possible for institutional investors focused on financial returns – not just ESG mandates – to support the activist.

**The Nominees.** Engine No. 1 nominated four director candidates, each with deep energy industry experience. Gregory Goff had led Andeavor, a major refining company. Kaisa Hietala had served as executive vice president of renewables at Neste, the Finnish oil refining company. Alexander Karsner had served as Assistant Secretary of Energy under President George W. Bush. Anders Runevad had led Vestas Wind Systems. These were not environmental activists. They were energy industry veterans with the strategic credibility to oversee an energy transition.

**The Coalition.** Engine No. 1's victory was built on institutional investor support. BlackRock, Vanguard, and State Street – ExxonMobil's three largest shareholders – each voted in favor of at least some Engine No. 1 nominees. CalPERS, the New York State Common Retirement Fund, and the Church of England Pensions Board added their support. The coalition was unprecedented in its breadth and in the scale of the company it challenged.

**The Outcome.** Three Engine No. 1 nominees won seats on Exxon-Mobil's board. The fourth fell short by a narrow margin.

**The Lessons.** First, no company is too large to be vulnerable. ExxonMobil's size, brand recognition, and decades of institutional relationships were insufficient to protect it when the governance case was strong enough. Second, credible analysis matters more than shareholding size. Engine No. 1 won not through the weight of its shares but through the quality of its argument and the credentials of its nominees. Third, institutional investors will abandon entrenched management when they believe the board has failed to adapt. The Big Three's decision to vote against ExxonMobil's incumbent directors was not casual – it reflected a deliberate judgment that the board had failed in its strategic oversight responsibilities. Fourth, framing matters. By positioning the campaign around financial returns rather than environmental advocacy, Engine No. 1 broadened its coalition beyond ESG-focused investors to include mainstream institutional holders.

For directors, the ExxonMobil case establishes a stark precedent: if your board's strategic oversight has resulted in sustained underperformance relative to peers, no defensive mechanism – not your company's size, not your shareholder rights plan, not your decades of institutional relationships – will protect you when a credible activist presents an alternative.

# Elliott Management vs. Starbucks (2024): The Campaign That Got More Than It Asked For

**The Setup.** Elliott Investment Management disclosed a stake of approximately $1.9 billion in Starbucks in July 2024. The coffee giant was struggling. Same-store sales were declining. The China business was underperforming. Customer traffic had fallen. CEO Laxman Narasimhan, who had been in the role for just over a year, was perceived by many analysts as failing to reverse the deterioration.

**The Thesis.** Elliott presented a detailed strategic overhaul plan to the Starbucks board in July 2024. The plan focused on operational efficiency, cost reduction, the lagging China business, and board composition changes. Notably, Elliott did not explicitly demand that the board replace the CEO. The fund's public posture was one of constructive engagement – we have concerns, here are our recommendations, we expect the board to act.

But the implicit message was unmistakable. Elliott had not built a nearly $2 billion position in a struggling company to watch the incumbent management team continue executing a failing strategy. And Starboard Value, another activist fund, held a separate position and added additional pressure.

**The Resolution.** On August 13, 2024 – barely two months after Elliott's stake disclosure – Starbucks announced that CEO Narasimhan was out. His replacement was Brian Niccol, the CEO of Chipotle Mexican Grill, who had transformed that company into one of the restaurant industry's strongest performers. Niccol was named CEO and chairman, effective September 9.

The market's verdict was immediate and overwhelming. Starbucks shares surged twenty-five percent on the news – the best single-day performance since the company's 1992 IPO.

**The Lessons.** First, implicit pressure can achieve explicit results. Elliott never publicly demanded a CEO change. The board acted preemptively, recognizing that the activist's presence – combined with deteriorating performance – made leadership change inevitable. This is the subatomic particle effect in its purest form: the observation changed the behavior. Second, boards that act quickly to address the underlying concern can resolve campaigns faster than boards that entrench. Starbucks went from stake disclosure to CEO replacement in approximately two months – a timeline that would have seemed impossibly fast even a few years ago. Third, the replacement matters as much as the removal. Niccol was a credible, high-profile hire who signaled to the market that the board was serious about transformation. A lesser appointment would not have produced the same market reaction. Fourth, the campaign created enormous shareholder value. The twenty-five percent stock surge represented billions of dollars in market capitalization – a concrete demonstration that the activist's pressure had been warranted.

For directors, Starbucks illustrates a governance reality that many boards resist: when the CEO is the problem, the board's fiduciary duty is to address the problem, not to defend the CEO. Elliott did not have to demand a CEO change. The board read the situation, assessed the evidence, and acted. That is governance.

# Trian Partners vs. Disney (2023-2024): The Most Expensive Proxy Fight

**The Setup.** Nelson Peltz and Trian Fund Management launched what would become the most expensive proxy fight in corporate history, with combined spending estimated at approximately $65 million. Trian sought two board seats, arguing that Disney had suffered from poor succession planning – the Bob Chapek debacle, Bob Iger's multiple retirements and returns – misdirected capital allocation, and sustained share price underperformance.

**The Thesis.** Peltz's campaign had two primary targets: the board's governance failures and the company's financial performance. Trian argued that Disney had destroyed billions in shareholder value through its streaming strategy, theme park investments, and content spending. Peltz nominated himself and former Disney CFO Jay Rasulo as director candidates.

**The Defense.** Disney's defense was perhaps the most aggressive and comprehensive ever mounted against an activist campaign. The company spent approximately $40 million – more than many companies' entire annual governance budgets – on proxy solicitation, communications, and advisor fees. But more importantly, Disney acted. Before the vote, the company announced significant cost-cutting initiatives, presented a credible path to streaming profitability, outlined a strategic plan for ESPN, and made board composition changes that addressed some of the governance concerns Trian had raised.

**The Outcome.** Peltz lost decisively. He was defeated by approximately a two-to-one margin. Rasulo lost by an even larger five-to-one margin. Bob Iger received ninety-four percent of the overall vote.

**The Lessons.** First, proactive transformation before the vote is the most effective defense strategy. Disney did not simply argue that Peltz was wrong. The company demonstrated – through specific actions announced before the vote – that it was already doing what the activist was demanding. This deprived Peltz of his strongest argument: that the board was failing to act. Second, retail shareholders matter. Disney's passionate retail investor base overwhelmingly backed the incumbent slate, offsetting the institutional investor votes that Peltz might have attracted. In companies with large retail bases, direct shareholder engagement – not just institutional investor outreach – can be decisive. Third, proxy advisory firms are not determinative. ISS supported one Peltz nominee; Glass Lewis supported neither. The split recommendation gave institutional investors permission to exercise independent judgment, and most chose the incumbent board. Fourth, the campaign itself can create value even in defeat. Disney's stock rose approximately fifty percent during the campaign period. Peltz claimed credit for this appreciation – and while Disney's management team certainly deserved credit for the operational improvements, it is difficult to argue that the activist pressure played no role in accelerating those improvements.

For directors, Disney demonstrates that proxy fights can be won –
but winning requires action, not just argumentation. A board that
responds to an activist campaign with defensive rhetoric will lose.
A board that responds with substantive governance and operational
improvements has a chance.

# Elliott Management vs. Southwest Airlines (2024): The Record-Setting Settlement

**The Setup.** Elliott disclosed an approximately $2 billion stake in
Southwest Airlines in June 2024, citing years of underperformance
and blaming CEO Bob Jordan and Executive Chairman Gary Kelly.

**The Thesis.** Elliott's analysis was operational and strategic. Southwest had lost its cost advantage – the foundation of its competitive
positioning for decades. Its fleet strategy had not kept pace with
competitors. Its revenue management systems lagged the industry.
Its financial performance, measured by every relevant metric, had
deteriorated relative to peers. Elliott argued that the underperformance was not cyclical – it was structural, and it required leadership
change.

**The Settlement.** On October 24, 2024, Southwest and Elliott
reached a settlement that represented the largest number of board
seats Elliott had ever obtained in a U.S. activist campaign: six. Five
Elliott nominees – David Cush, Sarah Feinberg, David Grissen,
Gregg Saretsky, and Patricia Watson – were appointed to the board
effective November 1. A sixth director was also added. Executive
Chairman Gary Kelly accelerated his retirement to November 1.
Six existing directors accelerated their own retirements. CEO Bob
Jordan, notably, kept his position.

**The Lessons.** First, record-setting settlements are possible
without a proxy vote. Southwest's board assessed the situation –
Elliott's stake, the quality of the activist's analysis, the strength of
the proposed nominees, the institutional investor sentiment – and
concluded that a negotiated outcome was preferable to a contested
vote. That is governance judgment in action. Second, the chairman
is not immune. Kelly had been Southwest's CEO for nearly two
decades before becoming executive chairman. His departure as

part of the settlement demonstrated that no role is protected when institutional investors have lost confidence. Third, the CEO can survive even when the chair does not. Jordan's retention – despite Elliott's initial criticism of his leadership – suggests that the board distinguished between governance failures attributable to the board's oversight structure and operational challenges attributable to management execution. Fourth, the speed of resolution continues to accelerate. From stake disclosure in June to settlement in October – four months. Companies no longer have the luxury of extended deliberation when an activist of Elliott's caliber arrives.

# Browning West vs. Gildan Activewear (2023-2024): The Total Board Replacement

**The Setup.** In December 2023, Gildan Activewear's board fired co-founder and long-time CEO Glenn Chamandy and replaced him with Vince Tyra, an executive from Houchens Industries. Browning West, a relatively small activist holding approximately five percent of Gildan's shares, immediately protested.

**The Thesis.** Browning West's campaign was unlike most activist efforts. The fund was not arguing that the CEO needed to be replaced – it was arguing that the CEO should never have been fired. Chamandy had built Gildan from a small Canadian underwear company into a major global apparel manufacturer. His termination, Browning West argued, was conducted without adequate shareholder input, without a credible succession plan, and without a compelling strategic rationale. The board had fired a founder-CEO who had delivered substantial long-term value and replaced him with an executive with no apparel industry experience.

**The Coalition.** What made Browning West's campaign devastating was not the fund's own shareholding – five percent is modest by activist standards. It was the breadth of institutional investor support. Major shareholders including Anson Funds and Janus Henderson backed the activist. Both ISS and Glass Lewis recommended in favor of Browning West's full eight-nominee slate. The alignment of both proxy advisory firms behind the activist – a relatively rare occurrence – sent an unambiguous signal to institutional investors.

**The Outcome.** On May 23, 2024, the entire board and CEO Vince Tyra resigned. All eight Browning West nominees were appointed. Glenn Chamandy was reinstated as CEO and director. Michael Kneeland, former CEO of United Rentals, became board chair.

**The Lessons.** First, firing a founder-CEO is extremely risky. Founder-CEOs typically command intense loyalty from both employees and shareholders. A board that fires a founder without overwhelming evidence of cause – and without a succession plan that shareholders find credible – invites exactly the kind of revolt that Gildan experienced. Second, a small stake can produce massive leverage when combined with institutional support. Browning West's five percent holding was not, by itself, threatening. But when that five percent was combined with ISS and Glass Lewis support, major institutional investor backing, and the emotional resonance of a founder's wrongful termination, the result was total board replacement. Third, complete board replacement is possible. This outcome is rare – in most campaigns, the activist wins a few seats and the remaining board members continue to serve. But Gildan demonstrated that when a board's decision is perceived as arbitrary, self-serving, and destructive to shareholder value, institutional investors will support the nuclear option. Fourth, both proxy advisory firms supporting the activist is devastating. When ISS and Glass Lewis align behind the activist, the institutional investor's decision calculus simplifies dramatically. The analytical burden shifts from the investor evaluating competing arguments to the board proving that two independent governance evaluation firms got it wrong.

# Ancora Holdings vs. Norfolk Southern (2024): The Post-Derailment Reckoning

**The Setup.** Ancora Holdings, a Cleveland-based activist that had carved a niche in transportation sector campaigns, targeted Norfolk Southern Corporation in early 2024. The campaign's catalyst was not primarily financial – it was the catastrophic train derailment in East Palestine, Ohio in February 2023, which resulted in a massive chemical spill that contaminated the surrounding area and became a national news story.

**The Thesis.** Ancora cited share price underperformance, deteriorating service metrics, and declining profitability – standard activist talking points. But the East Palestine derailment gave those arguments a visceral dimension that pure financial analysis cannot replicate. The derailment was a governance failure made visible – an operational catastrophe that raised fundamental questions about the board's oversight of safety, risk management, and operational performance. Ancora argued that the board needed new directors who would bring operational accountability and strategic focus.

**The Resolution.** Ancora won three board seats at Norfolk Southern's 2024 annual meeting. The board chair and two committee heads were effectively removed. Then, in an unexpected development, CEO Alan Shaw was removed after an internal investigation revealed an inappropriate personal relationship with the company's chief legal officer. Ancora subsequently secured a fourth board seat in a follow-up agreement.

**The Lessons.** First, operational crises create activist opportunities that are qualitatively different from purely financial campaigns. East Palestine gave Ancora a narrative that resonated with institutional investors, media, and the public in ways that a chart showing TSR underperformance never could. Boards that fail to manage operational risk are not just exposing the company to legal liability – they are creating the conditions for activist intervention. Second, CEO personal conduct is fair game. Shaw's removal was unrelated to the activist campaign's thesis, but it reinforced the activist's broader argument about governance failures at the company. The coincidence of the personal conduct issue and the activist campaign devastated management's credibility and accelerated the governance transformation. Third, campaigns can produce incremental results over time. Ancora did not win six seats in a single action. It won three at the annual meeting, contributed to the environment that led to the CEO's removal, and then secured a fourth seat. The trajectory – from initial campaign to gradual board transformation – reflects how many successful campaigns actually unfold.

For directors, Norfolk Southern illustrates a critical vulnerability: when operational failures become public, the activist's job becomes dramatically easier. The board's failure was not primarily one of financial oversight – it was one of operational oversight. Directors who view their role as limited to strategic and financial matters, who

do not scrutinize operational risk with the same rigor they apply to
the balance sheet, are leaving their companies exposed to exactly this
kind of campaign.

## Starboard Value vs. Pfizer (2024-2025): The Failed Campaign

**The Setup.** Starboard Value disclosed a $1 billion position in
Pfizer in October 2024. The pharmaceutical giant's stock had
fallen to roughly half its pandemic-era peak as COVID-19 vaccine
and treatment revenues declined sharply. Starboard recruited two
powerful allies: former Pfizer CEO Ian Read and former CFO Frank
D'Amelio.

**The Thesis.** Starboard argued that Pfizer's board had failed to manage the post-pandemic transition effectively, that capital allocation
decisions – including a series of large acquisitions – had destroyed
shareholder value, and that the board lacked the independence and
expertise needed to hold CEO Albert Bourla accountable. The recruitment of Read and D'Amelio was intended to provide both credibility and specific insider knowledge of Pfizer's operations and governance.

**The Collapse.** The campaign unraveled rapidly. On October 10,
Read and D'Amelio retracted their support for Starboard and publicly backed CEO Bourla. Starboard accused Pfizer's management
of forcing the retraction through threats of litigation, compensation
clawbacks, and the cancellation of unvested stock. The accusation
was damaging to Pfizer's reputation – but the practical effect was
devastating to Starboard's campaign. Without the former executives'
credibility, the activist's case for board-level change lost its most
compelling element.

Then, on October 29, Pfizer released third-quarter 2024 results that
significantly exceeded expectations, with revenue more than thirty
percent above the prior year's third quarter. The financial results
destroyed the activist's underperformance thesis. The stock had already begun recovering.

By the third quarter of 2025, Starboard had sold its entire 15.4 million share position. No board seats were gained. No visible opera-

tional changes were attributable to the campaign.

**The Lessons.** First, improving financial performance is the best defense. Pfizer's strong Q3 results eliminated the factual foundation of Starboard's campaign. An activist whose thesis depends on continued underperformance is vulnerable to any improvement in results – and the board that can demonstrate a turnaround in progress has the most powerful counter-argument available. Second, former executive allies can be neutralized. Read and D'Amelio's retraction – whatever the circumstances – eliminated the activist's most credible voices. Boards and companies have legitimate tools to remind former executives of ongoing obligations, including restrictive covenants, clawback provisions, and continuing compensation arrangements. Third, not every campaign succeeds. Starboard is one of the most experienced and successful activist investors in the world. Its founder, Jeffrey Smith, is widely regarded as one of the most feared activists in corporate governance. And yet the Pfizer campaign failed completely. The lesson is not that activism is unreliable – it is that activism requires the underlying thesis to be correct. When the facts change, even the most skilled activist must adapt or withdraw.

For directors, the Pfizer case offers reassurance – but only to boards that are actually delivering results. The defense that defeated Starboard was not a clever legal strategy or a slick communications campaign. It was financial performance. Everything else was secondary.

# Elliott Management vs. Honeywell (2024): The Mega-Cap Breakup

**The Setup.** Elliott disclosed a position exceeding $5 billion in Honeywell International in November 2024 – one of the largest activist positions ever taken. Honeywell, a diversified industrial conglomerate with operations spanning aerospace, building automation, industrial automation, and advanced materials, had a market capitalization well in excess of $100 billion.

**The Thesis.** Elliott's argument was the conglomerate discount thesis – the assertion that Honeywell's diversified structure obscured the value of its individual business segments and resulted in a val-

uation below the sum of its parts. The fund argued that separating
Honeywell into focused, standalone businesses would unlock significant shareholder value by allowing each business to be valued on its
own merits, attract specialized investors, and allocate capital more
efficiently.

Elliott estimated that a separation could produce up to seventy-five
percent upside over two years – a dramatic claim for a mega-cap
industrial company. The fund proposed splitting Honeywell into two
primary businesses: Aerospace and Automation.

**The Resolution.**    Honeywell did not resist.    The company
announced that it would split into three independently listed
companies – Aerospace, Automation, and a previously announced
Advanced Materials spin-off. The three-way split was actually more
aggressive than Elliott's two-way proposal, suggesting that the
board had independently concluded that the conglomerate model
was no longer serving shareholders.

The separations were structured as tax-free transactions for shareholders, with completion targeted for the second half of 2026.

**The Lessons.** First, no company is too large. Honeywell's market
capitalization – among the thirty largest companies in the United
States – did not deter Elliott or protect the incumbent structure. Size
is not a defense against a credible conglomerate discount thesis. Second, the conglomerate model is under sustained attack. General
Electric, Johnson & Johnson, and now Honeywell – the list of major conglomerates that have separated under activist pressure or in
anticipation of it continues to grow. Directors of diversified companies should assume that the sum-of-parts analysis will eventually
arrive at their boardroom table. Third, proactive breakups can pre-
empt activism. Honeywell's decision to propose a three-way split –
exceeding the activist's demand – allowed the company to control
the narrative and the timeline. A company that concludes its own
analysis that separation creates value can execute the transaction on
its terms, rather than ceding the initiative to an activist. Fourth, the
capital commitment signals intent. Elliott's $5 billion-plus position
was a statement that demanded engagement. At that scale, the activist's financial commitment to the outcome is so substantial that
dismissive responses are not credible.

# A Note on Campaigns Not Included

The seven campaigns profiled in this chapter are not the only important ones from this period. Elliott's campaign against Phillips 66 – which resulted in a rare proxy fight producing a split outcome of two seats for each side – illustrates what happens when initial settlements break down. Starboard Value's campaign against Kenvue – the Johnson & Johnson consumer health spin-off – demonstrates the vulnerability of newly public companies and the willingness of activist principals to take board seats personally. Elliott's roughly $4 billion position in PepsiCo, launched in 2025, represents the expansion of breakup activism from industrial conglomerates to consumer staples icons.

Each of these campaigns reinforces the patterns identified in this chapter. The activist landscape is not slowing down – it is accelerating, broadening, and becoming more consequential with each passing year.

# Cross-Campaign Patterns

Seven campaigns, seven different outcomes, seven different industries. And yet, viewed together, these cases reveal patterns that every director should internalize.

**The underlying thesis matters more than anything else.** In every successful campaign – ExxonMobil, Starbucks, Southwest, Gildan, Norfolk Southern, Honeywell – the activist's analysis was fundamentally correct. In the failed campaign – Pfizer – the underlying thesis was overtaken by improving results. No amount of tactical sophistication can compensate for an activist whose diagnosis is wrong. And no amount of defensive preparation can protect a board when the activist's diagnosis is right.

**Speed is accelerating.** Starbucks: two months from stake disclosure to CEO replacement. Southwest: four months to a six-seat settlement. Gildan: five months to total board replacement. Directors should assume that any activist engagement will move faster than they expect.

**Complete board replacement is a real possibility.** Gildan demonstrated that the nuclear option is not theoretical. The universal proxy card has lowered the barrier, and institutional investors have shown willingness to support sweeping change when the circumstances warrant it.

**The campaign creates value even when the activist loses.** Disney's stock rose fifty percent during the Trian campaign. The pressure of an activist campaign – even one that ultimately fails – forces boards to accelerate improvements, confront weaknesses, and communicate more effectively with shareholders. This is the subatomic particle effect applied to entire corporations.

The question is not whether your company will face a campaign. It is whether your governance is strong enough that, if a campaign arrives, your institutional investors will look at your board and conclude that you are already doing the work that needs to be done. If the answer is yes, you will survive. If the answer is no, the case studies in this chapter are your preview of what comes next.

# Chapter 18: The Activist Vaccine – Prevention Through Good Governance

Andrew Shapiro does something unusual for an activist investor. He consults with companies on how to prevent people like him from showing up at their door.

He calls the framework the "activist vaccine" – and the metaphor is precise. A vaccine does not build walls. It does not create barriers between the pathogen and the host. Instead, it strengthens the host's own immune system so that when the pathogen arrives – and it will arrive – the body is already equipped to respond. Shapiro's activist vaccine works the same way. It does not prevent activists from analyzing your company, accumulating shares, or drafting demand letters. What it does is make your governance so fundamentally sound that activism becomes unnecessary – or, if an activist does appear, ensure that your institutional investors have enough confidence in your board to support you.

The concept is simple. The execution is not. This chapter examines the four components of the activist vaccine, explains why each is necessary and none alone is sufficient, and provides a practical framework for boards to assess their own immunity.

# Component 1: Board Composition with an Investor Mindset

The first component of the activist vaccine is the most visible: a board composed of directors who think like investors.

This does not mean a board full of hedge fund managers. It means a board where every director understands capital allocation, scrutinizes strategy with the rigor of someone whose own money is at stake, and holds management accountable for results – not in the vague, ceremonial way that many boards practice, but with the specific, data-driven discipline that characterizes effective investment oversight.

Shapiro was blunt about what attracts activism on the board composition front. A proper governance and nomination process should assess the skills and capabilities that the board actually needs – not the skills and relationships that the CEO finds comfortable. When the nominating committee selects directors based on their relationship with the CEO, their social standing, or their willingness to go along, the resulting board sends a signal that is visible from a mile away. And activists are looking.

The question for every nominating committee is whether its process would survive external scrutiny. Does the board have a skills matrix that maps director qualifications to the company's strategic needs? Has the committee identified gaps in the board's expertise – and is it actively recruiting directors to fill those gaps? Are new directors selected because they will contribute to more effective oversight, or because they will maintain the existing power structure?

The Engine No. 1 case illustrates this principle with painful clarity. ExxonMobil's board included accomplished individuals, but Engine No. 1 argued – persuasively – that the board lacked directors with relevant experience in the energy transition. The nominees Engine No. 1 proposed were energy industry veterans with specific expertise in the strategic challenge facing ExxonMobil. When institutional investors compared the qualifications of Engine No. 1's nominees against the existing board's skills gaps, the activist's argument was difficult to refute.

A board that proactively addresses its own composition gaps – that recruits directors with the expertise the company needs, not just the experience the CEO prefers – deprives the activist of one of their most powerful arguments.

# Component 2: Disciplined Capital Allocation

The second component of the activist vaccine addresses what the board does with shareholder money.

Capital allocation is the most consequential decision a board oversees, and it is the area where boards most frequently fail the activist's test. Every dollar of retained earnings, every acquisition dollar, every capital expenditure represents a choice – a choice to deploy shareholder capital in a way that the board believes will generate returns exceeding the company's cost of capital. When that deployment is disciplined and transparent, institutional investors grant the board the benefit of the doubt. When it is not, activists fill the vacuum.

The red flags that attract activist attention on capital allocation are well established. Excess cash sitting on the balance sheet – earning treasury bill rates while shareholders demand equity returns – signals a board that lacks the discipline or the strategic imagination to deploy capital effectively. Money-losing divisions that persist year after year without a turnaround plan or a divestiture timeline signal a board that cannot make difficult decisions. Acquisitions that destroy value – the most expensive category of capital misallocation – signal a management team more interested in growth than in returns, and a board that either approved the deals without adequate scrutiny or lacked the expertise to evaluate them.

The discipline that the vaccine demands is not about returning all capital to shareholders. It is about demonstrating that every capital allocation decision has been subjected to rigorous analysis. Can the board articulate its return hurdle rate for acquisitions? Does the board track actual returns against the projections used to justify previous investments? When a division has underperformed for three consecutive years, does the board have a specific plan for remediation or divestiture – with a timeline and accountability?

These are not theoretical questions. They are the questions that activist investors ask when they build their campaigns. A board that can answer them credibly – because it has actually done the work – is a board that is difficult to attack. A board that cannot answer them is a board that will eventually face an activist who has done the analysis the board should have done itself.

# Component 3: An Investor Mindset in the Boardroom

The third component is the hardest to implement because it requires a cultural shift that most boards resist.

Here is the reality that many directors prefer not to confront: too many boards operate as though they are advisory bodies to the CEO rather than oversight bodies acting on behalf of shareholders. The meetings are cordial. The presentations are polished. The questions are gentle. The votes are unanimous. And the governance is illusory.

An investor mindset in the boardroom means that directors approach every decision with the question that an external investor would ask: Is this creating or destroying shareholder value? Not shareholder value in the abstract, long-term, eventually-if-everything-goes-right sense – but shareholder value in the measurable, benchmarkable, peer-comparable sense that institutional investors and activists use.

This means directors who know the company's return on invested capital – and who know how it compares to the peer group. Directors who scrutinize acquisition proposals not just for strategic rationale but for the specific financial assumptions underlying the valuation. Directors who ask management to explain why margins have compressed relative to competitors, why capital expenditures have increased without corresponding revenue growth, why the company's valuation multiple has diverged from its peer group.

Shapiro's observation was pointed: directors must understand that they are stewards of shareholder capital, not employees of the CEO. This is a distinction that governance education teaches in theory but that boardroom dynamics often erode in practice. The CEO controls the information flow, sets the meeting agenda, selects the advisors, and shapes the narrative. Directors who accept that information architecture without demanding independent analysis – from sell-side analysts, from institutional investors, from external governance advisors – are operating with an incomplete picture.

The practical test is straightforward. If an activist analyzed your company's financial performance, governance structure, and capital allocation decisions against the same peer group that your compensation committee uses, what would they find? If the answer is that they would find a company with competitive returns, disciplined capital deployment, and a board that asks hard questions – then the investor mindset is real. If the answer is that they would find a company with explanations for underperformance, justifications for questionable acquisitions, and a board that approves management's recommendations without visible dissent – then the investor mindset is a label, not a practice.

# Component 4: Transparency and Articulation

This is the component that Shapiro emphasized most forcefully – and the one that boards most consistently underestimate.

Transparency in the activist vaccine framework is not about meeting SEC disclosure requirements. Every public company meets those requirements. Transparency is about voluntarily providing the information that investors need to evaluate your company's governance, strategy, and performance – before they have to demand it.

Shapiro's warning about the bunker mentality was stark. When companies go into bunker mode – when they stop disclosing, become less transparent, block information flow – the effect on institutional investors is not neutral. It is actively destructive. Shapiro put it directly: when you stop communicating, investors do not assume the best. They assume the worst. And when they assume the worst, they become more receptive to the activist who is providing the analysis and transparency that the company has withheld.

The logic is inescapable. Institutional investors are making governance decisions about your company regardless of what you disclose. They are evaluating your board composition, your capital allocation, your executive compensation, and your strategic direction. If you provide them with detailed, credible, substantive information – through your proxy statement, your investor day presentations, your direct engagement with stewardship teams – you shape how they evaluate you. If you provide only the minimum required disclosures, you cede the narrative to whoever fills the information vacuum. And in an activist campaign, that someone is the activist.

The practical applications of transparency are specific and action-able. Your proxy statement should explain – not just disclose – your board composition. Why were these directors nominated? What skills do they bring? How does the board's composition address the company's strategic needs? Your investor communications should explain – not just announce – your capital allocation decisions. Why did you make this acquisition? What return hurdle did it clear? How will you measure success? Your shareholder engagement should explain – not just defend – your governance practices. Why does the CEO also chair the board? What role does the lead independent director play? How does the board evaluate its own effectiveness?

Companies that provide this level of transparency build the credibility reservoir that the activist vaccine depends upon. When an activist arrives with critiques of your governance, the institutional investors who have been receiving substantive disclosure from your board for years are equipped to evaluate those critiques in context. They have a basis for judgment that extends beyond the activist's presentation deck. And more often than not, they will give a transparent, communicative board the benefit of the doubt.

Companies that have not provided this transparency have no reservoir to draw upon. When the activist arrives with a detailed analysis and the company responds with generalities, the institutional investor's choice is obvious.

## Why Each Component Is Necessary and None Alone Is Sufficient

The four components of the activist vaccine work as an integrated system. A failure in any single component creates the opening that an activist needs.

Consider a company with excellent board composition – skilled, independent directors with relevant expertise – but poor capital allocation. The board's credentials will not protect the company when an activist demonstrates that management has destroyed value through undisciplined acquisitions and the board approved every one. The quality of the directors makes the capital allocation failure more damning, not less, because it raises the question of why qualified directors failed to prevent it.

Consider a company with disciplined capital allocation and strong financial returns – but a board dominated by long-tenured directors with close ties to the CEO. The financial performance may buy time, but the governance structure provides a compelling narrative for an activist who argues that the returns are happening despite the board, not because of it – and that better governance would produce even better returns.

Consider a company with strong governance practices across the board – but a bunker mentality when it comes to disclosure. The governance may be excellent, but if institutional investors cannot see it because the company will not show it, the company is vulnerable to an activist who presents a governance critique that the company's own disclosures fail to refute.

The vaccine works only when all four components are present and functioning. Board composition provides the human capital for effective oversight. Disciplined capital allocation demonstrates that the oversight is working. The investor mindset ensures that oversight is continuous and rigorous. Transparency makes the quality of governance visible to the people who will ultimately decide the outcome of any activist campaign.

Consider how the case studies from Chapter 17 map to the vaccine framework. ExxonMobil failed on components one and four – its board lacked energy transition expertise, and the company's engagement with institutional investors on strategic governance questions was perceived as dismissive. Gildan failed on component three – the board's decision to fire the founder-CEO without shareholder consultation revealed a board acting in its own interest rather than thinking like investors. Norfolk Southern's operational failures reflected weaknesses in component two – capital allocation and operational oversight. In each case, the activist targeted the specific vaccine component where the company was weakest.

The companies that survived – Disney, Pfizer – had the vaccine working when it mattered. Disney's board demonstrated proactive governance reform (component one), improving financial performance (component two), engaged board oversight (component three), and aggressive shareholder communication (component four). Pfizer delivered improving financial results (component two) that neutralized the activist's thesis. The vaccine is not theoretical. It is the framework that explains why some campaigns succeed and others fail.

## Shareholder Engagement as Ongoing Governance

The activist vaccine's transparency component deserves its own operational framework because it is the component most frequently neglected – and the one most likely to determine the outcome of an activist campaign.

Shareholder engagement should be a twelve-month governance practice, not a pre-annual meeting scramble. The engagement calendar should include regular touchpoints with the company's top institutional investors – not just the IR team communicating financial results, but independent directors discussing governance practices, strategic direction, and board priorities.

The engagement should be substantive. Institutional stewardship teams can distinguish immediately between a company that is genuinely interested in shareholder input and a company that is checking a governance box. A meeting where the lead independent director asks the institutional investor what governance concerns they have – and listens to the answer – builds credibility. A meeting where the general counsel reads prepared remarks about the board's strong governance practices builds nothing.

The results of shareholder engagement should be reported to the full board. Many boards delegate shareholder engagement to the IR function and never see the feedback. This creates the exact information asymmetry that makes boards vulnerable – management filters the investor feedback, emphasizing the positive and minimizing concerns, and the board makes governance decisions without the full picture. Shapiro's point about wanting to talk to sell-side analysts without management present applies equally to board access to investor feedback: the board needs unfiltered information to govern effectively.

## The Annual Governance Audit

A vaccine requires regular boosters. The annual governance audit is the mechanism by which boards evaluate their own immunity and identify vulnerabilities before an activist does.

The audit should be conducted annually – not as a crisis response but as a standing governance practice. It should be overseen by the nominating and governance committee, with input from the full board, and it should evaluate the company's position against each of the four vaccine components.

**Board composition assessment.** Does the board's skills matrix reflect the company's current strategic needs? Have those needs changed since the last assessment? Are there gaps in expertise that new director recruitment should address? Are any directors overboarded, disengaged, or compromised by relationships with management? Would any director be difficult to defend in a proxy contest?

**Capital allocation review.** How does the company's return on invested capital compare to its peer group? What returns have recent acquisitions generated relative to the projections used to justify them? Is excess cash being deployed productively? Are underperforming divisions being addressed with specific plans and timelines?

**Investor mindset evaluation.** Does the board regularly challenge management's strategic assumptions? Are directors accessing information sources beyond management's presentations – sellside analyst reports, institutional investor feedback, independent governance assessments? Is the board culture one of constructive challenge or comfortable consensus?

**Transparency audit.** Does the proxy statement provide substantive, specific disclosure about governance practices? Has the board engaged directly with major institutional investors in the past twelve months? Are shareholder proposals that received significant support being addressed with specific actions? If an activist presented a governance critique to your institutional investors, would those investors already have enough information from your own disclosures to evaluate it?

The output of the annual governance audit should be a specific action plan – not a general conclusion that "governance is strong." The action plan should identify the two or three areas where the company is most vulnerable and assign specific remediation actions with deadlines and accountability.

## The Self-Assessment: Would an Activist Find Ammunition?

The most powerful version of the governance audit is the self-assessment that asks the question every activist asks: Is this company's underperformance improvable?

This requires a degree of intellectual honesty that many boards find uncomfortable. It means looking at your own company through an adversarial lens – not to criticize for the sake of criticism, but to identify the specific data points, governance structures, and performance gaps that an activist would use to build a campaign.

The assessment should address Shapiro's four improvable problems – introduced in Chapter 4: low return on assets, suboptimal capital structure, governance and management failures, and transparency deficits. For each, the question is whether an activist analyzing your public filings would find exploitable weaknesses. If the honest answer to any is unfavorable, the follow-up question is not whether an activist will notice. It is when.

## Building the Credibility Reservoir

The activist vaccine is ultimately about credibility – the accumulated trust that comes from years of strong governance, transparent communication, and consistent performance.

Credibility cannot be manufactured in a crisis. It cannot be created by hiring the best proxy solicitor or producing the most polished investor presentation. It is built over time through the unglamorous work of genuine governance: recruiting strong directors, making disciplined capital allocation decisions, engaging substantively with shareholders, and communicating transparently about both successes and challenges.

The boards that have built deep credibility reservoirs – companies like Berkshire Hathaway, where Warren Buffett's decades of transparent communication and shareholder alignment have made the company essentially immune to activism – have done so through consistency over time. Not perfection. Consistency. Shareholders will tolerate occasional mistakes from a board they trust. What they will not tolerate is a pattern of opacity, defensiveness, and disregard for their concerns.

The practical implication for every director is this: the activist vaccine is not a program you implement in response to a threat assessment. It is a governance philosophy you adopt as the permanent operating standard of your board. Every meeting, every capital allocation decision, every director nomination, every shareholder communication is either building your credibility reservoir or draining it. The activist is not the threat. The threat is the governance practices that would give an activist ammunition.

Shapiro captured this with characteristic directness. The activist vaccine is not about building walls. It is about building a board that is so clearly doing its job – overseeing strategy with rigor, allocating capital with discipline, engaging with shareholders with transparency – that activism becomes unnecessary. When you are already doing what the activist would demand, the activist has nothing to demand.

The question for every director is not whether your board has adopted the activist vaccine. It is whether your board would pass the test that the vaccine is designed to prevent. And if it would not, the time to start building immunity is now – not after the 13D is filed.

## Putting the Vaccine to the Test

Appendix A provides a comprehensive vulnerability assessment checklist – a scored diagnostic tool that maps directly to the four vaccine components and the criteria that activists, proxy advisory firms, and institutional investors use when evaluating companies. Every board should complete that assessment annually, assigned to the nominating and governance committee and presented to the full board. The assessment covers financial performance, governance quality, board composition, capital allocation, transparency, and shareholder engagement – each scored against peer benchmarks.

The scoring is less important than the patterns. A company that scores well overall but has a cluster of weaknesses in a single category has a concentrated vulnerability that an activist will exploit. The goal is not a perfect score – it is the intellectual honesty to identify where your board is weakest and the discipline to address those weaknesses before someone outside the boardroom does it for you.

# Chapter 19: Running Your Own Activist Investor Tabletop Exercise

On December 9, 2025, I sat across a conference table from a team of aspiring directors who were playing the role of Flowers Foods' board of directors. I was on the activist investor team – Sterling Capital, we called ourselves – led by Taylor Price, with whom I co-led the overall tabletop exercise. For the previous eight weeks, our team had analyzed every public filing Flowers Foods had ever produced, benchmarked its financial performance against a carefully constructed peer group, mapped its governance vulnerabilities, and built a complete activist campaign from scratch. We had a thirteen-page demand letter. We had an investor presentation deck. We had proposed independent director candidates. We had a negotiation strategy.

We were ready. And we were terrified.

Not because the stakes were real – this was a simulation in the SLGI Board Readiness Program, not a real proxy fight. We were terrified because the people across the table had done the same amount of research from the opposite perspective, and we were about to find out whether our analysis would hold up under direct challenge from intelligent, motivated counterparts who had spent eight weeks preparing to take it apart.

The experience that followed was the most valuable governance education I have ever received. Not because it taught me the mechanics of an activist campaign – though it did. Because it forced me to exercise governance judgment under pressure, with imperfect information, against smart opposition, in real time. That experience – the gap between understanding concepts and applying them – is what every board should create for itself.

This chapter provides a complete guide to running your own activist investor tabletop exercise, drawing directly from the methodology and experience of the SLGI program.

# Why Every Board Should Run an Activist Simulation

Roosevelt Giles, the program's founder, had a phrase he returned to repeatedly when explaining the tabletop methodology. It captures something that governance professionals too often overlook.

The process is the key. It is the process.

Giles was not talking about the outcome – who wins, who loses, what settlement terms are negotiated. He was talking about the act of preparation itself. The eight weeks that teams spend researching a real company, building competing arguments from the same data, and developing strategies under time pressure produce learning that no lecture, case discussion, or governance manual can replicate.

Three specific learning objectives distinguish the tabletop from every other governance education method.

First, participants learn to see the company through multiple lenses simultaneously. The activist team discovers that building a credible case for change requires the same rigorous research that effective board oversight demands – financial benchmarking, governance assessment, competitive analysis, leadership evaluation. The management team discovers that defending against an activist requires honest self-assessment of the company's vulnerabilities, not reflexive dismissal. The board team discovers that its most important responsibility is evaluating the substance of both positions on their merits – independent of institutional loyalty to management or hostility toward the activist.

Second, participants experience the time pressure and information asymmetry that characterize real proxy contests. The eight-week preparation period compresses what activist funds spend months researching into a demanding but achievable timeline. The facilitator introduces unexpected developments that force teams to adapt their strategies in real time. The result is an emotional and intellectual intensity that mirrors what directors experience in actual campaigns.

Third, participants develop negotiation skills in a governance context. The settlement negotiation at the heart of the exercise requires participants to balance competing interests, make strategic concessions, and evaluate whether a deal serves shareholders better than a contested vote. These are skills that directors use in every dimension of board service – from CEO compensation negotiations to M&A decisions.

# Designing the Exercise: The Three-Team Structure

The exercise requires three teams, and the three-team structure is non-negotiable. Two-team simulations – activist versus management, or activist versus board – miss the governance dynamics that make the exercise valuable. It is the triangle of competing perspectives that produces the most important learning.

**The Activist Investor Team** plays the role of an activist hedge fund that has accumulated a significant position in the target company and is preparing to file a Schedule 13D. This team conducts the deepest financial and governance analysis, builds the campaign materials, and presents demands to the board. The activist team's job is to make the strongest possible case for change – supported by evidence, not rhetoric.

**The Company Management Team** plays the role of the target company's executive team and IR function. This team develops the company's defense strategy, prepares shareholder communications, and engages with the board on how to respond. The management team's most important challenge is intellectual honesty – acknowledging vulnerabilities while articulating a credible plan for addressing them without capitulating to activist demands.

**The Board of Directors Team** plays the role of the company's independent directors. This team must evaluate both the activist's case and management's defense independently. The board's job is the hardest: exercise fiduciary judgment under pressure, with incomplete information, while maintaining independence from both parties. The board team determines whether to engage the activist, what settlement terms are acceptable, and when to fight versus when to negotiate.

Team sizes of four to eight people work best. Smaller teams lack the diversity of perspective that makes deliberation productive. Larger teams diffuse accountability and make coordination difficult.

## Selecting the Right Target Company

The target company is the foundation of the exercise. A poorly chosen target will produce a superficial simulation regardless of how well the rest of the exercise is designed. The SLGI program's selection of Flowers Foods illustrates the five criteria that matter.

**Financial accessibility.** The target should have sufficient analyst coverage and publicly available data to support thorough research. SEC filings – 10-K, 10-Q, DEF 14A, 8-K – should be current and detailed. Earnings call transcripts should be available. Analyst reports and consensus estimates should be accessible through standard financial databases. Mid-cap and large-cap companies provide the richest material. Small-cap companies with limited coverage make the research phase frustrating rather than educational.

**Genuine governance issues.** The target should not be a company in crisis – that makes the exercise too easy for the activist team and too demoralizing for the management team. It should be a company with genuine but debatable governance issues – board tenure concerns, compensation questions, strategic ambiguity – where reasonable people could disagree about whether change is needed and what form it should take. Flowers Foods fit this criterion well. Its former CEO remained on the board years after stepping down from the executive role, creating legitimate independence questions. Several directors had served for more than a decade. But the governance was not egregious – it was the kind of nuanced situation where both sides could make reasonable arguments.

**Business model clarity.** Participants will spend eight weeks analyzing this company. If the business model requires deep technical expertise – pharmaceutical pipeline analysis, semiconductor manufacturing processes, financial services regulatory complexity – the exercise becomes an industry education program rather than a governance exercise. Consumer products, retail, industrial, and technology companies with clear revenue models work best. Flowers Foods – bread, baked goods, grocery distribution – was a business every participant could understand without specialized knowledge.

**Underperformance narrative.** The activist team needs a credible platform. A company whose stock has outperformed its sector by forty percent over three years provides no foothold for an activist campaign. The ideal target has a plausible underperformance story – flat total shareholder return against a rising sector index, margin compression while peers have maintained profitability, a valuation discount to peers – that the activist team can build a campaign around.

**No active proxy contest.** This is a practical requirement. Avoid companies currently under activist attack. Real-time developments would complicate the simulation, and participants might confuse the exercise with the actual campaign. Check 13D filings on SEC EDGAR and platforms like Insightia or SharkRepellent before finalizing the target.

# The Eight-Week Preparation Phase

The preparation phase is where the real learning happens. By the time the simulation sessions begin, participants should have developed a depth of knowledge about the target company that rivals what professional activist funds and corporate defense teams bring to actual campaigns. The preparation unfolds in three stages.

## Weeks 1-3: Research and Analysis

All three teams conduct independent research on the target company using the same publicly available sources. This parallel research structure is deliberate – it means that each team develops its own interpretation of the data, and the simulation reveals how the same facts can support different conclusions depending on the analytical lens.

Every team should complete a comprehensive research protocol: financial analysis with peer benchmarking, governance quality assessment from the proxy statement, competitive positioning analysis from industry data, and leadership evaluation from public sources.

In our Flowers Foods exercise, the research phase produced some of the most powerful learning moments. Team members who had never before analyzed a public company's proxy statement in detail discovered a world of governance information hiding in plain sight. Director biographies, committee assignments, tenure data, stock ownership – it was all there, and it told a story that the company's glossy investor presentations did not.

The research phase also surfaced the inevitable disagreements within each team about how to interpret the data. On my activist team, we debated whether Flowers Foods' dividend payout ratio was too high – a sign of capital allocation discipline or a sign that management was prioritizing income investors over growth investment. We debated whether the former CEO's continued board presence was a governance problem or a succession benefit. These internal debates – resolved through evidence, not authority – were as valuable as the eventual simulation itself.

## Weeks 4-6: Strategy Development and Deliverables

Each team transitions from analysis to strategy, developing the specific deliverables they will present during the simulation.

**Activist team deliverables.** The activist team must produce four core deliverables. First, a comprehensive analysis of the company's governance and financial vulnerabilities – the case for change, grounded in specific data. Second, a public letter to the board articulating specific demands. Not vague requests for improved governance – concrete actions with measurable outcomes. Separate the CEO and Chair roles. Replace specific long-tenured directors. Implement a capital return program of a specified size. Conduct a strategic review of underperforming business units with a defined timeline.

The letter is the centerpiece. Our Sterling Capital letter to the Flowers Foods board ran thirteen pages. Every claim was supported by a specific citation to a public filing. Every demand was tied to a specific governance improvement. Every proposed director candidate had qualifications that mapped to identified gaps in the existing board's skills matrix. The discipline required to build a letter of that specificity forced our team to separate what we could prove from what we merely suspected – a distinction that matters enormously in real campaigns.

Third, a slate of proposed director nominees with specific qualifications. Fourth, a shareholder presentation deck that could persuade institutional investors to support the activist's position.

**Management team deliverables.** First, a vulnerability assessment – an honest evaluation of where the activist's arguments are strongest. This is the hardest deliverable because it requires intellectual honesty about weaknesses that management instinctively wants to minimize. Second, a defense strategy that distinguishes between demands to resist and demands to accept or negotiate. Third, a shareholder letter presenting the case for continuity. Fourth, a proactive governance reform package – changes the company will implement regardless of activist pressure – that demonstrates responsiveness.

**Board team deliverables.** The board team occupies the most difficult position. It must produce an independent assessment of the company, evaluate each activist demand on its merits, and develop a negotiation mandate – the terms under which it would settle and the terms it would not accept. The board team must define its principles before the negotiation begins, not discover them during it.

## Weeks 7-8: Refinement and Preparation

Teams finalize materials, rehearse presentations, and prepare for the unexpected. The facilitator should schedule brief check-ins with each team to ensure preparations are on track and that all teams have developed substantive positions.

In our exercise, these final weeks were when the preparation shifted from analytical to emotional. We were no longer debating data – we were rehearsing arguments, anticipating counterpoints, and developing the confidence to present our case to a room full of skeptical, well-prepared adversaries. That shift – from analysis to advocacy – is one of the exercise's most important transitions.

# Scenario Injects: The Facilitator's Most Powerful Tool

Injects are unexpected developments introduced at critical moments that force teams to adapt their strategies. They transform the exercise from a structured debate into a dynamic simulation that mirrors the unpredictability of real governance crises.

**The earnings surprise.** The facilitator announces that the company has issued a preliminary earnings release showing quarterly results significantly below analyst expectations. This inject shifts momentum dramatically toward the activist – management's "stay the course" argument becomes harder to sustain when the current course is producing disappointing results. Alternatively, the facilitator can announce strong earnings, which undermines the activist's underperformance thesis and forces them to adapt.

**The media leak.** A financial journalist publishes a story revealing details of the activist's campaign before the formal public announcement. Both sides must manage the media narrative – the activist must decide whether to accelerate their timeline, and management must decide whether to respond publicly before their defense is ready.

**The ISS recommendation.** The facilitator announces that ISS has issued a report supporting some of the activist's director nominees. This inject alters the negotiation's power dynamics immediately. Management must contend with the reality that a contested vote may not go in their favor.

**The competing activist.** A second activist fund files a 13D with different demands. This complicates the negotiation for all parties and teaches participants about the multi-front dynamics that sometimes characterize real campaigns.

The timing of injects is as important as their content. A well-timed inject at a negotiation impasse can break the deadlock. An inject deployed too early can overshadow the teams' strategies before they have been articulated. The facilitator should prepare four to five injects before the simulation and deploy them based on how the exercise is unfolding rather than on a rigid schedule.

## The Negotiation Session

The negotiation is the exercise's centerpiece. All three teams come together for direct engagement – mirroring the private discussions that typically follow the public exchange in real proxy contests.

In our capstone session on December 9, the exercise unfolded over several hours. The Flowers Foods board team – led by Helen, playing the role of the lead independent director – opened by welcoming our Sterling Capital team and establishing the framework for discussion. We presented our demands: CEO and Chair separation, specific board member replacements, performance-linked compensation reform, and a comprehensive strategic operational plan with defined savings targets.

The negotiation that followed was intense. The board team pushed back on our demand to remove specific directors, arguing that recent board refreshment efforts had already addressed composition concerns. We countered with data on board expertise gaps – specifically the lack of directors with financial restructuring and divestiture experience. The board team challenged our proposed director nominees. We defended their qualifications with specific references to their track records.

Andrew Shapiro, the veteran activist investor who was observing and advising, intervened at key points. He pushed both sides toward substantive engagement rather than positional bargaining. When our team was too aggressive on CEO replacement demands, he steered us toward the more actionable objective of separating the CEO and Chair roles. When the board team was too dismissive of our capital allocation demands, he reminded them that the data supported the activist's case.

The negotiation eventually produced the outlines of a settlement – standstill terms, new board seats, governance reforms, a strategic review with a defined timeline. But the settlement itself was secondary to the process of reaching it. Every participant left the room with a visceral understanding of what governance judgment feels like when it is exercised under pressure.

Roosevelt Giles's reminder echoed throughout. The process is the key. What mattered was not who won the negotiation. What mattered was that every participant had experienced the process of evaluating competing claims, exercising fiduciary judgment, and negotiating on behalf of shareholders – skills that would transfer directly to every real boardroom they would eventually enter.

# The After-Action Review: Five Categories of Insight

The after-action review is the single most important element of the exercise. Without it, participants remember the competition. With it, they extract governance principles that will serve them for decades.

Our program's debrief consistently produced five categories of insight. These five insights – discovered through the exercise rather than taught before it – represent the deepest governance learning the simulation produces.

**The data was always there.** Across all three teams, participants reported the same revelation: the governance vulnerabilities the activist team identified were visible in public filings. They were not hidden. They were not obscure. They were sitting in the 10-K, the proxy statement, and the earnings call transcripts – available to anyone who took the time to look. The activist's advantage is not access to private information. It is the willingness to do the independent research that most directors do not do.

**Management's perspective is incomplete.** The management team participants consistently reported that the exercise forced them to confront weaknesses they would have preferred to explain away. The activist team's presentation of the same data through a different analytical lens – focusing on underperformance rather than stability, on governance gaps rather than institutional continuity – revealed blind spots that the management perspective naturally creates.

**The board's role is harder than it looks.** Board team participants consistently reported that evaluating competing claims under time pressure – with genuine uncertainty about who was right – was far more difficult than they had expected. The exercise demolished the comfortable assumption that governance judgment is obvious when the moment arrives. It requires preparation, analytical rigor, and the willingness to tolerate ambiguity.

**Negotiation is a governance skill.** Many participants entered the exercise viewing negotiation as separate from governance. The exercise demonstrated that negotiation pervades board service – every CEO compensation discussion, every M&A evaluation, every shareholder engagement. The settlement negotiation develops the same skills directors use in every boardroom decision.

**Intellectual honesty is non-negotiable.** The exercise's most powerful lesson was the importance of acknowledging when the other side has a point, when your own position has weaknesses, and when the data contradicts your assumptions. Participants who approached the exercise with fixed conclusions consistently underperformed those who let the evidence guide their analysis.

# The Flowers Foods Capstone: What Actually Happened

The December 9 simulation brought together three teams that had spent eight weeks preparing from different perspectives on the same company. The activist team – Sterling Capital – presented a comprehensive set of demands to the Flowers Foods board team. The management team was present to defend the company's current strategy and governance.

The topics negotiated were specific and substantive. CEO and Chair separation – whether to require it, when it would take effect, and who would fill the non-executive chair role. Board refreshment – which directors should be replaced, what qualifications the replacements should have, and how many seats the activist should receive. Compensation reform – tying executive pay more tightly to performance metrics the activist team had identified as lagging peers. Operational improvements – specific cost reduction targets, strategic review of underperforming divisions, and a timeline for implementation. Succession planning – ensuring that the board had a robust CEO succession process independent of the incumbent's preferences.

The negotiation involved evaluating specific board members by name, debating whether the lead independent director should be elevated to non-executive chair, assessing whether particular long-tenured directors should be asked to retire, and structuring standstill terms that gave the activist confidence the board would follow through while giving the board the operational flexibility to implement changes at its own pace.

Sheryl Palmer, the CEO and board chair of Taylor Morrison who wrapped up the session, brought a perspective that reframed everything the teams had experienced. Palmer emphasized corporate preparedness – the idea that the time to prepare for an activist campaign is before the letter arrives, not after. She stressed the importance of a skilled investor relations person who can serve as an early warning system and a bridge between the board and the investor community. And she underscored the deep technical expertise required for modern governance – not just financial literacy but fluency in governance structures, proxy mechanics, and institutional investor dynamics.

Palmer's closing point was the most important. The tabletop exercise is not a one-time event. It is a methodology that should be integrated into the board's ongoing governance practice. The companies that run these exercises regularly – that force themselves to see their own governance through an adversarial lens on a recurring basis – are the companies that build the activist immunity described in Chapter 18. The companies that treat the exercise as a novelty or a checkbox are the companies that remain vulnerable.

# Role Assignments and Team Dynamics

The internal dynamics of each team are as important as the inter-team competition. How participants are assigned to roles – and how those roles interact – shapes the quality of the exercise.

**Activist team roles.** The team lead serves as the campaign's principal spokesperson and chief strategist. A financial analyst role handles the quantitative case – peer benchmarking, TSR calculations, capital allocation analysis. A governance analyst role focuses on board composition, director qualifications, and governance structure. A communications role drafts the demand letter, investor presentation, and public messaging. In our Sterling Capital team, we also assigned a nominee recruitment role – someone responsible for identifying and presenting the qualifications of our proposed director candidates.

**Management team roles.** The CEO role is the most demanding – the person playing this role must defend the company's strategy while acknowledging genuine vulnerabilities. A CFO role handles the financial defense – explaining why the activist's benchmarking is misleading or incomplete, presenting forward-looking projections that justify the current strategy. An IR role manages the shareholder communication strategy. A general counsel role evaluates the legal dimensions – advance notice requirements, defensive measures, and the parameters of potential settlement terms.

**Board team roles.** The board chair or lead independent director role is the exercise's most consequential assignment. This person must manage the board's deliberation, maintain independence from both management and the activist, and ultimately lead the negotiation. Committee chair roles – nominating committee, compensation committee, audit committee – provide structure for evaluating specific activist demands within the committee's expertise. An independent director role allows participants to practice the hardest governance skill: exercising independent judgment when the institutional pressure is to align with management.

The team dynamics that emerge during the eight-week preparation often mirror real-world governance dynamics with surprising fidelity. On the activist team, the tension between aggressive demands and credible analysis mirrors the discipline that successful activists must maintain. On the management team, the tension between honest self-assessment and defensive instinct mirrors the challenge every management team faces when confronted with external criticism. On the board team, the tension between loyalty to management and fiduciary duty to shareholders mirrors the central governance dilemma that the exercise is designed to illuminate.

# Common Pitfalls to Avoid

Several pitfalls can undermine the exercise's learning value.

**Choosing a target that is too obvious.** A company in crisis with egregious governance makes the activist team's job too easy and the management team's job impossible. The best targets have genuine but debatable issues – the kind of company where the activist has credible arguments and management has credible defenses.

**Skipping the research phase.** Teams that jump from target selection to strategy development without thorough research produce superficial arguments that collapse under challenge. The research is the foundation. Without it, the simulation becomes an exercise in rhetoric rather than governance.

**Failing to introduce injects.** A predictable exercise without unexpected developments produces a structured debate, not a simulation. Injects transform the exercise by forcing adaptation under pressure – precisely the skill that directors need most.

**Neglecting the after-action review.** Without the debrief, participants remember who won and who lost. With it, they extract governance principles that last a career. The debrief is not an optional add-on. It is the exercise's most important component.

**Treating it as a performance rather than a learning exercise.** The temptation to "win" the exercise can overwhelm the learning objectives. The facilitator should consistently emphasize that the quality of analysis and the integrity of the process matter more than the outcome of any particular negotiation.

# Adapting the Exercise for Your Organization

The eight-week, three-team format produces the deepest learning. But the methodology can be adapted to different contexts and time constraints.

**Board retreat format.** For sitting boards, the exercise can be compressed into a half-day or full-day retreat using the board's own company – or a carefully selected comparable company – as the target. An external facilitator prepares the research materials and plays the

activist role, presenting a credible campaign to the board. The board
then deliberates and responds. This format is particularly valuable
for boards that have never experienced activist pressure.

**Corporate defense workshop.**   For management teams, the
exercise can focus exclusively on the defense perspective. An external team presents an activist campaign prepared in advance using
real company data, and management practices developing and
presenting its defense. This format is most valuable for companies
at elevated risk – those with underperforming stock prices, governance concerns flagged by proxy advisors, or significant ownership
by activist-friendly institutional investors.

**One-day intensive.** For governance education programs with limited time, the exercise can be compressed into a single day. The facilitator provides pre-prepared research packets, and teams spend the
morning developing strategy and the afternoon in simulation. This
format sacrifices depth but preserves the core learning objectives:
seeing the company through multiple lenses, negotiating under pressure, and exercising governance judgment.

**Recurring annual exercise.** The most valuable adaptation is the
recurring exercise – conducted annually as part of the board's governance calendar. Each year, the board selects a new target company
(or uses its own company with updated data) and runs the exercise
with fresh scenarios and injects. Over time, this practice builds institutional muscle memory for activist engagement and keeps governance skills sharp.

Regardless of format, one element is non-negotiable:  the after-
action review. Without the debrief, the exercise produces entertainment. With it, the exercise produces governance wisdom.

# The Standstill Negotiation:  The Exercise's Most Instructive Component

The standstill agreement negotiation deserves special attention because it is where governance theory meets practical deal-making –
and where participants consistently report the deepest learning.

In the Flowers Foods exercise, the standstill negotiation forced both sides to move from advocacy to compromise. Our Sterling Capital team had to decide which demands were essential and which were negotiable. We had to evaluate whether the board's proposed concessions – new director seats, governance reforms, a strategic review – were substantive enough to justify suspending our public campaign. We had to assess whether the standstill duration was long enough for the reforms to take effect and short enough to allow us to resume the campaign if the board failed to deliver.

The board team faced symmetrical challenges. They had to decide which activist demands to accept, which to modify, and which to reject. They had to evaluate our proposed director nominees against their own skills matrix. They had to structure standstill terms that gave us confidence in the board's commitment while preserving the board's operational flexibility.

The negotiation taught participants that every provision in a standstill agreement reflects a governance judgment. The number of board seats is not just a number – it determines the activist's ability to influence committee assignments, strategic decisions, and CEO evaluations. The standstill duration is not just a timeline – it determines how long the board has to demonstrate results before facing potential renewed pressure. The exception clauses are not just legal language – they define the circumstances under which the relationship can break down.

Participants who approached the standstill negotiation with principles rather than positions consistently outperformed those who took rigid stances. A board negotiator who said "we will consider nominees whose qualifications address specific gaps in our skills matrix" invited productive discussion. A board negotiator who said "we will not give any seats" invited escalation. The exercise demonstrated that principled negotiation – the same approach that works in M&A transactions and CEO compensation discussions – is the most effective approach to activist settlement.

# What I Learned Leading the Activist Tabletop

I will close this chapter with a personal reflection, because the most important lesson from the Flowers Foods tabletop was not about activist campaigns. It was about governance itself.

Leading the activist tabletop taught me something I could not have learned from any book – including this one. It taught me that the line between activist and director is much thinner than either side would like to admit. The research we did on the activist team – analyzing financial performance, scrutinizing governance structures, evaluating board composition, assessing capital allocation – was identical to the research that every effective independent director should be doing. The questions I asked were the questions that every board should be asking. The data I used was publicly available to anyone willing to look.

The difference was not knowledge or access. The difference was perspective. As the activist, I was incentivized to find problems – and I found them, because they were there. As a director, I would have been incentivized to explain them away – and I might have succeeded, because the explanations were also there.

The tabletop exercise closes that gap. It forces participants to inhabit both perspectives simultaneously – to see the company through the activist's eyes and through the board's eyes and through management's eyes. That multiplicity of perspective is not just useful for surviving activist campaigns. It is the foundation of effective corporate governance.

The moment that crystallized this lesson came during our final preparation session, two days before the capstone. We had been refining our presentation, debating which demands to prioritize and which to hold in reserve for the negotiation. One of my team members paused and said something that stuck with me: "If I were on this board, I would want to hear exactly what we are about to say. Because we are saying the things the board should have been saying to itself."

That observation captures the entire purpose of the tabletop exercise – and, in many ways, the entire purpose of this book.

The question is not whether to run a tabletop exercise. The question is whether your board can afford not to.

# Chapter 20: After the Campaign – Governance Transformation and the New Normal

The proxy fight is over. The settlement has been signed. The press releases have been issued. The activist's nominees have taken their seats at the boardroom table. For many directors, the instinct is to exhale – to treat the conclusion of the campaign as the end of the story.

It is not the end. It is a beginning.

What happens after an activist campaign – how the board integrates new directors, implements governance reforms, rebuilds cohesion, and sustains the momentum for improvement – determines whether the campaign produces lasting value or simply rearranges the deck chairs. The companies that treat the post-campaign period as a governance transformation opportunity become stronger. The companies that treat it as a return to the status quo waste the most expensive governance lesson their shareholders ever paid for.

## Integrating Activist-Nominated Directors

The most immediate challenge facing any post-campaign board is integrating the activist's director nominees. These new directors arrive under unusual circumstances. They were not recruited through the company's normal nominating process. They do not have pre-existing relationships with the other board members. They were nominated by a party that just spent months – and potentially millions of dollars – publicly criticizing the board they are now joining.

Here is the reality that every incumbent director needs to internalize: the activist-nominated directors are not adversaries. They are colleagues with a different lens. They bring exactly what the board was criticized for lacking – an investor's perspective, fresh analytical rigor, and an outsider's willingness to challenge assumptions. If the board treats them as hostile implants to be marginalized, the board is failing to capture the value that the campaign was meant to create. If the board embraces them as contributors who bring capabilities the existing board lacked, the post-campaign period becomes genuinely transformative.

The practical mechanics of integration matter. Structured onboarding for new directors – the same quality of onboarding that any new director should receive – is essential. New directors need access to the same information, the same committee materials, and the same management presentations as every other board member. They need introductions to key management leaders, facility tours, and deep-dive sessions on the company's strategy, financial structure, and competitive positioning.

Committee assignments are a particularly important integration tool. Assigning activist-nominated directors to committees where their specific expertise is most relevant – the finance committee for a director with capital allocation expertise, the nominating committee for a director with governance background – signals that the board values their contribution. Assigning them to committees where they will have minimal impact signals the opposite.

The board chair – or the lead independent director, if the roles are separated as part of the settlement – plays the pivotal role in building unity. A chair who creates opportunities for new and existing directors to work together on specific projects, who ensures that new directors' questions are welcomed rather than deflected, and who models the kind of constructive challenge that the activist was advocating – that chair is building a better board. A chair who creates an insiders-versus-outsiders dynamic is guaranteeing that the next activist campaign will be more damaging than the first.

# Governance Reforms Post-Settlement

Most activist settlements include specific governance reform commitments – CEO and Chair separation, board refreshment timelines, committee restructuring, enhanced disclosure practices, strategic reviews of underperforming business units. The board's obligation is not just to implement these reforms but to implement them with genuine commitment and on the agreed timeline.

Here is where post-campaign governance often fails. The settlement is signed. The immediate pressure abates. And the implementation of agreed reforms slows. The CEO and Chair separation is deferred to "a more appropriate time." The board refreshment timeline slips because the nominating committee "needs more time to identify qualified candidates." The strategic review of underperforming divisions produces a report that recommends no changes.

Activists notice. Institutional investors notice. And the standstill agreement that gave the board breathing room has an expiration date.

The Phillips 66 case is instructive. Elliott Management reached an initial settlement with Phillips 66 in February 2024 that included the addition of a new director and an agreement to add another together. But when former CEO Greg Garland, who had remained as chairman, retired and CEO Mark Lashier assumed the chair role – against Elliott's wishes – the relationship deteriorated. Elliott perceived the move as a violation of the settlement's spirit, even if not its letter. The result was a rare full proxy fight – Elliott launched a contested election that yielded mixed results but demonstrated that broken settlements escalate.

The lesson is clear: compliance with settlement terms must be genuine, not performative. The board that implements agreed reforms enthusiastically – because they improve governance, not because the activist demanded them – builds credibility with both the activist and the institutional investors who supported the settlement. The board that implements reforms grudgingly, partially, or on a delayed timeline is inviting the activist to return.

# Rebuilding Board Cohesion

Contested proxy campaigns create factions. Directors who were publicly criticized by the activist may harbor resentment toward new directors who arrived on the activist's slate. New directors who fought their way onto the board may carry adversarial instincts into boardroom deliberations. Management team members who spent months defending against the activist may view activist-nominated directors with suspicion.

These dynamics are natural and understandable. They are also destructive if allowed to persist.

Rebuilding cohesion requires deliberate effort. The chair's role is critical. Effective post-campaign chairs pursue several strategies.

**Structured social interaction.** Board dinners, off-site retreats, and informal gatherings provide opportunities for new and existing directors to build personal relationships outside the formal boardroom setting. These interactions – often dismissed as ceremonial – are where trust is built.

**Collaborative projects.** Assigning new and existing directors to work together on specific board initiatives – a strategic review, a governance improvement project, a compensation committee redesign – creates shared purpose and demonstrates that the board operates as a unified body.

**Open dialogue about the campaign.** The worst approach is to pretend the campaign never happened. The best approach is to acknowledge it – to discuss what the board learned, what the activist got right, and what the post-campaign board should do differently. This kind of candid reflection requires courage from the chair, but it produces the mutual respect that cohesion requires.

**Clear behavioral expectations.** The chair should establish from the outset that the boardroom is not a continuation of the proxy fight. All directors – incumbent and activist-nominated – are expected to contribute constructively, evaluate proposals on their merits, and act in the interest of all shareholders. Factional behavior that serves the activist's agenda or management's agenda at the expense of shareholder interests should be addressed directly.

# Management Transitions

In many post-campaign scenarios, the CEO changes – either as a direct result of the campaign or as a consequence of the governance dynamics it set in motion. Starbucks replaced its CEO with Brian Niccol. Southwest's executive chairman Gary Kelly departed. Norfolk Southern's CEO was removed for personal conduct issues discovered during a period of heightened governance scrutiny triggered by the activist campaign.

When the CEO changes, the board faces a governance challenge that is distinct from and more consequential than the activist campaign itself. The board must simultaneously support the new CEO through a leadership transition, maintain governance oversight during a period of organizational vulnerability, and demonstrate to shareholders that the transition is producing the improvements the campaign was meant to achieve.

The most effective post-campaign CEO transitions share several characteristics.

**Clear mandate from the board.** The new CEO should receive an explicit mandate from the board – specific priorities, measurable objectives, and a defined timeline for demonstrating progress. This mandate should be informed by the activist's critique and the board's own assessment, but it should be the board's mandate, not the activist's. The new CEO works for the board, not for the activist who pressured the board into making the change.

**Board support without board passivity.** The board should provide the new CEO with the resources, authority, and runway to implement changes. But support is not the same as passivity. The board's heightened governance oversight should continue – not as suspicion of the new CEO but as the standard of engagement that the activist campaign demonstrated the board should always have been providing.

**Communication with shareholders.** The institutional investors who were the decisive audience during the campaign remain the decisive audience during the transition. The board should communicate proactively about the CEO transition – what the new CEO's mandate includes, what milestones the board is tracking, and how the transition is progressing. Silence during a CEO transition invites speculation, and speculation favors the activist's narrative.

# Measuring Post-Campaign Governance Improvement

Post-campaign governance transformation is only meaningful if it is measurable. Boards that implement reforms without tracking their impact are engaging in governance theater – changes that look good in a press release but produce no measurable improvement for shareholders.

The board should establish specific metrics for evaluating the governance transformation's effectiveness. These metrics should be tied to the specific concerns the activist raised and the specific reforms the settlement requires.

**Financial performance metrics.** If the activist's campaign was built on underperformance, the post-campaign board must track whether financial performance improves. Total shareholder return relative to the peer group, return on invested capital, margin trajectory, and revenue growth should be benchmarked against pre-campaign baselines. Improvement validates the governance changes. Continued underperformance signals that the changes were insufficient – or that the wrong changes were made.

**Governance quality metrics.** Board composition should be evaluated against the skills matrix developed during or after the campaign. Director attendance, committee meeting frequency, and the substantiveness of board discussions should be tracked. The annual board evaluation – which should be conducted by an independent third party, not by the board itself – should assess whether the governance transformation has changed the board's culture and effectiveness, not just its composition.

**Shareholder engagement metrics.** The number and quality of direct engagements between independent directors and institutional investors should be tracked. Proxy voting results – particularly on say-on-pay and director elections – provide quantitative evidence of shareholder sentiment. The percentage of institutional investors who request governance meetings, and the nature of those requests, signals whether the board's enhanced engagement is producing results.

These metrics should be reported to the full board quarterly and disclosed to shareholders annually in the proxy statement. Transparency about post-campaign governance improvement builds the credibility that prevents the next campaign.

## Ongoing Shareholder Engagement

The activist campaign revealed something that the board should have known before the campaign began: your institutional shareholders are paying attention. They have governance expectations. They have analytical capabilities. And they will exercise their voting power when they believe the board is failing to meet their standards.

The post-campaign board's shareholder engagement should be qualitatively different from the pre-campaign engagement – not because the board is under heightened scrutiny, but because the campaign demonstrated what genuine engagement looks like.

Regular meetings between independent directors and institutional investors should become a standing governance practice. These meetings – structured to comply with Regulation FD – give institutional investors direct access to the people responsible for governance oversight. They also give directors unfiltered insight into investor sentiment that management's IR function may not fully convey.

Annual governance reviews should be communicated to shareholders through enhanced proxy disclosures. The board should explain – in specific, substantive terms – what governance improvements it has implemented, how it is tracking progress against the commitments made during the settlement, and what additional improvements it is pursuing.

Shareholder proposals that receive significant support should receive substantive responses. A board that ignores a shareholder proposal that received forty percent support after surviving an activist campaign is sending a message that the governance transformation was cosmetic.

# When the Activist Returns

Standstill agreements expire. And when they expire, the activist's options reopen.

A well-executed post-campaign governance transformation makes the activist's return unlikely. If the board has implemented agreed reforms, integrated new directors successfully, and demonstrated measurable improvement in the areas the activist targeted, the activist's basis for a renewed campaign is thin. The institutional investors who supported the activist the first time are unlikely to do so again if the board has delivered on its commitments.

But if the board has dragged its feet on implementation, marginalized activist-nominated directors, or failed to deliver the performance improvements that the governance changes were supposed to enable – the activist's return is not just likely. It is justified.

The Phillips 66 example bears repeating. When Elliott perceived that the initial settlement terms had been violated, the fund escalated to a full proxy fight – something Elliott rarely does. The result was a contested election that produced a split outcome but consumed enormous resources and management attention. The lesson is not that boards should fear activists. It is that boards should keep their commitments.

The best protection against an activist's return is the same as the best protection against the activist's initial appearance: governance so strong that activism is unnecessary. If the post-campaign board is genuinely governing with rigor – overseeing strategy, allocating capital, engaging with shareholders, maintaining transparency – the standstill expiration is a non-event. The activist has nothing to return to.

# The Governance Transformation Opportunity

Here is the perspective that separates boards that emerge stronger from campaigns from boards that merely survive them: an activist campaign is the most expensive governance audit your company will ever receive. An outside party with substantial financial incentives has spent months analyzing your governance structure, your financial performance, your board composition, and your strategic direction – and has presented its findings in a detailed, evidence-based format. The question is whether you treat that analysis as a threat to be repelled or an opportunity to be captured.

The evidence is clear that companies can emerge from activist campaigns in stronger governance positions. As noted in Chapter 12, academic research has consistently found that companies targeted by activists tend to experience governance improvements and, in many cases, improved financial performance in the years following a campaign. New directors bring fresh perspectives. Governance reforms create better structures. Enhanced shareholder engagement builds credibility. The catalyst may have been unwelcome, but the results can be genuinely positive.

Sheryl Palmer's emphasis during the SLGI program resonated with this theme. Palmer – who brought the CEO and board chair perspective to the program's activism discussions – stressed that corporate preparedness is a continuous practice, not a crisis response. She emphasized the importance of skilled investor relations professionals who can serve as early warning systems and bridges to the investor community. And she underscored the deep technical expertise that modern governance demands – not just financial literacy but fluency in governance structures, proxy mechanics, institutional investor dynamics, and the ever-evolving regulatory landscape.

Palmer's message was that the best boards are those that make activist campaigns unnecessary – but that when campaigns happen, they create opportunities for boards willing to learn from them. The companies that waste those opportunities – that return to the pre-campaign status quo the moment the standstill is signed – are the companies that will face the same problems again.

Palmer also delivered a warning that resonated with particular force. The governance environment is becoming more demanding, not less. Institutional investors are building more sophisticated stewardship capabilities. Proxy advisory firms are refining their analytical models. Activists are deploying more capital, conducting more rigorous research, and achieving results at an accelerating pace. The bar for what constitutes acceptable governance is rising every year. Boards that were adequate five years ago may be vulnerable today. Boards that are adequate today may be vulnerable in five years.

The implication is that post-campaign governance transformation is not a one-time initiative. It is a permanent change in the board's operating standard. The rigor, the transparency, the shareholder engagement, the intellectual honesty that the campaign forced the board to adopt – these must become the permanent baseline, not a temporary response to a temporary threat. The activist will not always be watching. But the institutional investors will be. And the question they will always be asking is whether this board is governing as though every decision will be scrutinized – because it will be.

## Lessons from Companies That Got It Right

Not every post-campaign story is one of dysfunction and delay. Some companies emerge from activist campaigns genuinely transformed – with stronger governance, better financial performance, and deeper institutional investor confidence than they had before the campaign.

The common thread among these success stories is not the specific reforms implemented – those vary by company and circumstance. The common thread is the board's attitude toward the campaign itself. Boards that viewed the campaign as a legitimate governance intervention – painful but informative – used the activist's analysis as a roadmap for improvement. Boards that viewed the campaign as an assault to be survived treated the settlement as the end of an unpleasant episode rather than the beginning of a transformation.

The attitude difference manifests in specific behaviors. Boards in the first category actively seek input from activist-nominated directors, proactively implement reforms beyond the settlement requirements, and communicate governance improvements to shareholders as evidence of the board's commitment to continuous improvement. Boards in the second category tolerate activist-nominated directors without integrating them, implement the minimum required by the settlement, and return to pre-campaign communication patterns as soon as the standstill is signed.

The market notices the difference. Companies where post-campaign governance transformation is genuine tend to experience sustained stock price improvement, reduced governance risk premiums, and improved proxy voting results. Companies where the transformation is cosmetic tend to experience the opposite – and eventually face renewed activist attention.

## The Closing Reflection

Shareholder activism is not a disease to be eradicated. It is a governance mechanism – imperfect, sometimes disruptive, occasionally self-serving, but fundamentally rooted in the principle that shareholders have the right to hold boards accountable.

Andrew Shapiro's subatomic particle analogy – borrowed from Nell Minnow and shared with our cohort in September 2025 – captures a truth that extends far beyond activist investing. The quality of oversight improves when someone is watching. Directors who know that their decisions will be scrutinized by investors with magnifying glasses, by proxy advisory firms with governance scorecards, and by activists with 13D filings make better decisions. Not because they are afraid, but because scrutiny imposes the discipline that all governance requires.

The directors who thrive in this environment – who build the boards described in this book – are not the ones who build the highest walls or adopt the most aggressive defensive measures. They are the ones who adopt the investor mindset within the boardroom. They ask the uncomfortable questions about capital allocation, governance structure, and management performance. They demand transparency and engagement rather than secrecy and entrenchment. They see the company through the eyes of the shareholders who own it – not just the management team that runs it.

In doing so, they provide the most effective defense any company can have: a board that is genuinely doing its job.

The question for every director is not whether activism is good or bad, or whether the next campaign will target your company, or whether your defensive mechanisms are sufficient. The question is simpler and more fundamental: Would your board pass the activist's test?

And if it would not – if an honest assessment would reveal the governance gaps, the capital allocation failures, the board composition weaknesses, and the transparency deficits that activists target – the question becomes: What are you going to do about it before someone outside the boardroom does it for you?

That question is where this book ends. And where your work begins.

# Appendix A: Activist Investor Vulnerability Assessment Checklist

Every company that trades on a public exchange is a potential activist target. The question is not whether an activist could build a case against your company – given enough creativity and capital, one almost certainly could. The question is whether that case would be compelling enough to attract serious capital, win institutional investor support, and produce governance changes that the board would rather have made on its own terms.

This checklist is a diagnostic tool. It is designed to help boards and management teams evaluate their own vulnerability honestly – before an activist does it for them. The scoring framework is not theoretical. It reflects the criteria that actual activists use when screening targets, the governance factors that proxy advisory firms weigh when making recommendations, and the financial metrics that institutional investors scrutinize when deciding whether to support an activist's campaign.

Use this assessment annually. Assign it to a committee – ideally the nominating and governance committee – and require that the results be presented to the full board. Do not delegate this to management alone. Management has an inherent conflict of interest in evaluating governance quality, since many of the items being assessed relate directly to their own accountability and oversight. The board must own this process.

This checklist maps directly to the "Four Improvable Problems" framework introduced in Chapter 4 and to the activist vaccine concept developed in Chapter 18. The five sections below correspond to the dimensions that activists evaluate when screening targets – and that your board should be evaluating continuously.

## How to Use This Checklist

Score each item on a scale of 1 to 5, where 1 represents the most vulnerable position and 5 represents the strongest. Be honest. The value of this exercise depends entirely on intellectual rigor. A board that grades itself generously is a board that will be surprised when an activist arrives with a different assessment.

After scoring all items, total the points in each section, then calculate the overall score. The interpretation guide at the end of the checklist provides a framework for understanding your results – but the numbers are less important than the patterns. A company that scores well overall but has a cluster of 1s and 2s in a single category has a concentrated vulnerability that an activist will exploit.

---

## Section 1: Financial Performance

Financial underperformance is the single most reliable predictor of activist targeting. An activist's fundamental thesis is that value is being left on the table – and financial metrics are how they prove it. Score each item relative to your industry peer group, not in absolute terms. A ten percent return on equity is strong in some industries and dismal in others. Context matters.

| # | Assessment Item | Score (1-5) |
|---|---|---|
| 1.1 | **Return on assets vs. peer group.** Is your ROA consistently at or above the median of your peer group? A persistent gap – particularly one that has widened over three or more years – is the first metric an activist screens for. Score 1 if your ROA trails peers by more than 300 basis points; score 5 if you consistently lead the peer group. | |
| 1.2 | **Return on equity vs. peer group.** ROE measures how effectively the company converts shareholder capital into returns. Activists distinguish between ROE driven by operational performance and ROE inflated by leverage. If your ROE looks strong only because of excessive debt, an activist will see through it. Score based on sustained, operationally driven ROE performance relative to peers. | |

| # | Assessment Item | Score (1-5) |
|---|---|---|
| 1.3 | **Revenue growth trajectory vs. peers.** Is the company growing at or above the rate of its peer group? Stagnant or declining revenue growth – particularly when competitors are growing – signals strategic stagnation. Activists use revenue trajectory as evidence that management lacks a credible growth strategy or is failing to execute one. | |
| 1.4 | **Margin trends (operating, EBITDA, net).** Margin compression over consecutive quarters tells an activist that the company is losing pricing power, failing to manage costs, or both. Evaluate three-year trends in operating margin, EBITDA margin, and net margin against peers. A company with flat revenue but declining margins is a particularly attractive target. | |
| 1.5 | **Free cash flow generation and deployment.** Strong free cash flow generation is a positive signal – unless the cash is being deployed poorly. Evaluate both the generation of free cash flow and the quality of its deployment. Is free cash flow being returned to shareholders, invested in high-return projects, or consumed by questionable acquisitions and overhead? | |

| # | Assessment Item | Score (1-5) |
|---|---|---|
| 1.6 | **Cash balance relative to market cap.** Excess cash on the balance sheet is one of the most reliable activist triggers. A company sitting on cash equal to fifteen or twenty percent of its market capitalization – without a clear, articulated rationale – is advertising that it does not have a disciplined capital allocation strategy. Activists will argue that excess cash should be returned through buybacks or special dividends. Score 1 if cash exceeds 20% of market cap with no articulated purpose; score 5 if cash levels are appropriate and the rationale is clearly communicated. | |
| 1.7 | **Capital allocation track record.** Review the last five years of major capital deployment decisions: acquisitions, divestitures, buybacks, dividends, and capital expenditures. Have acquisitions created or destroyed value? Have share buybacks been executed at reasonable valuations, or has the company been buying back stock at highs? Activists will reconstruct this track record in granular detail. | |

| # | Assessment Item | Score (1-5) |
|---|---|---|
| 1.8 | **Sum-of-parts analysis.** Is the company worth more broken up than as a combined entity? Conglomerates and multi-segment companies are especially vulnerable to this analysis. If a sum-of-parts valuation – applying appropriate peer multiples to each business segment – produces a value materially higher than the current enterprise value, an activist has a ready-made thesis: the conglomerate discount is destroying shareholder value. | |

**Section 1 Total:** _____ / 40

# Section 2: Governance Quality

Governance weaknesses are the second pillar of the activist's case – and often the more emotionally compelling one. Financial under-performance is abstract. Governance failures are personal. An over-boarded director, a CEO who chairs their own board, a compensation package that pays handsomely regardless of results – these are the stories that win shareholder votes and generate media coverage.

| # | Assessment Item | Score (1-5) |
|---|-----------------|-------------|
| 2.1 | **Board independence percentage.** What percentage of your directors are truly independent – not just technically independent under stock exchange listing standards, but substantively independent of management? Long tenure, personal relationships with the CEO, and consulting arrangements can compromise independence even when the technical definition is met. Score based on substantive, not merely technical, independence. | |
| 2.2 | **CEO/Chair separation.** Does the same person serve as both CEO and board chair? The governance community has moved decisively toward separation. ISS and Glass Lewis both view combined CEO/Chair roles as a governance risk. If your company combines these roles, do you have a truly empowered lead independent director with a clearly defined mandate – or is the lead director role cosmetic? | |

| # | Assessment Item | Score (1-5) |
|---|---|---|
| 2.3 | **Director tenure (average and longest-serving).** Average board tenure above twelve years raises questions about independence and refreshment. A director who has served for twenty or twenty-five years may be deeply knowledgeable about the company – but an activist will argue they have been captured by management and lack the fresh perspective that effective oversight requires. Score 1 if average tenure exceeds 15 years; score 5 if average tenure is 5-8 years with an appropriate mix of institutional knowledge and fresh perspectives. | |
| 2.4 | **Director overboarding.** Do any of your directors serve on four or more public company boards? ISS defines overboarding as serving on more than four boards for non-CEO directors, or more than two for sitting CEOs. Overboarded directors are easy targets – the activist's argument practically writes itself: a director serving on five boards cannot possibly devote adequate time and attention to any of them. | |

| # | Assessment Item | Score (1-5) |
|---|---|---|
| 2.5 | **Board refreshment rate.** How many new directors have joined the board in the past three years? A board that has not added a new director in three or more years signals entrenchment. Effective boards continuously evaluate their composition against the company's evolving strategic needs and refresh accordingly. Score based on the pace and quality of recent refreshment. | |
| 2.6 | **Annual vs. classified (staggered) board.** A classified board – where only one-third of directors stand for election each year – is the single most effective structural defense against activist campaigns. It is also increasingly viewed as a governance weakness by institutional investors and proxy advisory firms. If your board is classified, recognize that it provides defensive protection but creates governance perception risk. If your board is declassified, score higher for governance quality but recognize the reduced defensive posture. | |

| # | Assessment Item | Score (1-5) |
|---|---|---|
| 2.7 | **Advance notice bylaw reasonableness.** Review your advance notice provisions. Are they reasonable and standard – or have they been designed to make director nominations practically impossible? Bylaw provisions that require nominees to disclose unreasonable amounts of information, impose punitive qualification requirements, or create narrow filing windows are increasingly being challenged in court and criticized by proxy advisory firms. Punitive provisions score 1; reasonable provisions score 5. | |
| 2.8 | **Related-party transactions.** Are there any transactions between the company and its directors, officers, or their affiliates? Related-party transactions – even those conducted at arm's length and properly disclosed – create the appearance of self-dealing and are among the most damaging governance issues an activist can highlight. | |

| # | Assessment Item | Score (1-5) |
|---|---|---|
| 2.9 | **Executive compensation vs. performance alignment.** Review your most recent say-on-pay vote results. If your say-on-pay vote received less than seventy percent support, you have a compensation problem that an activist will weaponize. Even if the vote passed, evaluate whether your compensation structure truly aligns pay with performance – or whether it guarantees substantial payouts regardless of results. Examine the ratio of fixed to performance-based compensation, the rigor of performance targets, and whether the compensation committee has exercised discretion to increase payouts. | |

**Section 2 Total: _____ / 45**

# Section 3: Shareholder Composition

The composition of your shareholder base determines whether an activist can win. Financial underperformance and governance weaknesses create the thesis – but the shareholder base determines the verdict. Understanding who owns your shares, how they are likely to vote, and whether activist-friendly investors are already building positions is essential to assessing vulnerability.

| # | Assessment Item | Score (1-5) |
|---|---|---|
| 3.1 | **Top 5 shareholder concentration.** What percentage of outstanding shares is held by the five largest shareholders? High concentration can cut both ways. If the top five shareholders are long-term, engaged investors with strong relationships with management, concentration reduces vulnerability. If they are index funds with governance-focused stewardship teams – or if the activist is already among the top five – concentration increases vulnerability. Evaluate the identity and disposition of your largest holders, not just the percentage. | |

| # | Assessment Item | Score (1-5) |
| --- | --- | --- |
| 3.2 | **Insider ownership percentage.** What percentage of shares is held by directors and officers? High insider ownership – particularly ownership that reflects genuine investment rather than stock option exercises – signals alignment and reduces vulnerability. Very low insider ownership tells an activist that the people running the company do not have meaningful skin in the game. Score 1 if insider ownership is negligible; score 5 if insiders hold a substantial, genuinely invested stake. | |
| 3.3 | **Activist fund ownership (check 13F filings).** Are any known activist funds already among your shareholders? Review 13F filings quarterly to identify activist ownership. The presence of an activist fund in your shareholder register – even at a sub-5% level – is an early warning signal. Multiple activist funds holding positions simultaneously is a red alert. | |

| # | Assessment Item | Score (1-5) |
|---|---|---|
| 3.4 | **Index fund representation.** What percentage of your shares is held by index funds (BlackRock, Vanguard, State Street, and others)? Index funds cannot sell – they must hold your stock as long as it remains in the index. This makes them a permanent constituency that activists actively court. Index fund stewardship teams increasingly vote based on governance quality and proxy advisory recommendations, making them potential allies for well-constructed activist campaigns. Higher index fund ownership increases the importance of governance quality. | |

3.5     **Short interest as percentage of float.**
Elevated short interest signals that sophisticated investors are betting against the company. High short interest does not directly aid an activist campaign, but it creates a negative narrative environment and suggests that the market has concerns about the company's prospects. Short interest above five percent of float warrants attention; above ten percent signals serious concern.

---

**Section 3 Total: _____ / 25**

---

# Section 4: Defensive Posture

Structural defenses do not prevent activism – but they affect the campaign's timeline, tactics, and probability of success. A company with strong structural defenses forces an activist into a longer, more expensive campaign. A company with weak defenses – no poison pill, declassified board, low special meeting threshold – can be targeted and transformed in a matter of weeks.

| # | Assessment Item | Score (1-5) |
|---|---|---|
| 4.1 | **Poison pill status.** Does the company have a shareholder rights plan in place, a plan on the shelf ready for deployment, or no plan at all? A poison pill is the most direct structural defense against hostile accumulation – but adopting one in the heat of a campaign can create negative optics. Companies with shelf pills that can be deployed quickly have the strongest defensive posture. Score 1 if no pill exists and none is prepared; score 5 if a well-designed plan is ready for immediate deployment if needed. | |
| 4.2 | **Shareholder rights plan terms.** If a rights plan exists or is on the shelf, are its terms reasonable? Ownership thresholds, duration, and redemption provisions all matter. A plan with a ten percent trigger is standard; a plan with a five percent trigger may be viewed as punitive. Plans with sunset provisions and shareholder ratification requirements are viewed more favorably than plans adopted unilaterally without expiration. | |

| # | Assessment Item | Score (1-5) |
|---|---|---|
| 4.3 | **Bylaw provisions.** Beyond advance notice requirements (scored in Section 2), evaluate the full suite of bylaw provisions: special meeting call thresholds, written consent provisions, supermajority voting requirements, and board size flexibility. A high bar for calling special meetings (twenty-five percent or higher) reduces activist leverage. The ability to increase board size gives the board flexibility to add directors without removing incumbents. | |
| 4.4 | **State of incorporation.** Delaware incorporation provides access to the most developed and predictable body of corporate law, the most experienced judiciary (the Court of Chancery), and established precedents that generally – though not uniformly – support board authority. Other states offer different levels of protection. Some states have specific anti-takeover statutes that provide additional defenses. Score based on the legal environment of your state of incorporation. | |

| # | Assessment Item | Score (1-5) |
|---|---|---|
| 4.5 | **Dual-class share structure.** Does the company have a dual-class structure that gives insiders voting control disproportionate to their economic ownership? Dual-class structures are the ultimate activist defense – if insiders control fifty-one percent of the voting power, no activist campaign can succeed through shareholder votes alone. However, dual-class structures are increasingly criticized by governance advocates and may limit institutional investor support for other governance initiatives. Score 5 for defensive value, but recognize the governance trade-off. | |

**Section 4 Total: _____ / 25**

# Section 5: Communication and Transparency

The final dimension – and in many ways the most controllable – is the quality of the company's communication with its shareholders. Activists thrive in information vacuums. A company that communicates its strategy clearly, engages shareholders proactively, and provides substantive disclosure in its proxy materials makes it harder for an activist to construct a compelling narrative of boardroom failure.

| # | Assessment Item | Score (1-5) |
|---|---|---|
| 5.1 | **Investor day frequency and quality.** Does the company host regular investor days – and are they substantive? An annual investor day that provides a detailed strategic overview, specific financial targets, and direct access to management is a powerful defense against activism. An investor day that consists of vague platitudes about "long-term value creation" without specifics is worse than no investor day at all, because it signals that management either lacks a strategy or is unwilling to be held accountable for one. | |
| 5.2 | **Proxy statement substantiveness.** Is the proxy statement a compliance document or a communication tool? The proxy statement is the single most important governance document the company produces. Effective proxies include detailed director qualifications, thoughtful committee reports, clear compensation rationale, substantive shareholder engagement disclosures, and a coherent narrative about the board's governance philosophy. A boilerplate proxy is a missed opportunity – and an activist's invitation. | |

| # | Assessment Item | Score (1-5) |
|---|---|---|
| 5.3 | **Management accessibility to shareholders.** Can significant shareholders get meetings with management and independent directors? A company that makes its CEO, CFO, and independent directors accessible to major shareholders through regular non-deal roadshows, one-on-one meetings, and responsive investor relations builds relationships that matter when an activist comes calling. Shareholders who feel ignored are shareholders who will listen to an activist. | |
| 5.4 | **Long-term strategic plan articulation.** Has the company clearly articulated a long-term strategic plan – with specific, measurable objectives and a credible timeline for execution? The absence of a clear strategic narrative is one of the most common activist entry points. If the board and management cannot articulate where the company is going and how it plans to get there, an activist will provide their own narrative. Score based on the clarity, specificity, and credibility of the company's publicly communicated strategy. | |

| # | Assessment Item | Score (1-5) |
|---|-----------------|-------------|
| 5.5 | **Response to shareholder proposals.** How does the company respond to shareholder proposals? Does it engage constructively with proponents, address the substance of proposals in its opposition statements, and implement proposals that receive majority support? A company that dismisses shareholder proposals reflexively – or ignores them after they pass – signals that it does not take shareholder voice seriously. That signal is an activist's recruiting tool. | |

**Section 5 Total: _____ / 25**

# Scoring Interpretation

## Calculate Your Total Score

| Section | Maximum | Your Score |
|---------|---------|------------|
| 1. Financial Performance | 40 | |
| 2. Governance Quality | 45 | |
| 3. Shareholder Composition | 25 | |
| 4. Defensive Posture | 25 | |
| 5. Communication & Transparency | 25 | |
| **Total** | **160** | |

## Vulnerability Assessment

**128-160 (80-100%):  Low Vulnerability** Your company presents a difficult target for an activist. Financial performance is strong relative to peers, governance is robust, and communication with shareholders is substantive.  This does not mean you are immune – no company is – but it means an activist would struggle to build a compelling case.  Continue your annual self-assessment and do not become complacent. The companies that score highest on this checklist are the ones most likely to let their guard down.

**96-127 (60-79%): Moderate Vulnerability** Your company has strengths that would complicate an activist campaign, but also identifiable weaknesses that a sophisticated activist would exploit.  Review any section where your score falls below sixty percent of the maximum and develop a remediation plan.  The areas of weakness are likely the same areas an activist's analysts are already evaluating. Address them on your terms, before someone else forces the conversation.

**64-95 (40-59%):  Elevated Vulnerability** Your company presents multiple attack surfaces that an activist could exploit. One or more sections likely contain scores of 1 or 2, indicating serious weaknesses that would be featured prominently in an activist's presentation to your shareholders. This score demands immediate board attention.  Commission an independent governance review, engage proactively with your largest shareholders, and begin addressing the most significant weaknesses within the current quarter.

**Below 64 (Below 40%): High Vulnerability** Your company is an attractive activist target. Multiple dimensions of governance, financial performance, or shareholder communication are below acceptable standards. The probability that an activist is already evaluating your company – or has already begun accumulating shares – is significant. Treat this as a governance emergency. Engage specialized advisors, conduct an urgent board self-assessment, and develop a comprehensive vulnerability reduction plan.  Do not wait for the 13D filing to appear.

## A Note on Interpretation

The total score is less important than the pattern. A company with a total score of 110 but a governance section score of 15 out of 45 has a concentrated vulnerability that an activist can exploit regardless of the overall score. Activists do not build campaigns around companies that are mediocre at everything – they build campaigns around companies that have one or two glaring weaknesses they can dramatize for shareholders. Look for clusters of low scores. Those clusters are where your vulnerability lives.

Use this assessment as a starting point for a deeper governance review, not as a final verdict. And remember the fundamental lesson of this book: the best defense against activism is governance so strong that an activist's thesis collapses on first contact with the facts.

# APPENDIX A: ACTIVIST INVESTOR VULNERABILITY ASSESSMENT CHECKLIST

# Appendix B: The 13D Filing – Anatomy and Analysis Guide

The moment an activist investor crosses the five percent ownership threshold in a public company, the clock starts ticking. Under Section 13(d) of the Securities Exchange Act of 1934, any person or group that acquires beneficial ownership of more than five percent of a class of registered equity securities must file a Schedule 13D with the Securities and Exchange Commission – within ten calendar days of crossing the threshold.

That filing is the first public signal that something has changed. For the company's board, management, and existing shareholders, the 13D is a document of enormous consequence. It reveals who is accumulating shares, how they are funding the accumulation, and – most critically – what they intend to do with their position. Reading and interpreting a 13D filing correctly is one of the most important analytical skills a director or investor relations professional can develop.

This appendix provides a guide to understanding the Schedule 13D – what each section contains, how to distinguish routine filings from activist declarations of intent, and what the red flags look like when a campaign is escalating.

---

# Schedule 13D vs. Schedule 13G: The Critical Distinction

Not all five-percent ownership disclosures are created equal. The SEC provides two filing options for investors who cross the threshold, and the choice between them tells you everything about intent.

**Schedule 13G** is the short-form filing available to passive investors. Institutional investors – mutual funds, pension funds, registered investment advisors – who acquire shares in the ordinary course of business and have no intent to influence or control the issuer may file a 13G. The filing requirements are simpler, the disclosure obligations are lighter, and the filing deadlines are more relaxed. A 13G filing is, in effect, a declaration of passivity: the investor is saying they own the shares for investment purposes only.

**Schedule 13D** is required when the investor has an intent to influence or change control of the issuer. The word "intent" is doing significant work here. An investor does not need to have a fully formed campaign plan to trigger the 13D requirement – they need only the purpose of influencing the company's business, management, or governance. The 13D requires substantially more detailed disclosure than the 13G, including a narrative description of the investor's purpose and plans.

The conversion from 13G to 13D is itself a signal. An investor who originally filed a 13G – declaring passive intent – and subsequently amends to a 13D is announcing a change in posture. They arrived as an investor. They are now an activist.

**The ten-day filing window** is a frequent source of controversy. Critics argue that ten calendar days gives sophisticated activists too much time to continue accumulating shares after crossing the threshold but before the public knows. During that window, the activist is buying while the market lacks material information. Several legislative proposals have sought to shorten this window, and the SEC adopted amendments in 2023 requiring more detailed disclosure of derivative positions and group arrangements. Directors should be aware that by the time a 13D is filed, the activist's position may be materially larger than five percent.

———————————————

# Anatomy of the Schedule 13D: Item by Item

A Schedule 13D contains seven numbered items, each serving a specific disclosure purpose. Some items are administrative. One item – Item 4 – is where the campaign begins.

## Item 1: Security and Issuer

This section identifies the company being targeted and the class of securities being accumulated. It is straightforward: the company name, its principal offices, and the title and CUSIP number of the securities. No analytical value here – but confirm the details are accurate and that the filing pertains to the correct security class.

## Item 2: Identity and Background

This is where you learn who the activist is. Item 2 requires disclosure of the filer's name, address, principal occupation or business, and – importantly – any criminal convictions, civil judgments, or regulatory sanctions within the past five years. For funds, the filing must identify the controlling persons and principal executives.

**What to look for:** Research the activist's track record. How many campaigns have they waged? What were the outcomes? Do they have industry expertise relevant to your company? Are they a repeat player with a governance-focused approach, or a first-time activist with no track record? The identity of the activist shapes the likely trajectory of the campaign. An established fund like Elliott Management or Starboard Value brings different capabilities and credibility than an individual investor filing their first 13D.

Also examine the affiliations. Activist funds sometimes operate through multiple entities, and Item 2 may reveal connections to other investors, advisors, or operating partners who will be involved in the campaign.

## Item 3: Source and Amount of Funds

Item 3 discloses how the activist funded the share accumulation. Was the position built with the fund's own capital, or was it financed with borrowed money? The source of funds signals commitment and risk tolerance.

**What to look for:** A position funded entirely with the fund's own capital suggests conviction and staying power – the activist believes in the thesis enough to deploy their investors' money. A position funded heavily with margin debt or borrowed capital may indicate a more leveraged, shorter-term orientation. However, do not over-read this signal. Sophisticated funds use leverage routinely, and the presence of borrowed funds does not necessarily mean the activist lacks conviction.

The total amount of funds used to acquire the position provides a rough measure of the activist's financial commitment. Compare this to the fund's reported assets under management to understand what percentage of the fund is dedicated to your company. A fund that has concentrated ten or fifteen percent of its capital in your stock is deeply committed. A fund that has allocated two percent is testing the waters.

## Item 4: Purpose of Transaction

This is the most important section of the entire filing. Item 4 is where the activist discloses the purpose of the acquisition – their thesis, their demands, and their plans. Every word in this section has been drafted by securities lawyers who understand that the language will be scrutinized by the company, its advisors, the media, and the courts. Nothing in Item 4 is accidental.

**What to look for:**

*Specific demands vs. general language.* An activist who lists specific demands – particular governance reforms, named director candidates, a detailed strategic alternative, a specific capital return program – has a formed campaign strategy and is ready to execute. An activist who uses general language about "exploring ways to enhance shareholder value" or "evaluating strategic alternatives" is keeping options open. The more specific the language, the more advanced the campaign.

*Board representation requests.* If the activist names specific individuals they intend to nominate for board seats, a proxy contest is either imminent or being held in reserve as leverage. Named nominees mean the activist has already recruited director candidates, which requires substantial preparation.

*"Reserving all rights" language.* This standard legal phrase is a signal that the activist intends to escalate if the company does not engage. It preserves the activist's ability to launch a proxy contest, file additional demands, pursue litigation, or take other actions without being accused of failing to disclose their plans. Treat this language as a statement of intent to escalate, not as a formality.

*Strategic alternatives language.* Phrases like "exploring strategic alternatives," "evaluating whether the company would benefit from a sale," or "assessing the company's standalone value" signal that the activist may push for a sale, merger, or breakup. This language should trigger immediate engagement with the company's financial advisors to prepare a defense of the standalone strategy.

*References to prior engagement.* If the activist notes that they have previously communicated with the company's management or board, the filing is documenting that private engagement has failed. The 13D is now the public escalation.

## Item 5: Interest in Securities of the Issuer

Item 5 provides the detailed ownership disclosure – the exact number of shares, the percentage of the outstanding class, and the nature of the beneficial ownership. This section also discloses derivatives positions, including options, swaps, and other arrangements that give the activist economic exposure to the stock without direct ownership.

**What to look for:** The total economic exposure may be substantially larger than the direct share ownership. An activist who owns five percent of the shares directly but has swap agreements covering another three percent effectively controls an eight percent economic interest. Derivatives-heavy positions can signal sophisticated financial engineering and a focus on short-to-medium-term value extraction. They also indicate that the activist's voting power (which attaches only to actual shares, not to most derivatives) may be smaller than their economic interest suggests.

Also examine whether the position has been growing. Compare the current filing to any previous 13G filings and to the fund's historical 13F reports. A position that has grown from two percent to five percent over six months tells a different story than one that jumped to five percent in a single week.

## Item 6: Contracts, Arrangements, Understandings

Item 6 requires disclosure of any agreements between the filer and other parties regarding the company's securities. This includes voting agreements, joint filing agreements, standstill arrangements, and any understanding about the disposition of the shares.

**What to look for:** Group formations. If multiple investors have agreed to act together – sharing information, coordinating voting, or jointly pursuing governance changes – they may constitute a "group" under Section 13(d) and must aggregate their holdings for disclosure purposes. Evidence of group activity suggests a coordinated campaign with broader shareholder support than a single fund could provide.

## Item 7: Material to Be Filed as Exhibits

This section lists any documents attached to the filing. Exhibits frequently include the activist's letter to the board or management – often the most revealing document in the entire filing package.

**What to look for:** Read every exhibit. The activist's letter typically provides more detail than the formal Item 4 disclosure, including specific financial analysis, governance critiques, and the tone that will characterize the public campaign. The letter is where the activist makes their case to the market as much as to the board.

---

# Reading the Amendments: 13D/A Filings

The initial 13D is just the beginning. Any material change in the facts disclosed in the original filing – a change in ownership level, a change in plans or proposals, or a new agreement with other parties – triggers an obligation to file an amendment, designated 13D/A.

The cadence and content of amendments tell the story of the campaign's evolution. A single 13D with no subsequent amendments may indicate a passive posture or a quietly resolved engagement. A series of 13D/A filings over several months – each disclosing additional share purchases, escalating language, or new demands – signals an intensifying campaign.

**Key amendment signals:**

- **Increasing ownership.** Each amendment disclosing additional share purchases shows the activist is deepening their commitment and conviction. A rising position also increases the activist's credibility with other shareholders.
- **Escalating language in Item 4.** Compare the purpose language across successive amendments. If early filings use collaborative language and later filings shift to confrontational language – mentioning proxy contests, litigation, or public campaigns – the engagement has deteriorated.
- **Named director nominees appearing for the first time.** If an amendment adds specific nominee names that were absent from the original filing, a proxy contest has moved from theoretical to operational.
- **New group members.** An amendment disclosing additional parties to a group agreement means the activist is building a coalition.

---

# How to Find and Monitor 13D Filings

## SEC EDGAR

The primary source for all 13D filings is the SEC's Electronic Data Gathering, Analysis, and Retrieval system (EDGAR) at sec.gov. Search by company name or CIK number to find all ownership filings. Filter by filing type "SC 13D" to isolate activist-related disclosures. Set up EDGAR alerts to receive email notifications when new filings are made for your company.

## Company DEF 14A (Proxy Statement)

When reviewing your own proxy statement – or a competitor's – look for references to 13D filings in the beneficial ownership table. Companies are required to disclose any five-percent holders, and the proxy often provides context about engagement with those holders.

## Activist Tracking Services

Several commercial platforms track activist filings and campaign activity in real time. Insightia (formerly Activist Insight), 13D Monitor, Lazard's annual activism review, and Barclays' shareholder activism reports all provide curated analysis of 13D filings, campaign developments, and outcome tracking. These services are particularly valuable for identifying patterns across multiple campaigns by the same activist and for benchmarking your company's vulnerability against recent targets.

## 13F Filings

While not a substitute for 13D monitoring, the quarterly 13F filings required of institutional investment managers with $100 million or more in assets provide a broader picture of your shareholder composition. Review 13F filings quarterly to identify activist fund positions below the five-percent threshold – positions that may foreshadow a future 13D filing.

---

# The Board's Response to a 13D Filing

When a Schedule 13D appears, the board's response in the first hours and days sets the trajectory for the entire campaign. Chapter 6 describes the surveillance and detection systems that should flag activist accumulation before the 13D arrives. Chapter 11 provides the detailed response framework for when it does. At the filing-analysis stage, the critical steps are:

1. **Read the entire filing carefully** – every item, every exhibit, every word of Item 4.

2. **Identify the activist** – research their track record, recent campaigns, and typical playbook.
3. **Assess the substance** – separate the demands that have merit from those that do not.
4. **Evaluate the position** – understand the size, funding, and trajectory of the activist's ownership.
5. **Brief the full board** – ensure every director has read and understood the filing.
6. **Engage advisors** – retain or activate your financial advisor, legal counsel, proxy solicitor, and communications firm.
7. **Monitor for amendments** – the first filing is the opening move, not the last word.

The 13D is a document. How you read it is a choice. Read it defensively, and you will see only a threat. Read it analytically – with the intellectual honesty that this book advocates throughout – and you may find that the activist has identified real weaknesses that the board should have addressed on its own. The filing is the diagnosis. Whether you accept the activist's proposed remedy is a separate question entirely.

# Appendix C: Campaign Materials Templates

The documents that define an activist campaign – demand letters, board responses, standstill agreements, and settlement press releases – follow recognizable structural patterns. They are not form documents. Each one is crafted by securities lawyers and communications professionals for the specific circumstances of a particular campaign. But the underlying architecture is consistent enough that boards and management teams benefit from understanding what these documents look like before they encounter one under pressure.

This appendix provides structural frameworks for the four most common campaign documents. These are not fill-in-the-blank templates – no responsible advisor would use a generic template for documents this consequential. They are guides to the logic, sequence, and content that these documents typically contain. Understanding the architecture helps boards evaluate what they receive, draft what they need to send, and negotiate what they need to agree on.

---

## 1. Activist Demand Letter – Structural Guide

The activist demand letter is the opening salvo of a public campaign. It serves multiple audiences simultaneously: the target company's board, the company's institutional shareholders, the media, and the activist's own investors. Every sentence is calibrated to build a narrative of board failure and activist competence. Understanding the structure helps boards read the letter for what it is – a strategic communication, not a neutral assessment.

## Section 1: Establish Credibility and Ownership

The letter opens by establishing the activist's identity, track record, and economic stake. This section is designed to answer the board's first instinct – "Who are you, and why should we listen?" – before it can become a basis for dismissal.

**Typical elements:** - Fund name, assets under management, and investment track record - The specific ownership stake, including the date the position was established and the approximate dollar value - A statement that the fund is among the company's largest shareholders – this framing positions the activist as a concerned owner, not an outsider - Brief reference to prior campaigns and their outcomes, particularly successful ones - A note that the activist has attempted private engagement (if true) and that the letter represents an escalation after that engagement failed

**The strategic purpose:** Establish that the activist is a serious, well-capitalized investor with relevant experience – not a nuisance filer or an opportunistic trader.

## Section 2: The Investment Thesis – The Case for Underperformance

This is the analytical core of the letter. The activist presents their diagnosis of the company's problems, supported by financial data, peer comparisons, and governance analysis. This section is designed to be excerpted by journalists and circulated among institutional investors.

**Typical elements:** - Total shareholder return vs. peers over one, three, and five-year periods – the most common opening metric, because underperformance relative to peers is difficult to explain away - Specific financial metrics that demonstrate underperformance: ROA, ROE, margins, free cash flow yield, revenue growth - Analysis of capital allocation decisions: value-destroying acquisitions, excessive cash balances, poorly timed buybacks, dividend inadequacy - Sum-of-parts analysis demonstrating a conglomerate discount or breakup value premium - Governance failures: board tenure, overboarding, lack of independence, compensation misalignment, CEO/Chair combination - Direct quotes from the company's own filings, earnings calls, or proxy materials that contradict the company's narrative – activists are skilled at using management's own words against them - Comparison to specific peers by name, demonstrating that the underperformance is company-specific rather than industry-wide

**The strategic purpose:** Build an irrefutable case that the company is underperforming on both financial and governance dimensions – and that the underperformance is attributable to board and management decisions, not external factors.

## Section 3: Specific Demands

The demands section translates the thesis into action items. Specific demands are more powerful than general requests for "dialogue" because they give institutional investors concrete proposals to evaluate – and they give the board concrete items to respond to. Vague demands allow the board to delay. Specific demands force a substantive response.

**Typical categories of demands:**  - **Board composition changes:** A specific number of activist-nominated directors (usually two to four), named individuals with identified qualifications, and a rationale for why the current board composition is inadequate - **Governance reforms:** Declassification of the board, separation of CEO and Chair roles, elimination of the poison pill, adoption of majority voting, proxy access implementation, executive compensation restructuring - **Strategic changes:** Exploration of strategic alternatives (sale or merger), operational restructuring, divestiture of specific business units, cancellation of a pending acquisition - **Capital allocation changes:** Special dividend, accelerated buyback program, reduction of overhead and corporate expenses, monetization of non-core assets - **Management changes:** In more aggressive campaigns, direct calls for CEO replacement or management restructuring – though most activists frame this demand indirectly, requesting that the board "evaluate leadership" rather than demanding a termination

**The strategic purpose:** Create a public record of specific, measurable demands against which the board's response – or lack thereof – will be judged.

## Section 4: Timeline and Escalation

The letter typically concludes with a deadline for response and a statement of what the activist intends to do if the company does not engage.

**Typical elements:** - A specific deadline for a substantive response – usually two to four weeks - A request for a meeting with independent directors (not management alone) - "We reserve all rights" language – the standard legal formulation preserving the activist's ability to escalate to a proxy contest, public campaign, litigation, or other actions - A closing note expressing preference for constructive engagement, positioned as a final opportunity to resolve matters privately before the campaign becomes fully public

**The strategic purpose:** Create urgency and establish the consequences of inaction.

---

# 2. Board Response Letter – Structural Guide

The board's initial response to an activist demand letter is among the most consequential communications the company will produce during a campaign. It sets the tone for everything that follows – whether the engagement will be collaborative or adversarial, whether the board appears defensive or confident, and whether institutional investors perceive the board as responsive or entrenched.

The single most important principle: respond to the substance. Boards that dismiss the activist's claims without engaging with the specific financial and governance arguments lose credibility with institutional investors instantly. Even if the board disagrees with every demand, the response must demonstrate that the board has taken the time to understand and evaluate the activist's thesis.

## Section 1: Acknowledgment

Open by acknowledging receipt of the letter and the activist's status as a significant shareholder. This is not a concession – it is a signal of maturity and confidence.

**Typical elements:** - Acknowledgment of receipt, with the specific date of the activist's letter - Recognition of the activist's ownership stake and their right to express views as a significant shareholder - A statement that the board has reviewed the letter carefully and discussed it in a dedicated session - A tone that is respectful and substantive – not dismissive, defensive, or patronizing

**What to avoid:** Opening with language that characterizes the activist's letter as "disappointing" or "ill-informed." This kind of language reads as defensive and signals that the board is more interested in protecting its ego than engaging with the substance.

## Section 2: The Board's Current Actions

After acknowledging the concerns, present what the board is already doing. This section addresses the implicit accusation that the board has been passive or complacent.

**Typical elements:** - Specific governance improvements the board has made in recent years: new independent directors added, committee structure reforms, compensation redesign, strategic plan enhancements - Financial performance context that the activist's letter may have omitted – but only if the context is genuinely material, not cherry-picked - Strategic initiatives already underway that address one or more of the activist's concerns - Shareholder engagement activities: how many shareholders the board has met with, what feedback was received, and how it was incorporated

**What to avoid:** A laundry list of minor governance improvements that do not address the specific concerns raised. If the activist says ROA trails peers by 500 basis points, the response should not lead with the fact that the board adopted a new whistleblower policy.

## Section 3: Engagement Offer

The offer to engage is the centerpiece of the response. It demonstrates good faith, it puts the activist in the position of having to accept or reject a reasonable offer, and it creates a record that the board acted constructively.

**Typical elements:** - A specific offer to meet – not a vague expression of willingness, but a concrete proposal including dates, participants, and format - Identification of the independent directors who will participate – the activist has requested access to independent directors, not to management's defensive team - An agenda framework: the board is willing to discuss the specific concerns raised in the activist's letter - A suggestion that both sides agree to a confidentiality protocol for the discussions, preserving the ability to have candid conversations without public posturing

**What to avoid:** Conditions that make engagement impractical. Requiring the activist to sign a standstill agreement before the first meeting – or insisting that discussions be limited to pre-approved topics – will be interpreted as bad faith.

## Section 4: Closing – Constructive but Not Capitulatory

The closing sets the tone for the relationship going forward. It should convey confidence, openness, and a commitment to acting in the interests of all shareholders.

**Typical elements:** - A restatement of the board's commitment to maximizing long-term shareholder value - A genuine expression of interest in the activist's perspectives – directors should bring constructive ideas to the discussion, not just criticisms - A firm but non-aggressive statement that the board will continue to evaluate all strategic options and governance practices on an ongoing basis - An invitation for continued dialogue

**What to avoid:** Language that concedes the board has been deficient. The response should engage with the substance without accepting the activist's framing wholesale. It is possible to acknowledge that governance is an ongoing process of improvement without admitting that the board has failed.

# 3.   Standstill Agreement – Key Provisions Guide

When an activist campaign reaches a resolution through negotiation rather than a proxy contest, the terms are documented in a standstill agreement – sometimes called a cooperation agreement or a settlement agreement. This is a binding legal contract between the company and the activist that defines the terms of the truce: what the activist gets, what the company gets, and the rules that will govern the relationship for the duration of the agreement.

Standstill agreements are typically negotiated by outside counsel with significant input from the company's financial advisors and the activist's legal team. The provisions below represent the structural elements that appear in virtually every standstill agreement. The specific terms – duration, board seats, committee assignments, termination triggers – are negotiated for each situation.

## Voting Commitments

The activist agrees to vote their shares in favor of the company's director nominees and in accordance with the board's recommendations on other matters – for the duration of the standstill period. This provision prevents the activist from using their ownership position to support a second activist campaign or to vote against the board's slate at the next annual meeting.

**Negotiation considerations:** The scope of the voting commitment matters. Some agreements require the activist to vote with the board on all matters. Others carve out exceptions for extraordinary transactions – mergers, acquisitions, or significant asset sales – allowing the activist to vote independently on matters that fundamentally alter the company.

## Standstill Duration

The agreement specifies a period – typically twelve to twenty-four months – during which the activist agrees not to take certain actions:

launching a proxy contest, making public statements criticizing the board, increasing their ownership position beyond a specified cap, or seeking to influence other shareholders.

**Negotiation considerations:** Duration is one of the most heavily negotiated provisions. The activist wants the shortest possible standstill, preserving the ability to re-engage if the agreed-upon reforms are not implemented. The company wants the longest possible standstill, ensuring stability through at least one annual meeting cycle. Most agreements settle on a term that runs through the next annual meeting plus a buffer period – typically fifteen to twenty months.

## Board Seat Allocation

The agreement specifies how many board seats the activist receives, who the nominees are, and how long they will serve.

**Typical provisions:** - Number of activist-nominated directors (usually one to three) - Identification of the specific nominees by name - The term of service – often a minimum of one full election cycle - Board size provisions: the company may agree not to increase board size beyond a specified number during the standstill period, preventing dilution of the activist's board representation - Replacement provisions: if an activist-nominated director resigns or is unable to serve, the activist may have the right to designate a replacement, subject to the nominating committee's approval

## Committee Assignments

Activist nominees typically receive one or more committee assignments as part of the settlement. Committee seats give the activist's representatives meaningful influence over specific governance functions.

**Typical provisions:** - Assignment to at least one standing committee (audit, compensation, nominating/governance, or strategy) - The specific committee is identified in the agreement – activists typically seek representation on the committee most relevant to their thesis (strategy committee for operational activists, compensation committee for pay-focused campaigns) - The agreement may specify that the activist-nominated director will serve as committee chair – though this is less common and typically reserved for settlements where the activist has significant leverage

## Confidentiality Obligations

Both parties agree to keep board deliberations, non-public company information, and the terms of the standstill itself confidential.

**Typical provisions:** - The activist and their nominees agree not to disclose non-public information received through board service - The company agrees not to disclose the terms of the standstill beyond what is required by SEC filing obligations - Specific carve-outs for disclosures required by law, regulation, or legal process - Provisions addressing the activist's ability to share information with their investment team – this is heavily negotiated, as the activist fund needs to make investment decisions based on information its board nominees may possess

## Termination Triggers

The agreement specifies the circumstances under which either party may terminate the standstill before its scheduled expiration.

**Typical provisions:** - Material breach by either party, subject to a cure period (usually ten to thirty days) - The company entering into a definitive agreement for a change-of-control transaction - The board failing to nominate the activist's directors for re-election - The company increasing its board size in violation of the agreement - Appointment of a new CEO (in some agreements, a management change reopens the governance conversation) - The company's stock price falling below a specified threshold (in some agreements, deteriorating performance releases the activist from standstill obligations)

## Non-Disparagement Clauses

Both parties agree not to make disparaging public statements about each other for the duration of the standstill period.

**Typical provisions:** - The activist agrees not to publicly criticize the company's board, management, or strategy - The company agrees not to publicly characterize the activist negatively - Carve-outs for truthful statements required by law or regulation - Social media restrictions: some agreements specifically address public statements on social media platforms

## Expense Reimbursement

The company may agree to reimburse the activist for some or all of the campaign expenses – legal fees, advisory fees, proxy solicitation costs, and other out-of-pocket expenses.

**Typical provisions:** - A cap on reimbursable expenses (ranging from several hundred thousand dollars to several million, depending on the campaign's scope) - A requirement that the activist provide documentation of expenses - Payment timing – typically within thirty days of the agreement's execution

**Negotiation considerations:** Expense reimbursement is often the most emotionally charged provision for boards. Directors resist the idea of using shareholder money to fund the campaign against them. Activists argue that their efforts produced governance improvements that benefit all shareholders. The practical reality is that expense reimbursement is standard in the vast majority of settlement agreements, and refusing it on principle often impedes an otherwise constructive resolution.

---

# 4. Settlement Press Release – Structural Guide (Company Side)

When a settlement is reached, both the company and the activist typically issue press releases announcing the agreement. The company's release is a critical communication – it shapes how the market, the media, and the company's employees interpret the outcome. The goal is to present the settlement as a constructive governance evolution, not as a capitulation.

# Headline

The headline sets the framing. Effective settlement headlines emphasize collaboration, governance enhancement, and forward-looking strategy – not the activist's demands or the conflict that preceded the agreement.

**Structural pattern:** "[Company Name] Announces Governance Enhancements and Appointment of New Independent Directors"

or

"[Company Name] and [Activist Fund] Announce Cooperation Agreement"

**What to avoid:** Headlines that reference the campaign, the conflict, or the activist's demands. The headline should read as if the governance changes were the board's initiative – because from the market's perspective, a board that adopts good governance reforms is a board doing its job, regardless of who suggested the reforms.

# Opening Paragraph

The opening paragraph summarizes the agreement in one or two sentences: new directors are being appointed, governance reforms are being adopted, and the company and the activist have reached a mutual understanding.

**Typical elements:** - The company name and the activist fund name - The number of new directors being appointed - The headline governance reform (e.g., board declassification, CEO/Chair separation) - A characterization of the agreement as "cooperative" or "constructive"

# Board Quotes

Press releases typically include quotes from the board chair (or lead independent director) and from the activist fund's managing partner.

**Board chair quote structure:** - Acknowledge the value of shareholder engagement - Welcome the new directors by name and note their qualifications - Affirm the board's commitment to continuous governance improvement - Frame the agreement as consistent with the board's ongoing strategic review

**Activist quote structure:** - Express confidence in the company's leadership and strategic direction - Welcome the opportunity to contribute through board representation - Express support for the company's management team and long-term strategy

**What to avoid:** Quotes that sound forced, defensive, or inconsistent with the tone of the campaign that preceded them. If the activist spent three months publicly criticizing the CEO, a quote expressing full confidence in management's leadership will ring hollow. The quotes should be realistic – positive about the future without rewriting the past.

## New Director Biographies

Each new activist-nominated director receives a one-paragraph biography emphasizing their professional qualifications, relevant industry experience, and prior board service.

**Typical elements per biography:** - Current and most recent professional role - Industry experience relevant to the company - Prior public company board service - Educational credentials - The committee assignment they will receive

## Governance Reform Summary

If the agreement includes governance reforms beyond board composition changes, the press release summarizes them in a bulleted or short-paragraph format.

**Common items:** - Board declassification timeline - CEO/Chair separation - New committee structure or charter revisions - Enhanced shareholder engagement commitments - Executive compensation changes - Capital allocation framework updates

## Forward-Looking Statements

The release concludes with the standard forward-looking statements disclaimer required by securities law, and – in many cases – a brief statement about the company's strategic priorities going forward.

---

# A Final Note on Templates

These structural guides reflect the patterns that have emerged across hundreds of activist campaigns. They are analytical frameworks, not prescriptions. Every campaign has unique dynamics – the size of the company, the identity and style of the activist, the strength of the activist's thesis, the quality of the board's governance, and the composition of the shareholder base all shape the specific content and tone of campaign documents.

Use these guides to understand what you are looking at when campaign materials arrive on your desk, to prepare your team for the documents they may need to draft, and to ensure that your advisors are producing materials that meet the standards of current practice. Chapter 14 examines how actual settlement negotiations unfold and what makes them succeed or fail. And remember the principle that runs through this entire book: the best campaign materials are the ones you never need to use, because your governance made them unnecessary.

# Appendix D: The Activist Investor Tabletop Exercise Kit

This appendix provides a complete facilitator guide for running an activist investor tabletop simulation. Chapter 19 describes the methodology, the learning objectives, and the experience of the Flowers Foods capstone exercise in the SLGI Board Readiness Program. This appendix gives you everything you need to run one yourself.

Print this section. Distribute it to your facilitator. Adapt it to your organization. The format is deliberately prescriptive – because a well-structured exercise produces dramatically better learning than an improvised one.

---

## Exercise Overview

**Purpose:** Test board readiness for activist investor campaigns through a realistic, multi-team simulation that develops governance judgment, negotiation skills, and strategic thinking under pressure.

**Core Structure:** Three teams – Activist, Management, and Board – prepare independently, then engage in a facilitated simulation that mirrors the dynamics of a real proxy contest.

**Duration Options:**

| Format | Preparation | Simulation | Total Time | Best For |
|--------|-------------|------------|------------|----------|
| 8-Week Full Program | 8 weeks | 3-4 hours | ~10 weeks | Governance education programs, board fellowships |
| 4-Week Condensed | 4 weeks | 3 hours | ~6 weeks | Corporate board retreats, executive education |
| 1-Day Intensive | Pre-prepared packets | 3 hours | 1 full day | Law firm workshops, MBA courses, conference sessions |

The eight-week format produces the deepest learning. The one-day intensive preserves the core simulation dynamics but sacrifices the research depth that generates the most powerful insights. Choose the format that fits your organization – but do not skip the after-action review regardless of which format you select.

**Participant Count:** 12 to 24 participants, divided into three teams of 4 to 8 people each. Fewer than 12 limits the diversity of perspective within teams. More than 24 creates coordination problems that slow the exercise.

---

# Facilitator Requirements

The facilitator is the exercise's architect, referee, and debrief leader. This role demands a specific combination of skills.

**Required qualifications.** The facilitator should have working knowledge of corporate governance – board composition, proxy mechanics, institutional investor dynamics, and the general structure of activist campaigns. They do not need to be a governance expert. They need to understand enough to evaluate whether teams are producing substantive work and to lead a meaningful debrief.

**Helpful but not required.** Experience with activist campaigns – as an advisor, board member, or investor relations professional – makes the facilitator more effective at deploying injects and steering the debrief. Experience facilitating simulations or wargames in other contexts – military, cybersecurity, crisis management – also transfers well.

### The facilitator's responsibilities include:

- Selecting or approving the target company
- Providing research guidance during the preparation phase
- Designing and deploying scenario injects during the simulation
- Managing time and pacing during all simulation phases
- Maintaining neutrality between teams
- Leading the after-action review
- Ensuring the exercise produces learning, not just competition

The facilitator should not be assigned to any team. Their independence is essential to the exercise's credibility and learning value.

---

## Preparation Phase

### Target Company Selection

The target company is the exercise's foundation. A strong target makes every other element work. A weak target produces a superficial simulation regardless of how well the rest is executed.

### Selection criteria checklist:

- ☐ **Publicly traded** with full SEC filings available (10-K, 10-Q, DEF 14A, 8-K)
- ☐ **Mid-cap or large-cap** with sufficient analyst coverage and publicly available data

- ☐ **Clear business model** that participants can understand without specialized industry knowledge
- ☐ **Genuine but debatable governance issues** – board tenure concerns, compensation questions, capital allocation debates, or strategic ambiguity
- ☐ **Plausible underperformance narrative** – flat or lagging total shareholder return, margin compression, or valuation discount relative to peers
- ☐ **No active proxy contest** – check 13D filings on SEC EDGAR and activist tracking platforms before finalizing
- ☐ **Sufficient board disclosure** – proxy statement includes detailed director biographies, committee assignments, tenure data, and stock ownership

Companies in the consumer products, retail, industrial, and technology sectors with clear revenue models tend to work best. Avoid companies requiring deep technical expertise – pharmaceutical pipelines, semiconductor fabrication, financial services regulatory structures – unless your participants have that expertise.

## Research Assignments by Team

All three teams research the same company using publicly available sources. This parallel research structure is deliberate – it produces competing interpretations of the same data, which is precisely what happens in real campaigns.

### Activist Team Research Protocol:

1. Financial analysis with peer benchmarking (revenue growth, margins, ROE, ROA, TSR vs. peers and index)
2. Capital allocation assessment (dividend payout ratio, share repurchase history, M&A track record, capex efficiency)
3. Governance vulnerability analysis from DEF 14A (board tenure, independence, committee composition, skills gaps, director stock ownership, related-party transactions)
4. Compensation analysis (CEO pay vs. performance, pay ratio, peer benchmarking, incentive structure alignment)
5. Ownership analysis from 13F filings (top institutional holders, activist-friendly investors, insider ownership levels)
6. Competitive positioning from 10-K and industry data

## Management Team Research Protocol:

1. Same financial and governance analysis as the activist team – but with an emphasis on identifying which criticisms are legitimate and which are defensible
2. Strategic narrative review – how does the company explain its strategy in SEC filings, earnings calls, and investor presentations?
3. Vulnerability self-assessment – where is the company most exposed to activist criticism?
4. Defense inventory – what structural defenses exist (staggered board, advance notice provisions, poison pill authorization)?
5. Shareholder base analysis – which institutional investors would support management in a proxy fight, and which might side with an activist?

## Board Team Research Protocol:

1. Independent governance assessment – evaluate the board's composition, independence, and effectiveness without reference to either side's framing
2. Director-by-director evaluation – qualifications, tenure, committee contributions, attendance, stock ownership
3. Fiduciary framework – what outcome would best serve all shareholders, not just management or the activist?
4. Negotiation mandate development – before the simulation begins, define what terms the board would accept, modify, or reject

## Source materials for all teams:

| Filing | Source | Key Information |
|---|---|---|
| 10-K (Annual Report) | SEC EDGAR | Financial performance, business segments, risk factors |
| DEF 14A (Proxy Statement) | SEC EDGAR | Board composition, compensation, governance structure |
| 10-Q (Quarterly Reports) | SEC EDGAR | Recent financial performance and trends |

| Filing | Source | Key Information |
|---|---|---|
| 8-K (Current Reports) | SEC EDGAR | Material events, executive changes |
| Earnings Call Transcripts | Investor relations website or financial platforms | Management commentary, analyst questions |
| 13F Filings | SEC EDGAR | Institutional ownership |
| Peer Company Proxies | SEC EDGAR | Benchmarking data for compensation and governance |

---

# Role Assignments

## Activist Team

| Role | Responsibilities |
|---|---|
| **Lead Activist / Campaign Manager** | Overall campaign strategy, primary spokesperson during simulation, leads negotiation |
| **Financial Analyst** | Peer benchmarking, TSR analysis, capital allocation case, financial projections |
| **Governance Analyst** | Board composition critique, director evaluations, governance structure analysis |
| **Communications Lead** | Drafts demand letter, investor presentation, press statements, campaign website content |
| **Nominee Coordinator** (optional) | Identifies and presents qualifications of proposed director candidates |

## Management Team

| Role | Responsibilities |
|------|------------------|
| **CEO** | Defends company strategy, leads management response, negotiates with board and activist |
| **CFO** | Financial defense – challenges activist's benchmarking, presents forward projections |
| **General Counsel** | Evaluates legal dimensions, advises on defensive measures, reviews settlement terms |
| **Head of Investor Relations** | Shareholder communication strategy, institutional investor outreach, media management |

## Board Team

| Role | Responsibilities |
|------|------------------|
| **Board Chair / Lead Independent Director** | Manages board deliberation, leads engagement with activist, controls negotiation |
| **Nominating/Governance Committee Chair** | Evaluate activist's director nominees against board skills matrix |
| **Compensation Committee Chair** | Evaluates activist's compensation reform demands |
| **Audit Committee Chair** | Evaluates financial claims from both sides, assesses capital allocation arguments |
| **Independent Director(s)** | Practice independent judgment – evaluate both positions on their merits |

# Simulation Flow: The Three-Hour Exercise

The following schedule structures a three-hour simulation. Adjust timing as needed, but preserve the sequence – each phase builds on the previous one.

## Phase 1: The Activist's Opening (30 minutes)

The activist team presents its demand letter and investment thesis to the full room. This mirrors the real-world moment when an activist makes its case public – or presents it privately to the board for the first time.

The presentation should include: the financial underperformance case, the governance critique, specific demands with supporting evidence, and proposed director nominees if applicable.

The board and management teams listen. Questions are permitted but should be limited – the purpose is to hear the activist's full case before responding.

## Phase 2: Board and Management Caucus (30 minutes)

The board and management teams retreat to separate rooms to develop their initial response. The board team evaluates the activist's demands on their merits. The management team prepares its defense and recommendations to the board. The board may consult with management but should maintain its independence.

The activist team uses this time to prepare for the negotiation – anticipating counterarguments, identifying which demands are priorities and which are negotiable.

## Phase 3: Board's Initial Response (20 minutes)

The board team delivers its initial response to the activist team. This may include: areas of agreement, areas of disagreement with specific reasons, questions requiring additional information, and the board's proposed framework for continued engagement.

The management team may present supporting arguments at the board's invitation – but the board, not management, controls the response.

## INJECT 1 (Facilitator deploys at this transition)

The facilitator introduces the first unexpected development. See the Scenario Inject Library below. Allow five minutes for teams to absorb and discuss the inject's implications before proceeding.

## Phase 4: Second Round of Engagement (30 minutes)

Both sides engage in substantive negotiation. The inject has shifted the dynamic – one side now has more leverage, or both sides face a new variable they must accommodate. The negotiation should address specific terms: board seats, governance reforms, standstill duration, strategic review commitments.

## INJECT 2 (Facilitator deploys at this transition)

The facilitator introduces a second development. This inject should increase urgency – a media leak, a proxy advisory recommendation, or an institutional investor declaration.

## Phase 5: Final Negotiation Round (20 minutes)

The decisive phase. Both sides must determine whether a settlement is achievable or whether the campaign will proceed to a proxy fight. The board team drives this decision. The terms discussed should be specific enough to form the outline of a standstill agreement.

## Phase 6: Resolution Announcement (15 minutes)

Both sides present the outcome – either a settlement with specific terms or a declaration that the campaign will continue to a proxy contest. Each side explains its reasoning.

## Phase 7: After-Action Review (35 minutes)

The facilitator leads a structured debrief. This is the most important phase. See the After-Action Review Framework below.

---

# Scenario Inject Library

Prepare four to five of the following injects before the simulation. Deploy two to three during the exercise based on how the negotiation is unfolding. Time injects to moments of impasse or complacency – they should force adaptation, not merely add noise.

**1. Earnings Miss.** The company issues a preliminary earnings release showing quarterly results significantly below analyst expectations. Revenue down eight percent. Operating margins compressed. Full-year guidance revised downward. *Effect:* Strengthens the activist's underperformance narrative. Forces management to defend the current strategy with deteriorating results.

**2. Proxy Advisory Firm Recommendation.** ISS issues a report recommending shareholders vote "Against" the re-election of two incumbent directors identified in the activist's campaign materials. *Effect:* Shifts negotiation leverage toward the activist. Forces the board to consider whether a contested vote is winnable.

**3. Media Leak.** A financial journalist publishes a story revealing the activist's campaign demands before the formal public announcement. The article includes details from the demand letter and quotes from anonymous institutional investors expressing sympathy with the activist's position. *Effect:* Accelerates the timeline for both sides. Forces management to respond publicly before its defense is fully developed.

**4. Second Activist Accumulates Position.** A second activist fund files a Schedule 13D disclosing a significant ownership stake and different – potentially conflicting – demands. *Effect:* Complicates the negotiation for all parties. Forces the board to manage multiple activist relationships simultaneously.

**5. Key Executive Departure.** The company's CFO announces resignation for "personal reasons" effective in thirty days. *Effect:* Creates leadership uncertainty. Reinforces the activist's narrative about management instability or governance weakness.

**6. Institutional Investor Declaration.** The company's largest institutional shareholder – holding nine percent of outstanding shares – issues a public statement expressing support for "meaningful board refreshment and enhanced shareholder engagement." The statement does not explicitly endorse the activist but echoes several of its demands. *Effect:* Signals that the shareholder base may not support management in a contested vote. Increases pressure on the board to negotiate.

**7. Shareholder Lawsuit Filed.** A derivative lawsuit is filed alleging breach of fiduciary duty related to one of the governance issues identified in the activist's campaign. *Effect:* Introduces legal risk. Forces the board to consider litigation exposure in its response calculus.

**8. Competitor Acquisition Offer.** A strategic competitor announces an unsolicited acquisition offer at a modest premium to the current stock price. *Effect:* Transforms the campaign dynamics entirely. Both the activist and management must evaluate whether the offer serves shareholders, and the board faces a dual crisis – activist engagement and M&A evaluation simultaneously.

**9. Strong Earnings Surprise.** The company reports quarterly results that significantly exceed expectations. Revenue growth accelerates, margins expand, and the stock price jumps twelve percent. *Effect:* Undermines the activist's underperformance thesis. Forces the activist team to adapt its narrative or shift emphasis to governance issues that persist regardless of financial performance.

**10. Director Resignation.** One of the incumbent directors targeted in the activist's campaign resigns from the board, citing "a desire to allow for board refreshment." *Effect:* Partially satisfies one of the activist's demands without negotiation. Forces both sides to reassess their positions.

---

# After-Action Review Framework

The debrief should be facilitator-led, structured, and focused on extracting transferable governance principles – not rehashing who won the negotiation.

**Duration:** 35 to 45 minutes minimum. Do not cut this short.

**Structure the debrief around five questions:**

### 1. What surprised you?

Ask each team to identify the single most surprising moment of the exercise. Surprises reveal assumptions that the exercise challenged – and assumptions are where governance failures begin.

## 2. Where were the governance gaps?

Ask the board team and management team to identify specific governance weaknesses that the exercise exposed – not weaknesses in the target company, but weaknesses in their own preparation, analysis, and decision-making processes. Ask the activist team to identify which of their arguments were strongest and which were weakest.

## 3. What would you do differently?

Ask each team to identify one strategic decision they would change if they could run the exercise again. This question forces participants to distinguish between decisions that failed because of execution and decisions that failed because of flawed analysis.

## 4. What should your real board implement?

This is the most important question. Ask every participant – regardless of team assignment – to identify one governance improvement that should be implemented at a board they currently serve on or aspire to join. The answers to this question are the exercise's practical output.

## 5. What did this exercise teach you about governance that a lecture could not?

This reflective question helps participants articulate the experiential learning that distinguishes the simulation from every other governance education method. Their answers will consistently center on the gap between understanding concepts and applying them under pressure.

**Facilitator notes for the debrief:**

- Call on participants from all three teams. Do not let one team dominate.
- Push past surface-level answers. When someone says "communication was important," ask them to identify the specific communication failure and what they would do differently.
- Connect observations back to real-world governance. Every lesson from the simulation has a direct parallel in actual board service.
- Close with Roosevelt Giles's framing: *The process is the key*. What matters is not who won. What matters is that every par-

ticipant has exercised governance judgment under pressure –
and can now do it better.

---

# Adaptation Guide

## For Corporate Boards

Use your own company as the target – but only with appropriate
confidentiality protections. An external facilitator prepares the activist case using public filings, and the board practices responding.
This format produces the most directly actionable learning because
the governance issues are real and the improvements can be implemented immediately. Engage your general counsel to establish appropriate information barriers.

## For Governance Education Programs

The eight-week format with an external target company is the gold
standard. Assign teams early, provide research guidance, and schedule regular check-ins during the preparation phase. The SLGI Board
Readiness Program model – with a capstone simulation followed by
expert commentary – is the most effective structure.

## For Law Firm Client Development

Offer the tabletop exercise as a value-added service for corporate
clients. The firm's governance attorneys can serve as facilitators and
inject designers, and the exercise creates natural opportunities to
discuss preparedness measures. A half-day format works well for
this purpose.

## For MBA and Executive Education Courses

The one-day intensive format preserves the core learning objectives
within academic scheduling constraints. Provide pre-prepared research packets so students can focus on strategy development and
simulation rather than primary research. Use the exercise to bridge

theory and practice – assign governance readings before the simulation and debrief the experience through a governance theory lens
afterward.

## Scale Options

| Element | 1-Day Intensive | 4-Week Condensed | 8-Week Full |
|---|---|---|---|
| Research | Pre-prepared packets | 2 weeks independent | 3 weeks independent |
| Strategy development | Morning session (2 hrs) | 1 week | 3 weeks |
| Refinement | None | 1 week | 2 weeks |
| Simulation | Afternoon (3 hrs) | 3 hours | 3-4 hours |
| Injects | 1-2 | 2-3 | 3-4 |
| Debrief | 30 minutes | 35 minutes | 45-60 minutes |
| Learning depth | Moderate | Strong | Maximum |

Regardless of format, three elements are non-negotiable: the three-
team structure, at least one scenario inject, and the after-action review. Remove any of these and the exercise loses its distinctive value.

---

The tabletop exercise is the single most effective governance education tool available to boards today. It costs nothing but time. It requires no special technology. It produces learning that no lecture,
case discussion, or governance manual can replicate.

The question is not whether your board should run one. The question is when you will start.

# Appendix E: Key Governance and Activism Research Sources

This appendix provides a curated directory of the essential resources for monitoring activist campaigns, researching governance quality, engaging with proxy advisory firms, and building the institutional knowledge that effective board service requires. These are the tools and platforms that professional activist investors, governance advisors, and sophisticated boards use daily. They are available to any director willing to invest the time.

---

## SEC Filings and Tools

The Securities and Exchange Commission's EDGAR database is the foundation of all governance research. Every public company filing is available at no cost, and the system's full-text search capabilities – often overlooked – make it a powerful intelligence tool.

**EDGAR Full-Text Search** (efts.sec.gov/LATEST/search-index) – Search across all SEC filings by keyword, company name, or filing type. This is the single most underused governance research tool available. Search for your company's name combined with terms like "13D," "proxy contest," "shareholder proposal," or "board nominee" to identify activist activity before it becomes public news.

**Schedule 13D / 13G Filings** – Filed when an investor acquires more than five percent of a company's outstanding shares. The 13D is the activist's calling card – Item 4 describes the filer's intentions regarding the company, and it is where activists first signal their demands. Monitor these filings for your company and peer companies. A 13G filing indicates passive investment intent; an amendment converting a 13G to a 13D signals that a previously passive investor has become an activist.

**DEF 14A (Definitive Proxy Statement)** – The richest single source of governance intelligence for any public company. Contains director biographies, compensation tables, committee assignments, stock ownership data, related-party transactions, and the company's governance structure. Read your own company's proxy cover to cover at least once a year. Read your peer companies' proxies to benchmark governance practices.

**Form 3 / Form 4 (Insider Trading Reports)** – Filed when directors and officers buy or sell company stock. Patterns of insider selling – particularly by multiple insiders simultaneously – can signal governance concerns. Patterns of insider buying can signal confidence. Activists monitor these filings closely.

**Setting up EDGAR alerts.** SEC EDGAR allows users to subscribe to email notifications for specific companies. Navigate to the company's filing page on EDGAR, and use the RSS feed or email subscription feature to receive automatic notifications whenever a new filing is posted. Set alerts for your own company, your peer group, and any known activist funds that operate in your sector. This is a five-minute setup that provides continuous early warning.

---

# Activist Tracking Platforms

These commercial platforms aggregate and analyze activist campaign data. They are expensive – annual subscriptions typically run from five thousand to fifty thousand dollars depending on the platform and access level – but they provide intelligence that would take hundreds of hours to compile manually.

**Insightia** (formerly Activist Insight) – The most comprehensive activist campaign database available. Tracks campaigns globally, maintains detailed profiles of activist investors, and provides analytics on campaign outcomes, settlement terms, and governance changes. The platform's campaign alerts notify subscribers when new activist positions are disclosed. Insightia is the platform most frequently referenced by governance professionals and proxy solicitation firms.

**13D Monitor** – Specializes in real-time tracking of Schedule 13D filings and activist campaign developments. Provides daily alerts on new 13D filings, amendments, and campaign milestones. The editorial commentary contextualizes filings within broader campaign dynamics. Particularly valuable for investor relations teams that need early warning of activist accumulation.

**SharkRepellent** (Diligent) – Focused on governance defense analytics. Provides detailed data on companies' structural defenses – poison pills, advance notice provisions, classified boards, voting standards – and benchmarks them against peer companies and market norms. Useful for boards conducting vulnerability self-assessments and for activists evaluating target defensibility.

**Diligent Market Intelligence** – Board-level governance data and analytics platform. Provides director profiles, board composition analysis, compensation benchmarking, and shareholder voting analytics. Integrates with Diligent's board portal products, making it particularly useful for boards already using Diligent for meeting management.

**FactSet SharkWatch** – Activist campaign tracking integrated within the broader FactSet financial data platform. Useful for institutional investors and analysts who already use FactSet for financial analysis and want activist campaign intelligence within their existing workflow.

---

# Proxy Advisory Firms

Proxy advisory firms analyze governance practices and issue voting recommendations that influence how institutional investors vote their shares. Their recommendations do not determine outcomes – but they significantly influence them, particularly among smaller institutional investors that rely on advisory firm guidance rather than conducting independent analysis.

**ISS (Institutional Shareholder Services)** – The largest and most influential proxy advisory firm. ISS evaluates director elections, executive compensation, shareholder proposals, and contested elections. Their voting recommendations are followed – in whole or in part – by institutional investors controlling trillions of dollars in assets.

*Engagement process:* Companies can submit supplemental materials to ISS analysts two to four weeks before ISS publishes its report. ISS analysts will typically hold a call with the company to discuss governance issues flagged in their analysis. This engagement window is critical – once the report is published, changing a recommendation is extremely difficult. Contact ISS through your proxy solicitor or directly through the issuer engagement portal on their website.

**Glass Lewis** – The second-largest proxy advisory firm, with growing influence particularly among international institutional investors. Glass Lewis's methodology differs from ISS in several areas – notably on executive compensation and board independence thresholds – so companies should understand both firms' standards and tailor engagement accordingly.

*Engagement process:* Similar to ISS. Glass Lewis accepts supplemental materials and holds engagement calls. Submit materials early – Glass Lewis analysts work under tight deadlines during proxy season, and late submissions may not receive full consideration.

**Egan-Jones Proxy Services** – Smaller than ISS and Glass Lewis but influential among certain institutional investor segments. Egan-Jones positions itself as providing more independent analysis, less reliant on formulaic governance scoring models. Worth engaging if your shareholder base includes investors that follow Egan-Jones recommendations.

**Important Note for 2027 and Beyond:** Beginning with the 2027 proxy season, Glass Lewis will no longer issue a single benchmark voting recommendation. Companies will need to understand which of Glass Lewis's four research perspectives – management-aligned, governance fundamentals, sustainability, or active owner – their institutional investors have selected. Engagement strategy must be tailored accordingly, as different investors may receive different Glass Lewis recommendations on the same issue. ISS maintains its benchmark policy but offers products (Gov360, Custom Lens) that allow investors to bypass standard recommendations. The engagement best practices below remain valid but must be supplemented with research into which advisory frameworks your specific investors use. See Chapter 9 for a detailed analysis of these changes.

**Best practices for proxy advisory firm engagement:**

- Submit supplemental materials two to four weeks before the proxy advisory firm's publication deadline
- Request an engagement call – do not rely on written submissions alone
- Address specific governance concerns the firm has flagged in prior years
- If facing a contested election, prepare a dedicated supplemental filing that addresses the activist's claims point by point
- Monitor both ISS and Glass Lewis – their recommendations may differ, and understanding the differences helps you prioritize engagement

---

# Institutional Investor Stewardship

The largest asset managers maintain dedicated stewardship teams that evaluate governance practices and engage directly with portfolio companies. Understanding their priorities – and building relationships before a campaign begins – is one of the most effective governance preparedness measures available.

**BlackRock Investment Stewardship** – BlackRock publishes annual voting guidelines and stewardship priorities. Their stewardship team engages with thousands of companies annually on governance topics including board quality, climate risk, executive compensation, and shareholder rights. BlackRock's voting decisions are influenced but not determined by proxy advisory firm recommendations. Access their published priorities and engagement framework through the Investment Stewardship section of blackrock.com.

**Vanguard Investment Stewardship** – Vanguard's stewardship principles emphasize board composition, oversight effectiveness, and shareholder rights. As one of the largest holders of U.S. equities, Vanguard's voting decisions carry significant weight. Their published stewardship principles are available on the Investment Stewardship section of vanguard.com.

**State Street Global Advisors** – Known for the "Fearless Girl" governance framework emphasizing board diversity and governance quality. State Street's stewardship team publishes voting guidelines and engagement priorities annually. Their governance scoring framework influences voting decisions across their portfolio.

**CalPERS (California Public Employees' Retirement System)** – One of the most activist-minded public pension funds. CalPERS publishes detailed governance principles and maintains a focus list of companies with governance concerns. Their governance standards often exceed minimum market norms and signal where institutional investor expectations are heading.

**Finding stewardship team contacts.** Most large institutional investors list their stewardship team and engagement process on their corporate website. Your proxy solicitation firm can provide direct contacts. Investor relations professionals should maintain a relationship map of the stewardship contacts at your top twenty institutional holders and engage them at least annually – during the off-season, not just during proxy season.

---

# Industry Organizations and Standards

**Council of Institutional Investors (CII)** – An association of institutional investors focused on governance best practices. CII publishes corporate governance policies that represent the consensus view of major institutional investors. Their positions on board independence, shareholder rights, and executive compensation are widely referenced as benchmarks. CII's annual conference is a valuable venue for board members and governance professionals.

**National Association of Corporate Directors (NACD)** – The primary professional association for corporate directors in the United States. NACD provides board education, governance research, and peer networking. Their annual governance surveys and director compensation reports are essential benchmarking resources. NACD's Blue Ribbon Commission reports address emerging governance topics with practical recommendations.

**The Conference Board** – Publishes governance research including the annual Corporate Governance Handbook, studies on board practices, and analyses of institutional investor voting patterns. Their research is academically rigorous while remaining accessible to practitioners.

**Harvard Law School Forum on Corporate Governance** – A daily online publication featuring short-form analysis from governance practitioners, academics, and law firms. The Forum publishes timely commentary on activist campaigns, SEC regulatory developments, proxy advisory firm policies, and emerging governance issues. It is the single best free resource for staying current on governance developments. Available at corpgov.law.harvard.edu.

---

# Recommended Reading

These books provide foundational context for understanding the history, dynamics, and evolving practice of shareholder activism.

**Dear Chairman** by Jeff Gramm – A history of shareholder activism told through the actual letters that activists wrote to boards. Covers campaigns spanning decades, from Benjamin Graham to Carl Icahn to Daniel Loeb. Essential reading for understanding how activist rhetoric, strategy, and legitimacy have evolved over time.

**The Shareholder Value Myth** by Lynn Stout – A counterpoint to the shareholder primacy model that underlies most activist campaigns. Stout argues that the legal obligation of boards is broader than maximizing shareholder value – a perspective that every director should understand, whether they agree with it or not. This book will sharpen your thinking about whose interests the board serves.

**King Icahn** by Mark Stevens – A biography of Carl Icahn that provides insight into the mind and methods of the most famous activist investor in history. Though Icahn's era and methods differ from to-day's governance-focused activism, the strategic thinking and psy-chological dynamics remain relevant.

**Barbarians at the Gate** by Bryan Burrough and John Helyar – The definitive account of the leveraged buyout of RJR Nabisco. While the LBO era differs from modern activism, this book captures the board dynamics, management incentives, and institutional in-vestor behavior that continue to shape contested corporate control situations.

------

These resources are your intelligence infrastructure. An activist fund considering a campaign against your company will use every one of them. A board that familiarizes itself with these tools – and uses them proactively – will identify vulnerabilities before an activist does, engage with institutional investors before proxy season, and respond to campaigns from a position of preparation rather than surprise.

The information asymmetry that gives activists their advantage is not a function of access. Every resource listed here is available to every director. The asymmetry is a function of effort. Close the effort gap, and you close the vulnerability gap.

# Appendix F: Glossary of Activist Investor and Proxy Contest Terms

The language of shareholder activism borrows from securities regulation, corporate governance, investment banking, and – occasionally – military strategy. This glossary covers the key terms that board directors, executives, and investor relations professionals will encounter throughout an activist campaign. Definitions are written for practitioners, not lawyers. For regulatory precision, consult legal counsel.

---

**13D Filing (Schedule 13D)** – The SEC filing required when an investor acquires beneficial ownership of more than five percent of a public company's voting securities with the intent to influence or change control. Item 4 of the filing – the "Purpose of Transaction" section – is where activists signal their intentions. Shapiro calls Item 4 an "entertaining love letter" to the company.

**13D/A (Amendment)** – An amendment to a previously filed Schedule 13D. Activists must file amendments promptly when there are material changes to their position, plans, or intentions. A 13D/A often signals an escalation – new demands, increased ownership, or the addition of director nominees.

**13F Filing** – A quarterly report filed by institutional investment managers with more than $100 million in qualifying assets. 13F filings disclose long equity positions but not short positions, options strategies, or the timing of trades. They are useful for identifying who owns a company's shares but provide only a lagging, incomplete picture.

**13G Filing (Schedule 13G)** – A shorter alternative to Schedule 13D available to investors who acquire more than five percent of a company's shares but do so in the ordinary course of business without intent to influence control. Passive investors – index funds, for example – typically file 13Gs. When an investor converts a 13G to a 13D, it signals a shift from passive ownership to active engagement.

**Activist Investor** – An investor who acquires a significant ownership stake in a public company and uses that position to advocate for changes in governance, strategy, operations, or capital allocation. Activists range from single-issue governance reformers to large multi-strategy hedge funds running billion-dollar campaigns.

**Advance Notice Bylaws** – Provisions in a company's bylaws that require shareholders to provide advance notice – typically 60 to 120 days before the annual meeting – when nominating directors or proposing business. These provisions are standard corporate hygiene. When they are drafted to be unreasonably burdensome or to trap unwary challengers, they become a defensive weapon – and a potential liability if challenged in court.

**Annual Meeting** – The annual gathering of shareholders at which directors are elected, auditors are ratified, and shareholder proposals are voted upon. For most companies, the annual meeting is a formality. When an activist is running a proxy contest, it becomes the decisive event.

**Beneficial Owner** – The person or entity that ultimately owns or controls securities, even if those securities are held in the name of a broker, bank, or other nominee. Beneficial ownership is the trigger for 13D and 13G filing requirements. The calculation includes shares held directly, shares over which the investor has voting or investment power, and – in some cases – shares subject to derivative contracts.

**Board Observer** – A non-director individual who is granted the right to attend board meetings, receive board materials, and observe deliberations, but who cannot vote. Board observer seats are sometimes offered to activists as part of settlement agreements when the company is unwilling to grant a full board seat.

**Board Refreshment** – The process of systematically evaluating board composition and bringing in new directors with relevant skills, experience, and perspectives. Companies that demonstrate genuine board refreshment – through regular assessments, mandatory retirement ages, and term limits – are harder for activists to attack on governance grounds.

**Bylaw Amendment** – A change to a company's governing bylaws, which can typically be made by either the board or the shareholders (depending on the company's charter and state law). Activists sometimes propose bylaw amendments – such as allowing shareholders to call special meetings or reducing supermajority voting thresholds – as part of their campaigns.

**Capital Allocation** – The process by which a company deploys its financial resources across organic investment, acquisitions, dividends, share repurchases, and debt reduction. Flawed capital allocation is one of the four improvable problems that activists target most frequently. Companies that hoard cash, overpay for acquisitions, or fund value-destroying projects are prime activist targets.

**Caremark Claims/Duties** – Derived from the 1996 Delaware Chancery Court decision *In re Caremark International Inc.*, Caremark duties require that boards implement and monitor systems of compliance and reporting. A Caremark claim alleges that directors failed in their duty of oversight – that they either never established a monitoring system or consciously disregarded red flags. These claims were historically difficult to win but have gained traction in recent years.

**Classified Board (Staggered Board)** – A board structure in which directors are divided into classes (typically three) and only one class stands for election each year. This means an activist cannot win control of the board in a single election cycle – they would need to win at least two consecutive annual meetings. Classified boards remain the single most effective structural defense against activism, but they have fallen out of favor with institutional investors and proxy advisory firms.

**Consent Solicitation** – A process by which shareholders can take action – including removing directors or amending bylaws – by written consent, without waiting for an annual meeting. Not all companies permit consent solicitations; the availability depends on the company's charter and bylaws. When available, consent solicitations allow activists to move on an accelerated timeline.

**Control Premium** – The additional price per share that a buyer pays to acquire a controlling interest in a company, above the company's current market price. Control premiums typically range from 20 to 50 percent and reflect the value of having authority over the company's strategy, management, and capital allocation.

**Corporate Raider** – A term from the 1980s describing investors who acquired controlling stakes in companies through hostile means – leveraged buyouts, greenmail, or forced asset sales. The term carries negative connotations and is largely outdated as a description of modern activism, though it still shapes how some boards perceive any activist engagement.

**Cumulative Voting** – A voting system in which each shareholder receives a number of votes equal to the number of shares owned multiplied by the number of directors being elected. Shareholders can then concentrate all their votes on a single candidate. Cumulative voting makes it easier for minority shareholders to elect at least one director, which is why it is increasingly rare – most companies have eliminated it.

**DEF 14A (Definitive Proxy Statement)** – The final version of a company's proxy statement filed with the SEC and sent to shareholders in advance of an annual or special meeting. The DEF 14A contains the company's director nominees, executive compensation disclosures, shareholder proposals, and voting instructions. It is the company's primary communication vehicle with shareholders during proxy season.

**Director Interlock** – A situation in which a director or executive of one company serves on the board of another company whose director or executive simultaneously serves on the first company's board. Director interlocks can create conflicts of interest and are restricted under antitrust laws (specifically Section 8 of the Clayton Act) when the companies are competitors.

**Dissident Proxy Statement** – The proxy statement filed by an activist or dissident shareholder group in connection with a proxy contest. The dissident proxy statement presents the activist's case for change, introduces their director nominees, and solicits shareholder votes on the universal proxy card.

**Dual-Class Share Structure** – A capital structure in which a company issues two or more classes of stock with different voting rights. Typically, founders and insiders hold high-vote shares (10 votes per share, for example), while public investors hold low-vote shares (one vote per share). Dual-class structures effectively insulate management from shareholder accountability and make proxy contests mathematically unwinnable for activists.

**Engagement (Shareholder)** – The process of communication between shareholders and company leadership – including directors, management, and investor relations – on matters of governance, strategy, and performance. Effective engagement is the first line of defense against activism. Companies that refuse to engage, or engage only superficially, invite escalation.

**ESG (Environmental, Social, Governance)** – A framework for evaluating a company's practices across environmental impact, social responsibility, and governance quality. ESG has become both a basis for activist campaigns (Engine No. 1's climate-focused ExxonMobil campaign) and a target of anti-ESG activism (Strive Asset Management's campaigns against perceived ESG overreach).

**Exempt Solicitation** – A solicitation that is exempt from the full SEC proxy filing requirements. Under Rule 14a-2(b), shareholders who are not seeking proxy authority and who own more than $5 million in securities can communicate with other shareholders without filing a proxy statement. Activists often use exempt solicitations to rally support before launching a formal proxy contest.

**Fiduciary Duty** – The legal obligation of directors and officers to act in the best interests of the corporation and its shareholders. Fiduciary duties include the duty of care (informed decision-making), the duty of loyalty (no self-dealing), and – in certain contexts – the duty of good faith. Activists frequently frame their demands as holding boards accountable for fiduciary failures.

**Form 8-K** – A current report filed with the SEC to announce material events – leadership changes, acquisitions, financial restatements, settlements with activists, and other developments that shareholders need to know about promptly. Settlement agreements with activists are typically disclosed via 8-K.

**Full Slate** – An activist's nomination of candidates for every board seat up for election. Running a full slate signals an attempt to gain working control of the board. Full slates are aggressive, expensive, and relatively rare – most activists run minority or short slates.

**Golden Parachute** – A contractual provision guaranteeing substantial compensation to executives upon termination following a change of control. Excessive golden parachutes are a frequent target of activist criticism and say-on-pay campaigns, because they can entrench management by making leadership changes prohibitively expensive.

**Governance Score** – A composite rating assigned to a company by proxy advisory firms or governance research organizations that assesses the quality of the company's governance practices. ISS's Governance QualityScore and Glass Lewis's ratings are among the most influential. Low governance scores attract activist attention.

**Greenmail** – The practice of buying enough shares in a company to threaten a takeover, then selling those shares back to the company at a premium in exchange for an agreement to withdraw the threat. Greenmail was common in the 1980s and has been curtailed by tax penalties and shareholder activism. The concept survives in modified forms when companies pay activists to go away through settlements that include stock repurchases.

**Hart-Scott-Rodino (HSR) Filing** – A pre-merger notification filing required under the Hart-Scott-Rodino Antitrust Improvements Act when an investor's acquisition of voting securities exceeds certain dollar thresholds. The HSR filing provides the FTC and DOJ an opportunity to review acquisitions for antitrust concerns before they are completed. HSR thresholds adjust annually.

**Hostile Takeover** – An acquisition attempt made directly to a company's shareholders – typically through a tender offer – without the approval of the target company's board. Hostile takeovers are distinct from activist campaigns, which seek to change governance or strategy rather than acquire the company outright. However, the threat of a hostile takeover can be an implicit or explicit component of an activist's leverage.

**Institutional Investor** – A large organization that invests on behalf of others – including pension funds, mutual funds, insurance companies, endowments, and sovereign wealth funds. Institutional investors typically own 70 to 80 percent of the shares of large public companies, making their voting decisions the most important variable in any proxy contest.

**Interlock (Board/Director)** – See *Director Interlock*.

**Investment Stewardship** – The governance engagement activities conducted by asset managers – particularly large index fund managers like BlackRock, Vanguard, and State Street – to promote long-term value creation at the companies they own. Investment stewardship teams vote proxies, engage with boards, and publish voting guidelines that shape governance expectations across the market.

**ISS (Institutional Shareholder Services)** – The largest proxy advisory firm, providing voting recommendations and governance research to institutional investors worldwide. An ISS recommendation in favor of an activist's nominees significantly increases the likelihood of a favorable vote outcome. ISS evaluates campaigns based on its own analytical framework, not automatically on the merits of either side's arguments.

**Material Definitive Additional Information** – Supplemental proxy materials filed with the SEC that provide additional information beyond the initial proxy statement. Both companies and activists file supplemental materials as a campaign progresses, often in response to the other side's claims.

**Minority Slate** – See *Short Slate*.

**Nominating/Governance Committee** – The board committee responsible for identifying, evaluating, and recommending director candidates and overseeing governance policies. A well-functioning nominating committee is one of the strongest defenses against activism, because it demonstrates that the board takes its own composition and governance seriously. Activists often target this committee when arguing that the board has failed to refresh itself.

**Non-Disparagement Clause** – A provision in a settlement or standstill agreement that prohibits both the company and the activist from making negative public statements about each other. Non-disparagement clauses are standard in settlement agreements and provide a cooling-off period after a contentious campaign.

**Overboarded Director** – A director who serves on more boards than proxy advisory firms consider appropriate – typically more than four public company boards for a non-executive, or two for a sitting CEO. Overboarded directors are flagged by ISS and Glass Lewis as a governance concern and may receive negative vote recommendations.

**Passive Investor** – An investor who holds shares without intent to influence or change the company's governance or strategy. Index fund managers are the archetypal passive investors, though their investment stewardship activities increasingly blur the line between passive ownership and active governance engagement.

**Poison Pill (Shareholder Rights Plan)** – A defensive mechanism that allows existing shareholders to purchase additional shares at a steep discount if any single investor's ownership exceeds a specified threshold (typically 10 to 20 percent). Poison pills make hostile acquisitions prohibitively expensive and prevent activists from accumulating dominant positions. They are effective but controversial – proxy advisory firms and institutional investors generally oppose long-duration pills.

**Pre-IPO Planning** – The process of designing a company's governance structure before it goes public, including board composition, voting structures, and defensive provisions. Decisions made at the IPO stage – such as whether to adopt a dual-class share structure or classified board – have lasting implications for the company's vulnerability to activism.

**PRELIM 14A (Preliminary Proxy Statement)** – A draft proxy statement filed with the SEC for review before the definitive version (DEF 14A) is distributed to shareholders. The SEC may comment on the preliminary filing, requiring changes before the company or activist can mail the definitive proxy.

**Proxy Access** – A bylaw provision that allows qualifying shareholders (typically those owning at least three percent of shares for at least three years) to nominate a limited number of director candidates (typically up to 20 percent of the board) on the company's own proxy card. Proxy access is a governance reform frequently demanded by activists and institutional investors.

**Proxy Advisory Firm** – A firm that provides voting recommendations and governance research to institutional investors. ISS and Glass Lewis are the two dominant proxy advisory firms. Their recommendations significantly influence voting outcomes, particularly at companies where institutional investors rely on advisory firm guidance for routine voting decisions.

**Proxy Contest (Proxy Fight)** – A contested election in which an activist solicits shareholder votes for its own director nominees in opposition to the company's slate. Proxy contests are the highest-stakes, most expensive form of shareholder activism. The introduction of the universal proxy card in 2022 made proxy contests more accessible to activists and more difficult for companies to win through structural advantages alone.

**Proxy Statement** – See *DEF 14A*.

**Record Date** – The date established by the board that determines which shareholders are entitled to notice of, and to vote at, a shareholder meeting. Only shareholders who owned shares as of the record date can vote. Setting the record date is a procedural but important step in the proxy contest timeline.

**Revlon Duties** – Derived from the 1986 Delaware Supreme Court decision *Revlon, Inc. v. MacAndrews & Forbes Holdings*, Revlon duties require that when a company is for sale, the board's obligation shifts from preserving the company as a going concern to maximizing the sale price for shareholders. Revlon duties are triggered by certain change-of-control transactions and limit the board's discretion to favor one bidder over another.

**Say-on-Pay** – An advisory shareholder vote on executive compensation, required at least once every three years under the Dodd-Frank Act. While the vote is non-binding, a failed say-on-pay vote is a significant governance signal – it indicates that shareholders believe the board's compensation committee is not aligning executive pay with performance. Failed say-on-pay votes often precede or coincide with activist campaigns.

**Schedule TO** – The SEC filing required when a person or entity makes a tender offer to acquire shares of a public company. The Schedule TO discloses the terms of the offer, the offeror's plans for the company, and the source of funding. It is the regulatory mechanism for hostile and friendly tender offers alike.

**Section 220 Demand** – A demand made under Section 220 of the Delaware General Corporation Law (or equivalent provisions in other states) by a shareholder to inspect a company's books and records. The shareholder must demonstrate a proper purpose – such as investigating potential mismanagement or waste. Section 220 demands are a powerful pre-litigation tool for activists, and Delaware courts have generally been receptive to them.

**Shareholder Activism** – The use of an equity position to influence a company's governance, strategy, or operations. Shareholder activism encompasses a wide spectrum – from private engagement letters to full-scale proxy contests – and is pursued by a diverse range of investors including hedge funds, pension funds, individual investors, and social advocacy organizations.

**Shareholder Proposal (Rule 14a-8)** – A proposal submitted by a shareholder for inclusion in the company's proxy statement. Rule 14a-8 proposals are advisory – even if they receive majority support, the board is not legally required to implement them. However, proposals that receive strong shareholder support create significant pressure on boards to act.

**Shareholder Rights Plan** – See *Poison Pill*.

**Short Slate** – An activist's nomination of fewer candidates than the total number of seats up for election – for example, nominating two candidates when five seats are available. Short slates signal a desire for board representation rather than board control. Most activist campaigns run short slates. Also called a *minority slate*.

**Solicitation** – The process of requesting shareholders' proxy votes in connection with a meeting. Both the company and the activist engage in solicitation – the company through its proxy statement and the activist through its dissident proxy statement. Proxy solicitation is governed by SEC rules that require the filing and distribution of specified disclosure documents.

**Special Meeting** – A shareholder meeting called outside the regular annual meeting cycle, typically to address a specific issue – such as removing a director, approving a merger, or voting on a shareholder proposal. The right to call special meetings varies by company; some require a petition from shareholders holding 10 to 25 percent of shares, while others reserve the right exclusively for the board.

**Standstill Agreement** – A contract between a company and an activist in which the activist agrees, for a specified period, to limit their ownership stake, refrain from launching proxy contests, and cease public criticism of the company. In exchange, the activist typically receives board seats, governance reforms, or other concessions. Standstill agreements are the most common resolution to activist campaigns.

**Staggered Board** – See *Classified Board*.

**Strategic Alternatives** – A process in which a company's board evaluates a range of options – including a sale, merger, spinoff, recapitalization, or management changes – in response to underperformance or activist pressure. Announcing a review of strategic alternatives is sometimes a defensive tactic (signaling that the board is acting), but it can also create genuine outcomes (including a sale at a premium).

**Supermajority Voting Requirement** – A charter or bylaw provision that requires more than a simple majority – typically two-thirds or 80 percent – of shareholder votes to approve certain actions, such as merging the company, amending the charter, or removing directors. Supermajority provisions are defensive in nature and are increasingly targeted for elimination by activists and proxy advisory firms.

**Tender Offer** – An offer made directly to a company's shareholders to purchase their shares at a specified price, typically at a premium to the current market price. Tender offers can be friendly (board-approved) or hostile (opposed by the board). Activists occasionally launch tender offers as an alternative or supplement to a proxy contest.

**Universal Proxy Card (UPC)** – Adopted by the SEC in November 2021 and effective for shareholder meetings held after August 31, 2022, the universal proxy card requires that in a contested elec-

tion, both the company and the activist include all director nominees
– from both sides – on a single proxy card. This allows shareholders
to mix and match nominees, eliminating the structural advantage
companies previously held by forcing an all-or-nothing choice. The
UPC is the most consequential regulatory change in proxy contests
in decades.

**White Paper Activist** – An activist who presents a detailed operational or strategic analysis – a "white paper" – alongside their
campaign demands. White paper activists tend to have deep industry expertise and propose specific operational improvements rather
than generic governance changes. Their credibility comes from the
quality of their analysis.

**Withhold Campaign** – A campaign in which shareholders are
urged to withhold their votes from one or more of the company's
director nominees rather than voting against them. Withhold
campaigns do not require a proxy contest – they work within the
company's own proxy card. A director who receives a majority of
withheld votes faces a governance embarrassment and, under many
companies' majority voting policies, must tender their resignation.

**Wolf Pack** – An informal, often uncoordinated group of activist
and activist-sympathetic investors who accumulate positions in the
same company around the same time. Wolf packs are controversial
because they may allow investors to collectively exert influence without triggering the 13D disclosure requirements that would apply to a
formal group. Regulators have debated – but not yet adopted – rules
to address wolf pack behavior.

---

*This glossary covers the terms most frequently encountered in ac-
tivist investor campaigns and proxy contests. For additional regulatory definitions, consult the SEC's online glossary at sec.gov or
your legal counsel.*

# Appendix G: Resource Directory

The organizations, platforms, and firms listed below represent the ecosystem that shapes activist campaigns, proxy contests, and corporate governance. This is not an exhaustive list – the governance landscape evolves continuously – but it provides a practical starting point for boards and executives who need to engage quickly with credible resources.

---

## Governance Organizations

These organizations provide education, research, networking, and best-practice guidance for directors and governance professionals.

- **National Association of Corporate Directors (NACD)** – nacd.org – The leading membership organization for corporate directors. Offers board education programs, governance research, peer forums, and the annual NACD Summit. Their Directorship certification program is widely recognized.

- **Council of Institutional Investors (CII)** – cii.org – A nonprofit association of pension funds, endowments, and other institutional investors focused on shareholder rights and corporate governance. CII publishes governance policies and best practices that many institutional investors reference when evaluating proxy votes.

- **Society for Corporate Governance** – societycorpgov.org

– A professional membership organization for corporate secretaries, in-house counsel, and governance professionals. Strong focus on the operational side of governance – meeting management, SEC compliance, and proxy mechanics.

- **Boardroom INSIDERS** – boardroominsiders.com – Provides intelligence profiles on corporate directors and executives, useful for understanding board composition and identifying potential vulnerabilities.

- **The Conference Board** – conferenceboard.org – Publishes research on CEO succession, executive compensation, ESG, and shareholder engagement. Their ESG Center and Governance Center produce reports frequently cited in proxy contests.

---

# Regulatory Bodies

Understanding the regulatory framework is essential for both sides of an activist campaign.

- **SEC Division of Corporation Finance** – sec.gov/corpfin – Oversees the proxy process, reviews proxy filings, and issues guidance on disclosure requirements. The Division's staff no-action letters on Rule 14a-8 shareholder proposals are critical reference points.

- **NYSE Listed Company Manual** – nyse.com – Governance requirements for NYSE-listed companies, including board independence, audit committee composition, and shareholder approval requirements.

- **NASDAQ Listing Rules** – nasdaq.com – Comparable governance requirements for NASDAQ-listed companies, with some differences from NYSE standards.

- **Delaware Division of Corporations** – corp.delaware.gov – Most large public companies are incorporated in Delaware. The Delaware General Corporation Law and the Chancery Court's rulings on fiduciary duties, defensive measures, and shareholder rights define the legal landscape for the majority of activist campaigns.

---

# Data and Research Platforms

These platforms provide the data infrastructure for activist campaigns, proxy advisory, and governance research.

- **SEC EDGAR** – sec.gov/edgar – The SEC's Electronic Data Gathering, Analysis, and Retrieval system. The primary source for all public filings including 13D, 13F, DEF 14A, and 8-K filings. Free and publicly accessible.

- **Insightia** – insightia.com – The leading database for tracking activist campaigns, shareholder proposals, and governance trends. Provides campaign histories, activist profiles, and outcome data. Essential for any company monitoring activist activity in their sector.

- **ISS Governance Solutions** – issgovernance.com – Provides governance scoring, peer benchmarking, and compensation analytics in addition to proxy voting recommendations. ISS's Governance QualityScore is widely referenced by institutional investors.

- **Glass Lewis** – glasslewis.com – The second-largest proxy advisory firm, providing independent voting recommendations and governance analysis. Their approach differs from ISS in methodology and emphasis, and some institutional investors subscribe to both services.

- **Diligent Market Intelligence** – diligent.com – Governance analytics platform offering board composition analysis, peer benchmarking, and vulnerability assessments. Their activism preparedness tools help companies identify and monitor potential threats.

- **FactSet** – factset.com – Financial data and analytics platform widely used for ownership analysis, peer benchmarking, and the financial modeling that underlies both activist theses and company defense materials.

- **S&P Capital IQ** – capitaliq.com – Comprehensive financial intelligence platform used for company screening, ownership analysis, and the financial benchmarking that drives activist target selection.

---

# Law Firms Specializing in Activism Defense

The following firms are frequently retained for activism-related matters. This is not an endorsement but a starting point for companies seeking counsel. Firm selection should be based on relevant experience with your specific situation, industry, and jurisdiction.

- **Wachtell, Lipton, Rosen & Katz** – The firm that invented the poison pill. Widely considered the preeminent advisor on hostile takeover defense and activist response. Known for aggressive defense strategies.

- **Sullivan & Cromwell** – Full-service firm with a leading M&A and governance practice. Frequently advises companies on activist defense, proxy contests, and settlement negotiations.

- **Skadden, Arps, Slate, Meagher & Flom** – Major presence in proxy contests, hostile defense, and shareholder activism. Advises both companies and, in some cases, activists.

- **Sidley Austin** – Strong governance and securities practice with significant experience in proxy contests and shareholder engagement strategy.

- **Gibson, Dunn & Crutcher** – Active in shareholder activism defense, SEC regulatory matters, and corporate governance litigation. Known for their securities regulation expertise.

---

# Investment Banks with Activism Advisory Practices

These firms provide strategic advisory services to companies facing activist campaigns, including financial analysis, shareholder identification, and defense strategy.

- **Goldman Sachs (Strategic Advisory)** – One of the most frequently retained advisors in high-profile activism situations. Provides shareholder analysis, valuation defense, and strategic alternatives review.

- **Morgan Stanley (Shareholder Advisory)** – Dedicated shareholder advisory practice focused on activism preparedness, institutional investor engagement, and proxy contest strategy.

- **Lazard (Shareholder Advisory & Activism Defense)** – A leading independent advisory firm with one of the busiest activism defense practices. Known for providing candid strategic advice and managing complex multi-stakeholder situations.

- **Evercore (Shareholder Advisory)** – Independent advisory firm with a growing activism defense practice. Frequently engaged for valuation opinions and strategic review processes.

- **Moelis & Company** – Independent advisory firm that advises on both activism defense and activist-side engagements, providing perspective from both sides of the table.

---

# Proxy Solicitation Firms

Proxy solicitors manage the mechanics of reaching shareholders, soliciting votes, and tracking voting results during proxy contests.

- **Innisfree M&A** – One of the most active proxy solicitation firms in contested situations. Specializes in high-stakes proxy fights and has extensive experience with institutional investor engagement.

- **Morrow Sodali** – Global proxy solicitation and governance advisory firm. Provides shareholder identification, proxy solicitation, and ESG advisory services.

- **Okapi Partners** – Specializes in proxy solicitation, information agent services, and shareholder identification for contested and uncontested situations.

- **MacKenzie Partners** – Full-service proxy solicitation firm with experience in proxy fights, tender offers, and shareholder engagement campaigns.

- **D.F. King** – Part of AST, providing proxy solicitation, corporate governance consulting, and information agent services for both companies and activists.

---

# Board Education Programs

These programs offer governance training, networking, and professional development for current and aspiring board directors.

- **NACD Board Leadership Programs** – nacd.org – The most widely recognized director education programs in the United States, offering foundational and advanced courses on governance, audit, compensation, and risk oversight.

- **Stanford Directors' College** – gsb.stanford.edu – An intensive multi-day program for sitting directors, hosted annually at Stanford University. Known for its case-study approach and access to leading governance scholars.

- **Harvard Corporate Governance Executive Education** – exed.hbs.edu – Programs offered through Harvard Law School and Harvard Business School, covering governance, fiduciary duties, and board leadership.

- **Wharton Boardroom Programs** – executiveeducation.wharton.upenn.edu – Programs focused on board effectiveness, financial oversight, and strategic governance, leveraging Wharton's finance and management faculty.

- **SLGI Board Readiness Program** – The board readiness program described throughout this book, which includes the activist investor tabletop simulation. Provides comprehensive governance training with an emphasis on practical application and experiential learning.

---

# Media and Publications

These sources provide ongoing coverage of activist campaigns, governance trends, and proxy season developments.

- **Harvard Law School Forum on Corporate Governance** – corpgov.law.harvard.edu – The leading academic forum for governance commentary. Publishes daily articles from law firms, academics, proxy advisors, and governance practitioners. Free and essential reading during proxy season.

- **The Deal** – thedeal.com – Covers activism, M&A, and corporate governance with detailed campaign tracking and analysis. Subscription-based with deep coverage of activist campaigns.

- **Activist Insight (Insightia)** – activistinsight.com – Publishes research reports, league tables, and newsletters tracking activist campaigns globally. Their annual review of activism provides comprehensive year-over-year data.

- **Wall Street Journal** – wsj.com – Covers major activist campaigns, proxy contests, and governance controversies. Their Heard on the Street and Business & Finance sections regularly feature activism analysis.

- **Bloomberg** – bloomberg.com – Real-time coverage of activist campaigns, 13D filings, and proxy contests. Bloomberg Terminal users have access to additional ownership analytics and filing alerts.

---

*Resources current as of publication date. URLs and organizational details are subject to change. For the most current information, visit the organizations directly.*

# About the Author

**Brian R. Miller** is a technology executive, CISO, and author who brings more than 25 years of leadership experience to the intersection of AI systems, cybersecurity, and corporate governance.

A recognized Top 100 CISO, Brian has led enterprise security programs and advised boards on cyber risk, AI governance, and digital transformation across government, defense, IT, and healthcare sectors – including 13 years at Booz Allen Hamilton serving DoD, NSA, and NIST. He serves on venture capital technical advisory boards for Viola Ventures and Glilot Capital Partners, and has served as a customer advisory board member for Wiz and CyberArk.

Brian is the founder of Synthetic Insights, where he publishes practical guides and builds AI systems that augment human capability. His books include *Agentic Development: The Complete Guide to AI-Assisted Coding, The Board Director's Operating Manual, The 75% Secret*, and *AI for the Rest of Us*. He holds an Executive Certificate in Public Policy from Harvard Kennedy School, an MS from Johns Hopkins University Carey Business School, an MA in Global Leadership from Fuller Theological Seminary, and professional certifications including CISSP.

Brian is a graduate of the SLGI Board Readiness Program and an Activist Investor Fellow. During the program's capstone exercise – an eight-week activist investor tabletop simulation targeting a real public company – Brian co-led the tabletop exercise and served on the activist investor team, helping build the investment thesis, draft campaign materials, and conduct the negotiation that culminated in a settlement agreement. That experience – seeing a company through an activist's eyes while simultaneously understanding the board's responsibilities – became the foundation for this book.

**Connect with Brian:** - LinkedIn: linkedin.com/in/brianrmiller - Publisher: synthetic-insights.ai

# About Synthetic Insights Publishing

**Synthetic Insights** is an independent publishing and advisory firm that produces practical, research-driven guides for business leaders navigating complex challenges. Founded by Brian R. Miller, Synthetic Insights combines deep domain expertise with modern analytical capabilities to deliver content that is substantive, actionable, and grounded in real-world experience.

## Our Mission

We believe that the most valuable business knowledge is practical — drawn from direct experience, tested in realistic scenarios, and presented in frameworks that leaders can apply immediately. Every Synthetic Insights publication follows this principle: concept, framework, application.

## Our Publications

- **The Activist Investor Campaign: A Board and Executive Survival Guide** — The complete guide to understanding, preparing for, and navigating activist investor campaigns from both sides of the table.

- **Agentic Development: The Complete Guide to AI-Assisted Coding** — The definitive framework for integrating AI tools into professional software development workflows.

- **The 75% Secret** — The hidden job market and a definitive guide to landing your next role.

- **AI for the Rest of Us** — A practical, non-technical guide to understanding and leveraging artificial intelligence in everyday professional life.

- **The Board Director's Operating Manual** — The essential field guide for new and aspiring board directors navigating their first years of corporate governance.

- **The Activist Investor Tabletop Exercise Workbook** — A participant's guide to running the eight-week governance simulation.

## Our Approach

Synthetic Insights publications are distinguished by:

- **Insider perspectives** — Direct insights from practitioners, not secondhand analysis
- **Practical frameworks** — Step-by-step playbooks that leaders can implement immediately
- **Real-world grounding** — Case studies, simulations, and examples drawn from actual experience
- **Both sides of the table** — Understanding every stakeholder's perspective, not just one

## Contact

- **Website:** synthetic-insights.ai
- **Email:** brian@synthetic-insights.ai

———————————————

*Synthetic Insights Publishing — Practical intelligence for business leaders.*

www.ingramcontent.com/pod-product-compliance
Lightning Source LLC
Chambersburg PA
CBHW070409290526
45791CB00005B/1686